**Prehistoric Households at
Turkey Creek Pueblo, Arizona**

ANTHROPOLOGICAL PAPERS OF
THE UNIVERSITY OF ARIZONA
NUMBER 54

Prehistoric Households at Turkey Creek Pueblo, Arizona

Julie C. Lowell

THE UNIVERSITY OF ARIZONA PRESS
TUCSON
1991

About the Author

Julie C. Lowell earned a B.A. degree from Ohio Wesleyan University in humanities in 1967, a M. Ed. degree from Boston University in education of the deaf in 1969, and a Ph.D. degree from the University of Arizona in anthropology in 1986. Her research focus is the prehistoric pueblo Southwest. She has participated in excavations in Grasshopper, Arizona; near Chaco Canyon, New Mexico; and in Harappa, Pakistan; and has analyzed data from excavations carried out by the University of Arizona Archaeological Field School at Point of Pines, Arizona. Her publications focus on prehistoric pueblo household and community organization as reflected in architecture and on finding new ways of using early ethnographic information to sharpen archaeological inferences. Dr. Lowell is an Assistant Professor in the Department of Sociology and Anthropology at the University of Northern Iowa in Cedar Falls.

Contribution to Point of Pines Archaeology Number 30.

Cover: Room 257 showing access into storage room(*inset*) at Turkey Creek Pueblo

THE UNIVERSITY OF ARIZONA PRESS

Copyright © 1991
The Arizona Board of Regents
All Rights Reserved

This book was set in 10/12 Times Roman
♾ This book is printed on acid-free, archival-quality paper.
Manufactured in the United States of America.

95 94 93 92 91   5 4 3 2 1

Library of Congress Cataloging-in-Publication Data

Lowell, Julie C. (Julie Carol). 1945–
   Prehistoric households at Turkey Creek Pueblo, Arizona / Julie C. Lowell
      p. cm.—(Anthropological papers of the University of Arizona : no. 54)
   Includes bibliographical references and index.
   ISBN 0-8165-1238-8
   1. Turkey Creek Pueblo (Ariz.) 2. Pueblo Indians—Social life and customs. 3. Pueblo Indians—Antiquities. 4. Social archaeology—Arizona. I. Title. II. Series.
E99.P9L68 1991
917.91'55—dc20   90-48539
                                                  CIP

Contents

FOREWORD: Archaeological Approaches to Prehistoric Social Organization *Jeffrey S. Dean*	ix
PREFACE	xiii
Acknowledgments	xiii
1. THE ARCHAEOLOGICAL HOUSEHOLD	**1**
Why are Households Important?	1
Household Definitions	3
Household Classification Systems	3
Archaeological Approaches to the Household	3
Household size	4
Household configuration and descent systems	5
Household function	6
Control of time	7
Ethnoarchaeological approaches to understanding activities in space	7
Conclusion	8
2. TURKEY CREEK PUEBLO	**9**
Excavation	9
Assessment of the Value of the Turkey Creek Pueblo Data	10
Other Studies that Include Data from Turkey Creek Pueblo	11
Environment and Subsistence	11
Agricultural features	11
Hunting	15
Dating Turkey Creek Pueblo	15
Tree-ring dates: dating the construction of the pueblo	15
The ceramic sequence: dating the occupation span of the pueblo	15
Who Lived at Turkey Creek Pueblo?	15
3. TURKEY CREEK PUEBLO DATA ANALYSIS	**17**
The Room Sample	17
The Room Variables	17
Definitions of architectural attributes and features	17
Definitions of portable artifacts	20
Computer Procedures	20
Organization of the Analysis	21
4. TOWARD THE IDENTIFICATION OF DWELLINGS	**22**
A Functional Room Typology for Turkey Creek Pueblo	22
Rooms without Hearths (Storage Rooms)	24
Rooms with Circular Hearths (Miscellaneous Activity Rooms)	24
Rooms with Rectangular Hearths (Habitation Rooms)	26
Comparisons between Habitation Rooms and Miscellaneous Activity Rooms	27
Room Size	28
Inferences Regarding the Nature of Dwellings at Turkey Creek Pueblo	29
Inferences about dwellings from room types	29
Access to and communication within dwellings: hatches, doors, and vents	31
Conclusion: Turkey Creek Pueblo Dwellings	31
5. TEMPORAL CONSIDERATIONS	**32**
The Sterile-Trash Dichotomy: A Measure of Relative Room Construction	32
Sequence of construction	32
Relationship between the Turkey Creek Pueblo construction sequence and its tree-ring dates	35

Temporal changes in room construction	36	Room Group and Room Placement Analysis: Conclusion	55
Temporal Implications of Rooms with Multiple Floors: A Study in Remodeling	36	The Dual Division	56
Conversions involving storage rooms	36	Structural indicators of duality	56
Conversions involving miscellaneous activity rooms	38	North-South room attribute contrasts	56
Conversions involving habitation rooms	38	North-South Analysis: Conclusion	58

7. THE HOUSEHOLD AT TURKEY CREEK PUEBLO: SYNTHESIS AND CONCLUSIONS — 59

The Sherd Density Index: A Measure of Relative Room Abandonment — 38

Sequence of abandonment — 38

Relationships between the SDI and other variables — 40

Sherd density, portable artifacts, and patterns of abandonment — 40

Dwellings at Turkey Creek Pueblo: Inferences about Households — 59

Variability among households — 59

The developmental cycle of households and architectural constraints — 60

Mortality and fertility — 60

Household level activities — 61

6. VARIABILITY ACROSS SPACE AT TURKEY CREEK PUEBLO AND THE DUAL DIVISION — 43

The Room Group Analysis — 43

Groups A, I, and B: the early basalt groups — 43

Groups G and H: expansion eastward in the northern rooms — 46

Groups E, D, and C: late construction to the northeast — 50

Groups F and J: the constriction of Plaza 2 — 50

Group L: constriction of an early plaza — 50

Groups M and S: early groups to the southwest — 51

Group N: some fill-in rooms — 51

Groups O, Q, and T: the late south-central groups — 51

Group R: the late southeast section — 52

Groups K and P: the Kiva Room Groups — 52

Room Placement — 53

Room placement and the postabandonment deterioration of walls — 53

Room placement and function — 55

Supradwelling Divisions: Inferences about Suprahousehold Units — 61

Suprahousehold level activities — 61

The Dual Division at Turkey Creek Pueblo: Inferences about Dual Organization — 61

Dual unit activities — 62

The Village Unit — 62

Turkey Creek Pueblo aggregation — 62

The abandonment of Turkey Creek Pueblo — 63

Conclusions — 64

APPENDIX A: DEFINITIONS OF VARIABLES — 67

APPENDIX B: TURKEY CREEK PUEBLO DATA BY ROOM NUMBER AND ROOM GROUP — 69

APPENDIX C: FREQUENCY TABLE FOR TURKEY CREEK ROOM VARIABLES — 77

APPENDIX D: CONTINGENCY TEST RESULTS — 79

REFERENCES — 85

INDEX — 91

ABSTRACT — 95

FIGURES

1.1.	Location of Turkey Creek Pueblo	2
2.1.	Aerial view of Turkey Creek Pueblo	9
2.2.	Pit House 1 under Room 40	10
2.3.	Turkey Creek Pueblo, showing the surrounding trash mounds and locations of burials	13
2.4.	Plan of Turkey Creek Pueblo showing room numbers	14
4.1.	Hearth category of rooms	23
4.2.	Doors, vents, and hatches	30
5.1.	The Sterile-Trash dichotomy	33
5.2.	Room Groups	34
5.3.	Room floor transitions	37
5.4.	Sherd density index groups	39
5.5.	Jars, bowls, and artifacts on room floors	41
6.1.	Long walls in the pueblo	44
6.2.	Plastered and basalt-based walls	45
6.3.	Posthole locations	47
6.4.	Rooms with trough metates	48
6.5.	Height of pueblo walls	49
6.6.	The North-South pueblo division and the locations of burned rooms	54
6.7.	Rooms with storage bins	57

TABLES

2.1.	Turkey Creek Pueblo tree-ring dates	15
4.1.	Average room area by hearth category	22
4.2.	Numbers and percentages of rooms by hearth category and room size	22
4.3.	Rooms with no hearth and continuous variables	24
4.4.	Rooms with no hearth and nominal variables	24
4.5.	Rooms with circular hearths and continuous variables	25
4.6.	Rooms with circular hearths and nominal variables	25
4.7.	Rooms with rectangular hearths and continuous variables	26
4.8.	Rooms with rectangular hearths and nominal variables	26
4.9.	Contingency table summary of room type variables by room size and hearth category	28
4.10.	Number and percent of rooms with hearths by class	29
5.1.	Relative construction sequence by room group	35
5.2.	Transitions between floor levels	36
5.3.	Summary of room floor transitions	36
5.4.	Frequencies and percentages of rooms in each SDIGP	38
5.5.	Relative abandonment sequence by room group and location in the North and South sides of the pueblo	40
6.1.	Number of rooms in each room group	43
6.2.	Frequency and percent of rooms in the room placement categories	53
6.3.	Contingency table summary for room placement	55
6.4.	Presence of projectile points and antler flakers in kiva placement rooms and in kiva room groups K and P	56
7.1.	Summary of archaeological evidence for a four-level hierarchy of social groups at Turkey Creek Pueblo	59
7.2.	Reasons for village moves	63
7.3.	Evidence for defense and conflict	64
D.1.	Contingency test results for fixed attributes	80
D.2.	Contingency test results for portable artifacts with fixed attributes	81
D.3.	Contingency test results for portable artifacts with individual artifacts	81
D.4.	Contingency test results for individual artifacts with other individual artifacts, using the total room sample	82
D.5.	Contingency test results for individual artifacts with other individual artifacts, using the limited room sample	82
D.6.	Contingency test results for individual portable artifacts with fixed attributes, using the total room sample	82
D.7.	Contingency test results for individual portable artifacts with fixed attributes, using the limited room sample	83

Foreword: Archaeological Approaches to Prehistoric Social Organization

A concern for prehistoric social phenomena has inspired Southwestern archaeologists virtually since the middle 19th century when the formal study of the abundant and often spectacular ancient remains of the region began. This precocious interest in prehistoric society can be attributed to two principal factors. First, the abundance, visibility, and excellent preservation of sites presented archaeologists with an expansive array of data that virtually compelled consideration of the organization of the people who had lived in them. Second, and more important, the extant native populations of the region provided convenient living analogues for the striking similarities between the products of the prehistoric inhabitants of the region and their modern counterparts. These factors were nowhere more compelling than on the Colorado Plateau where the archaeological manifestations of prehistoric societies were explained in terms of the attributes of the modern Puebloan groups. The absence of clear modern analogues for the archaeological remains of the Sonoran Desert accounts for the fact that a strong concern for Hohokam social organization did not materialize until the advent of the "new archaeology" in the 1960s.

Early efforts to comprehend prehistoric social organization in the Southwest are exemplified by the work of Prudden and Fewkes. Prudden (1903, 1914, 1918) approached the problem from the perspective of the archaeological record. He identified a consistent patterning of masonry roomblock, a kiva, and a trash mound that he called a "unit pueblo." He inferred that these "small house ruins," which were ubiquitous in the northern San Juan area, sheltered small residential groups he identified as "families" or "clans." Prudden recognized that sites composed of two or more roomblock-kiva units or of more amorphous agglomerations of rooms and kivas implied the existence of communities composed of multiple residence groups, but he did not venture an opinion on the nature of these more complex configurations. A number of Prudden's contemporaries (Kidder 1924: 207–211) and successors (Beals and others 1945: 14–15; Mc.Gregor 1941: 259–260; Roberts 1930: 6–7; 1931: 111) applied his typology and reasoning in the context of their own excavations. Indeed, Roberts (1935: 11) and Gladwin (1957: 208) refer to this configuration as, respectively, "unit-type structures or one-clan houses," and the "single family unit-type."

Prudden's empirical approach to prehistoric social organization contrasted with Fewkes' method, in which inferences derived from the actual archaeological data were replaced by the imposition of modern Puebloan organizational principles on the archaeological record. Fewkes' approach was to interpret the archaeological record in terms of Puebloan (primarily Hopi) social divisions and Puebloan (again, primarily Hopi) mythology. These dual objectives led to the disregard of chronology, the rejection of any notion of change, and the focus on sociocultural categories that were thought to be elemental units of Puebloan (that is, Hopi) organization, lineages and clans. Fewkes (1896, 1897, 1900a, 1900b) and others (Cummings 1915) devoted considerable energy to defining the archaeological counterparts of such kinship units, to identifying particular clans, and to tracing their movements from various points of origin to their modern locations. One outcome of these procedures was the convergence of archaeological and ethnographic research represented by the Mindeleffs' work on Puebloan architecture (C. Mindeleff 1895; V. Mindeleff 1891) and social organization (C. Mindeleff 1900). Later studies, such as Steward's (1937, 1955) analysis of room-kiva ratios and Ellis' (1951, 1964; Hawley 1937) detailed considerations of potential relationships between Pueblo social organization and archaeology continued the trend established by Fewkes and his colleagues. Eventually, however, the realization that nonlocalized units such as lineages and clans were extremely difficult to recognize archaeologically caused interest in this type of research to flag.

During the interval from 1930 to 1960, little systematic attention was devoted to prehistoric social organization as archaeologists concentrated on determining the spatial and temporal parameters of the Southwestern archaeological record. As data accumulated, the notion of a Puebloan archetype for prehistoric Southwestern societies gave way to the realization that several distinct archaeological configurations existed. They were given separate status by the terms Anasazi, Mogollon, Hohokam, and Patayan (Dean 1986). Only the first of these was recognized as fully representative of the ancestral Puebloan patterns. At the same time, the refinement of dating techniques—stratigraphic analysis, ceramic cross dating, and, especially, dendrochronology—intensified concern for the chronology of Southwestern prehistory and effectively put an end to the atemporal aspects of the "Fewkes approach" to prehistoric social organization. Not until the late 1950s, when the spatial and chronological limits of Southwestern prehistory were well in hand, was serious attention redirected to social matters.

Once again, two general approaches to social organization developed that exhibited some similarities to the Prudden and

Fewkes dichotomy. Both approaches are well represented in Longacre's (1970b) seminal edited volume on "Prehistoric Pueblo Societies" that resulted from a School of American Research Advanced Seminar held in 1968. The first approach developed from architectural studies of well-preserved cliff dwellings. Faced with the consistent grouping of storage chambers and living rooms into distinct architectural units ("suites" at Mesa Verde, "room clusters" in the Kayenta area), Rohn (1965), Dean (1969, 1970), and Lindsay (1969) found an analog for these habitation units in the Puebloan household. Agglomerations of these minimal units into larger configurations were identified as subvillage residential units in the Mesa Verde area and hamlets or villages in the Kayenta area. Several studies in the volume edited by Upham and others (1989) expand the evaluation of the social implications of architectural and artifact patterns.

Simultaneously, the advent of the "new archaeology" led to a different perspective on prehistoric social organization in the Southwest. Working out of the Chicago Museum of Natural History field camp at Vernon, Arizona, Paul Martin and his associates sought to identify material correlates of the social units that comprised modern Puebloan societies. The archaeological record was examined for the occurrence of architectural and artifact correlates in order to delimit prehistoric social units and to define the cultural constraints that structured them (Hill 1966, 1970a, 1970b; Longacre 1964, 1966, 1970b). Once again, the household was identified as a fundamental building block of prehistoric as well as modern Puebloan communities.

Recently, dissatisfaction with the results of these analyses has stimulated a somewhat different tactic. Prefigured in Martin and Rinaldo's (1950) study of settlement in the Pine Lawn Valley, this method utilizes large samples of societies rather than relying on specific groups thought to be the direct descendants of the prehistoric populations. World-wide anthropological surveys, such as Murdock's (1949) cross-cultural sample or the HRAF, commonly are used to derive expectations of the archaeological data. This technique, which makes analogy to general human behavior rather than to a few selected societies, helps control biases caused by archaeological formation processes (Schiffer 1987) and major behavioral disjunctions between the prehistoric populations and their putative descendants (Wilcox 1981).

The global sample approach has serious drawbacks that must be carefully controlled if the method is to realize its full potential for illuminating prehistoric social phenomena. First, there is little reason to believe that the world ethnographic sample adequately represents all the sociocultural configurations that have existed throughout time. Too rigid an application of this method may prevent the detection of prehistoric social patterns absent from the ethnographic record. Second, ethnographically documented societies, by definition, have been impacted to a greater or lesser degree by contact with more complex societies, that is, literate western and eastern civilizations. Few descriptions can be considered to reveal "pristine" conditions, and most reflect colonial relationships of dominance and subordination that may not have prevailed in the past. Third, merely scouring the ethnographic data for patterns thought to resemble those of the past is not sufficient to elucidate the latter. Control samples representing situations from which the target patterns are absent must be examined to determine the sociocultural and environmental limitations on the configuration of interest. Great care and methodological rigor, therefore, must be exercised in applying this particular approach to prehistoric social organization.

Given these theoretical, methodological, and empirical considerations, what can be said about the archaeological investigation of prehistoric social organization and the household in the Southwest? Several anthropological and archaeological issues are relevant to this question. First is the general anthropological issue of the position of the household in human societies. Is it a universal and fundamental element of human social systems (Wilk and Netting 1984), or do structural and compositional inconsistencies, functional variations, and amorphous attributes vitiate the utility of the concept (Hammel 1984; Roseberry 1985)? Carefully conceived and executed archaeological studies like that reported in this volume have the potential to aid materially to the resolution of this problem in two principal ways. First, definitions of "household" that possess both anthropological and archaeological verity and relevance cannot fail to sharpen the concept through the excision of extraneous elements. Second, archaeology can provide a much more comprehensive idea of the structural, spatial, and temporal boundaries of household distributions than can be achieved through ethnographic data alone.

Lowell's detailed analysis of Turkey Creek Pueblo makes several important contributions to the archaeological study of the household and its place in communities that no longer exist. Building on Rohn's (1965) contention that the archaeological visibility of the household is predicated on two aspects of past human behavior—residential exclusivity and economic cooperation—she makes a strong case for function as the principal behavioral locus for the archaeological recognition of households. A thorough survey of the ethnographic record and the literature on households isolates the major functions that characterize most such units: shelter; procreation; implement manufacture and maintenance; and food production, preparation, and consumption. Lowell correctly identifies the observable residues of food preparation and consumption as the archaeologically most visible functional manifestation of the household. To this should be added the material results of the household's shelter function, which, at least in pueblos, produces perceivable spatial boundaries. Analysis of a wide range of architectural, artifactual, and ceramic variables specifies the spatial loci of the food storage, preparation, and consumption activities that identify households. The isolation of individual household units leads directly to the delineation of three higher levels of organization at Turkey Creek Pueblo: suprahousehold units, a dual division, and the pueblo as a whole. The analysis constitutes an excellent case study of the ways in which archaeological data can be used to establish the presence and configuration of households and to clarify the mechanisms by which these units are integrated into more encompassing groups up to the level of the village itself. In conclusion, the study described here develops a solid theoretical and methodological foundation for future archaeological research on the form, nature, and role of households in prehistoric communities throughout the world.

Jeffrey S. Dean

May 10, 1990
Tucson, Arizona

Preface

Turkey Creek Pueblo is a thirteenth-century ruin of some 335 rooms located in the Point of Pines region of the San Carlos Apache Reservation in Arizona. It was excavated by the University of Arizona Archaeological Field School, which was based in Point of Pines from 1946 through 1960 (Haury 1989). Excavations at Turkey Creek were carried out by Alfred Johnson in the summers of 1958, 1959, and 1960, during which time the school was under the direction of Emil W. Haury and Raymond H. Thompson. A grant from the National Science Foundation (No. G–5549) made it possible to hire a crew of Apache workers to augment student labor in the excavations (Haury 1989: 100).

I first became familiar with the Turkey Creek Pueblo collection, housed at the Arizona State Museum, when looking for a set of prehistoric burials to use in dissertation research. I intended to investigate social structure through variability in burial patterns. The excavated Turkey Creek burial population is extensive and appeared promising for my purposes. While looking through the materials from Turkey Creek, I was struck by several outstanding aspects of its excavation. An extraordinary 314 of its approximately 335 rooms were excavated or trenched. Furthermore, brief but remarkably consistent records were kept of the architectural attributes of each of the rooms. From several summers of work at the University of Arizona Archaeological Field School at Grasshopper, I was familiar with the lively interest among many archaeologists in the structure and functions of prehistoric households. It occurred to me that the broad Turkey Creek architectural data provided a uniquely rich source of information about prehistoric pueblo household organization and function. Therefore, I abandoned my plan to analyze the burial data and began to study the architecture.

A second and ethnographic component of my research was a study of historic Hopi and Zuni use of space. I poured through early ethnographic materials on these Western Pueblo groups, gathering and tabulating information on the activities by sex and social unit that occurred within the various physical spaces of the villages. By developing a solid understanding of the social use of space in some of the living pueblos, I expected to improve the soundness of my inferences about the use of space at prehistoric Turkey Creek. Although this study proved to be an essential addition to my research, I found crucial contrasts between the organization of the ethnographic and the archaeological villages. Most notably, Turkey Creek Pueblo was organized into a moiety system and therefore was probably more similar in its organization to the historic Eastern Pueblos, who have moieties, than to the Hopi and Zuni, who do not.

My dissertation (Lowell 1987) included separate analyses of these two sets of data. In the present monograph the archaeological portion has been reworked and the most pertinent ethnographic information has been integrated into the text.

Acknowledgments

Several institutions have been extremely helpful to my research and to the production of this text. The Arizona State Museum provided access to the records and artifacts from the Turkey Creek Pueblo excavations, and gave me work space and a research assistantship in 1983–1984 that allowed me to concentrate fully on the data analysis. The Department of Anthropology at the University of Arizona provided me with additional work space, computer access, and a scholarship to help cover miscellaneous expenses. Finally, the University of Northern Iowa has provided work space and computer access for undertaking the revisions resulting in this monograph.

Many individuals deserve mention for their assistance. The encouragement, guidance, and insights of J. Jefferson Reid and Keith Kintigh were essential to the completion of this project. Raymond H. Thompson, Director of the Arizona State Museum, was an invaluable source of information about the Turkey Creek Pueblo excavation and about research in the Point of Pines region. Jeffrey Dean's expertise on prehistoric pueblo architecture and social organization made his comments on various drafts of this project especially useful. I had many helpful conversations with Alexander Lindsay, who is investigating the Maverick Mountain ceramics from Point of Pines Pueblo. Michael Jacobs also offered thought-provoking suggestions and graciously helped me find my way around the collections of the Museum. Emil Haury discussed certain aspects of this research with me and offered valuable insights that only someone directly involved in the excavations could have provided. Robert Netting and Jerrold Levy furnished numerous suggestions about the ethnographic components of the research. I am indebted to Michael Faught, who did an archaeologically perceptive job of drafting the maps. Ron Beckwith (Arizona State Museum) revised certain figures for publication, and Carmen Prezelski (Southwest Studies Center, University of Arizona) translated the Abstract into Spanish.

CHAPTER ONE

The Archaeological Household

Traditionally, social scientists have tended to ignore the household as a social unit, perhaps finding it too ordinary to study. In recent years, however, this universal social phenomenon has become a vital focus of interest. Social scientists now view the household as the basic unit of human social organization. It is considered a complex and flexible aspect of human interaction that must be understood before certain other aspects of social organization can be approached.

In the Pueblo Southwest, a region with both excellent archaeological preservation and a rich prehistory, archaeologists have made important contributions to the burgeoning social science literature on household organization and function. At Grasshopper Pueblo, a large ruin excavated by the University of Arizona Archaeological Field School, researchers have recognized that the household is the building block of social organization, and they are developing techniques toward identifying and understanding its organization and functions within the challenging framework of archaeological data (Ciolek-Torrello 1978, 1985; Ciolek-Torrello and Reid 1974; Reid and Whittlesey 1982). My study of household organization and function centers on Turkey Creek Pueblo, a large thirteenth-century ruin located in the Point of Pines region of the San Carlos Apache Reservation in east-central Arizona (Fig. 1.1). It was excavated during the summers of 1958 through 1960 by the University of Arizona Archaeological Field School, under the direction of Emil W. Haury, Raymond H. Thompson, and Alfred E. Johnson.

WHY ARE HOUSEHOLDS IMPORTANT?

In the introduction to a collection of papers on households, Netting, Wilk, and Arnould (1984: xiii–xix) review the history of social thought related to households. During the nineteenth century, the nuclear family household was assumed to be the apex of a unilinear evolutionary trend that began with large kin groups. Because it was thought that progress would naturally result in the predominance of nuclear family households, the household was not considered to be an interesting focus of study. A second misconception also contributed to a lack of interest in household units. The forms that households took were thought to be the result of the application of rules of kinship, marriage, inheritance, and residence. These rules were studied, but not the households that were thought to result from their application.

Social scientists have shifted away from both a unilinear evolutionary approach to social organization and a focus on cognitive systems. Instead, social arrangements are perceived as flexible and responsive to changing socioeconomic circumstances. Households are basic units in such adaptations. The way a household is organized and the activities it takes on are the result of a complex interplay of influences that include, but go far beyond, the simple application of rule systems. As Wilk and Rathje argue, "Households are the level at which social groups articulate directly with economic and ecological processes. Therefore, households are a level at which adaptation can be directly studied. In fact, we define the household as the most common social component of subsistence, the smallest and most abundant activity group" (Wilk and Rathje 1982: 618; see also p. 631). Households are basic social units because so much happens within this smallest of social units. They are "a primary arena for the expression of age and sex roles, kinship, socialization, and economic cooperation where the very stuff of culture is mediated and transformed into action" (Netting and others 1984: xxii).

In addition to being primary and adaptive, households are ubiquitous (Netting and others 1984: xxi). This is not to say that households are easy to identify, define, or classify. On the contrary, the more one looks at households, the more complicated definition and classification become. Nevertheless, because household units are found in every society, they are reasonable units of analysis to use in cross-cultural comparisons of human social organization.

Another reason that households are a focus of social science interest is a practical one. The household is a natural unit of analysis when certain sources of data are used. The old census records used by some social historians interested in literate societies are one such source. Blocks of names from these censuses are interpreted to represent units of individuals who lived together as household units. Censuses of living peoples are another source. Researchers gathering census material in a community move from dwelling to dwelling and generate lists of groups of individuals who reside in discrete houses. Some archaeological data also produce information about household units. Discrete prehistoric dwellings are often distinguishable by architectural boundaries, by identification of cooking facilities, or by both (Chang 1958: 302).

In sum, households are pivotal social units. First, they are adaptive units that respond to a variety of socioeconomic influ-

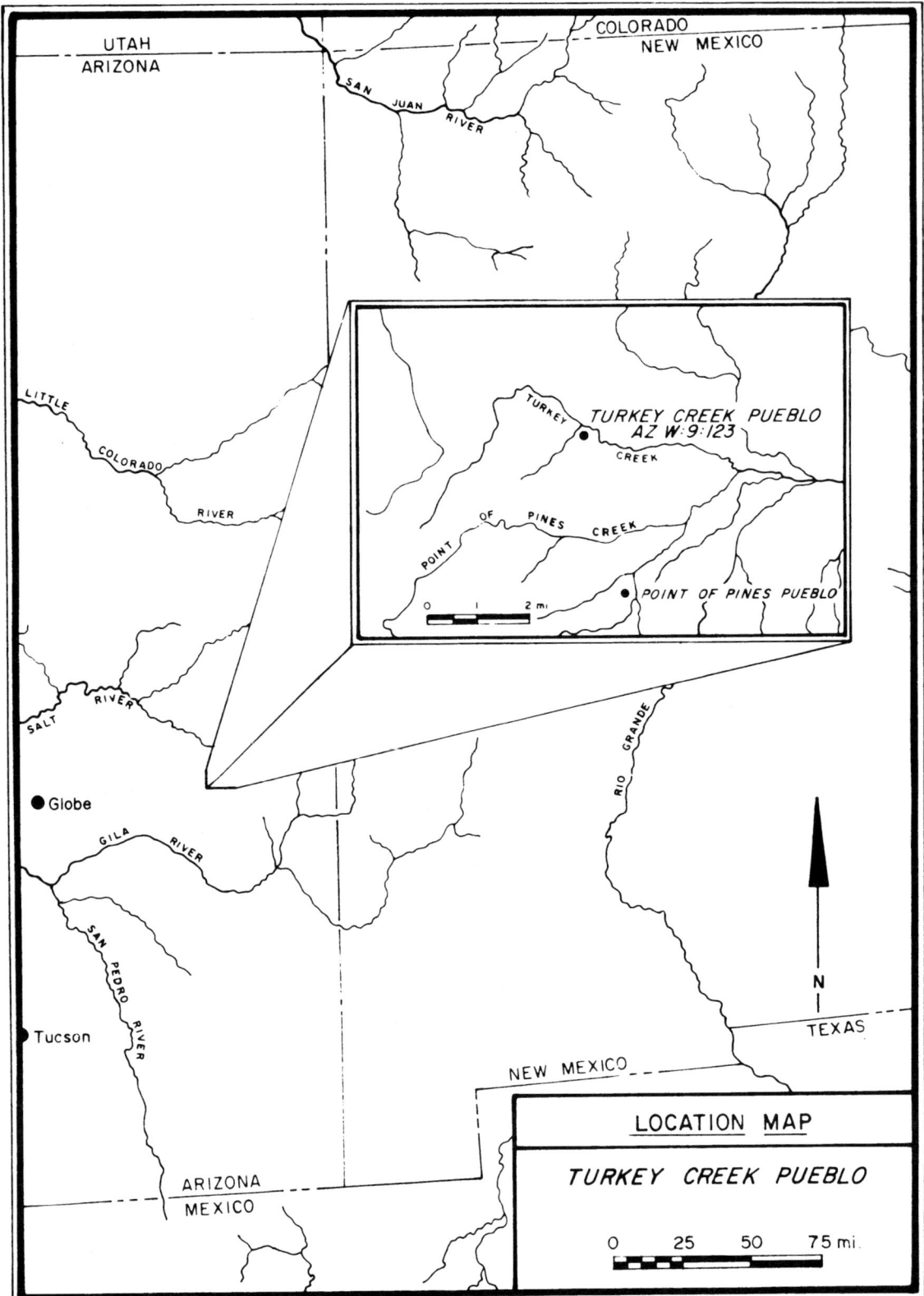

Figure 1.1. Location of Turkey Creek Pueblo.

ences; second, they are basic social entities that provide a foundation for more inclusive units; third, they are probably universal; and, fourth, they form a natural unit of analysis, amenable to identification given certain accessible data sources. The current social science research thrust toward understanding the dynamics of household organization and function, past and present, in a variety of cultural and environmental circumstances, holds much promise for elucidating the complexities of human organizational strategies.

HOUSEHOLD DEFINITIONS

A cross-cultural definition of the household is not easily achieved (Woodford-Berger 1981; Yanagisako 1979). Furthermore, the various current definitions of households are not equally applicable to archaeological data. Three frequently used defining characteristics of household groups are kinship, shared residence, and cooperation in domestic activities. Of these only two, shared residence and domestic activities, are likely to leave interpretable preserved remains in the archaeological record. Inferences about kinship or household configuration are particularly difficult to draw from archaeological data. Archaeologists can most easily define households by function rather than by form.

Households as units of people who carry out domestic activities are definable archaeologically insofar as these activities and their spatial locations are preserved. Goody (1972) presents a functional scheme for defining households that is useful from an archaeological perspective. He argues that the activities of domestic groups center on four processes: consumption, production, reproduction, and shelter. Four units of people with varying degrees of overlap in membership take responsibility for these functions. These units are the consumption unit, the production unit, the reproduction unit, and the dwelling unit.

The consumption unit, to Goody, is the household unit. This minimal definition of the household is useful for archaeologists, since the material remains of the preparation of food for consumption are often preserved as hearths, grinding equipment, storage facilities, cooking and serving pots, and so on. Production activities, too, may leave a record archaeologically whenever animal and plant remains, extraction tools, manufacturing debris, traces of field systems, and sexual division of labor as seen in burial tool kits are preserved. However, because the material remains of production activities are likely to be more spatially dispersed than are consumption activities, production units are difficult to analyze at the household level. The reproductive unit is not easily distinguished in the archaeological record, but some hint of its functioning may be drawn from evidence such as inferred labor needs, dwelling size, and child burials. In contrast to the reproduction unit, the dwelling unit may leave clear material evidence as a discrete house. Unfortunately, fuzzy boundaries between dwellings often make distinction of this unit difficult.

Our best course as archaeologists is to focus on the consumption unit, with its comparatively clear material correlates, as the basic household unit. Where possible, we should also try to discern production and residence units. Once this is accomplished, we may begin to present interpretations concerning how these various domestic groups operated in relation to each other and in relation to more inclusive social units in a particular archaeological situation.

HOUSEHOLD CLASSIFICATION SYSTEMS

Archaeologists may be able to identify some of the activities that took place in a given space but are rarely able to offer an accurate interpretation of the actual interrelationships of the individuals who occupied and functioned within that space. Therefore, morphologically based schemes for classifying households, such as those of Hammel and Laslett (1974), Wheaton (1975), and Bohannan (1963) are not directly useful in archaeological analysis, whereas functional approaches to household classification, as suggested by Wilk and Netting (1981) and Sanjek (1982), are.

Of potential interest to archaeologists is Bohannan's suggestion that the relative complexity of societies might be classified according to the functions that households take on within them. He seems to view the household as a kind of waste basket for the functions that other institutions in a particular society do not fulfill. "It may well be...," says Bohannan, "that a classification of societies on the basis of how many and which functions are carried out by the household, and the moral dimensions given to the basic family relationships that lie behind each would provide a sensible scale for the complexity of society" (Bohannan 1963: 99). The concept of moral dimensions is archaeologically elusive, but the idea that the range of activities carried on at the household level is broad in simpler societies, and narrow in more complex societies in which other institutions carry out the remaining functions, is worthy of consideration. Furthermore, this type of contrast is amenable to study with archaeological data. Many basic activities, including the grinding, cooking, and storing of food, the manufacture of tools, and the observation of religious rites, can be carried out either within small spatial units such as individual dwellings, or within larger units such as compounds, villages, or regions. Both the activities and the spatial units in which they took place may leave preservable remains available for archaeological interpretation.

In sum, a functional approach to defining and classifying prehistoric households is preferred over a morphological approach, because the activities of households are more clearly reflected in archaeological data than their configurations.

ARCHAEOLOGICAL APPROACHES TO THE HOUSEHOLD

Archaeological interest in household units is by no means new. Early in the history of Southwestern archaeology researchers noted architecturally discrete but repetitious architectural forms and attempted to correlate these with social groups that might have occupied them. Especially well known in this regard is T. Mitchel Prudden, who defined the "unit pueblo" type of site that is so common during the Pueblo II period on the Colorado Plateau. A "unit pueblo" consists of a set of contiguous surface rooms, a kiva, and a trash and burial mound (Prudden 1903: 234–235). By analogy with contemporary Pueblo social structure, Prudden suggested that these architectural units were occupied by family, or perhaps clan, units (Prudden 1914: 34).

Unfortunately from the perspective of household research, archaeologists studying prehistoric Pueblo social organization, along with cultural anthropologists studying historic Pueblo social organization, became preoccupied with the development and role of the matrilineal clan in Pueblo society. Steward, for example, created an elaborate reconstruction for the prehistoric development of the Pueblo clan system. He based his reconstruction on kiva-to-house ratios (Steward 1955). Since it is not clear, even historically, if, or in what way, kivas were tied to clans, Steward's interpretation is not solid.

A major difficulty with attempts to study prehistoric Pueblo clans is that clans are not physically localized within Pueblo villages, nor do they function as discrete groups of people that carry out activities together (Lowell 1987). Instead, the clan is a cognitive phenomenon. It is an organizational principle regulating ownership and inheritance procedures, avenues of rights and duties involving mutual assistance, and other essential social functions. Such a cognitive system is unlikely to leave archaeologically discernible traces in the record, since neither architecturally distinct structures, nor the preserved artifacts reflecting distinct clan-related activities, result from such a system.

In recent years the concern with social organization as it is reflected in the archaeological record has taken a more realistic turn, and the household has begun to receive the attention it deserves. Three trends have converged to spark this current research thrust. The first trend involves the practical realization that the nature of archaeological data often lends itself to identification of dwelling units, reflected in houses (Chang 1958: 302–303; Goody 1972: 4, 13; Wilk and Rathje 1982: 618–620), or of food preparation units, reflected in cooking features. Such physical reflections of social units form a natural starting point for archaeological investigations of prehistoric social organization.

The second trend stems from the recognition that households are particularly sensitive instruments for adaptation, and thus are intrinsically worthwhile units of analysis (Wilk and Rathje 1982: 631).

The final trend involves the study of complex cultures. Archaeologists first exploring such cultures naturally tended to excavate temples and palaces, the structures that were large, impressive, clearly preserved, and filled with exotic artifacts. However, as archaeologists began to ask serious questions about "culture process—the general principles of social structure and economics that describe the rise and fall of specific civilizations" (Rathje 1980: 1), it became obvious that such understanding could only be achieved if the average people were studied along with the elites. In order to learn about these average people, it was necessary to find and excavate their dwellings. Thus, for archaeologists interested in function and change in both complex and simple cultures, the realization has finally come that households are both a practical and an essential focus of study.

The following paragraphs provide a brief review of the questions archaeologists ask about prehistoric household organization and function and the approaches they take to answer such questions. In addition, suggestions are presented both toward broadening the range of archaeological research related to households, and toward limiting it, so that prehistoric household research conforms in a realistic way to the character of archaeological data. Southwestern Pueblo archaeology is emphasized in this discussion.

Household Size

A number of attempts have been made to estimate household size from prehistoric architectural data. An early example of such an estimate was by Harold S. Colton (1936). Colton tried to compute prehistoric Pueblo population over time, working from an assessment of average nineteenth-century Hopi household size and from counts of ground floor rooms in prehistoric sites.

More recently, Naroll (1962: 587–588), using cross-cultural data, estimated prehistoric site population as one-tenth of the floor area in square meters. LeBlanc (1971) expanded on Naroll's work with data from several additional cultural groups. He found that only when living area was isolated from other types of functional space could the estimate of population size based on 10 square meters per person be computed (LeBlanc 1971: 211). Moreover, Naroll's data show much intercultural variability in the average amount of space allocated to each person (Naroll 1962: 588), and LeBlanc's data show much intracultural variability (LeBlanc 1971: 211; see also Watson 1978). Charles Kolb (1985) looks at ethnohistoric and ethnographic data on the relationship between floor area and household size in Mesoamerica and finds that the variables impacting on this relationship are many and complex.

In sum, the use of floor area to calculate household size can provide only an extremely rough estimate. There are tremendous contrasts both within villages and between cultures in such use. Furthermore, it is necessary to differentiate floor area by function before even coarse estimates of household size can be attempted in this way.

Turner and Lofgren (1966) depart from a focus on architectural and ethnographic data to estimate household size. Reasoning that the capacity of a cooking jar reflects the relative size of the household eating food from that jar, they analyze changes in the average size of Kayenta cooking jars over time. They conclude that, since the average jar size increases over time, the average household size among the Kayenta also increases over time.

Nelson (1981), using ethnographic data collected among

the Maya, tests Turner and Lofgren's hypothesis concerning the relationship between cooking vessel size and household size. He concludes that cooking vessel size has multivariate causes, only one of which is household size. Other determinants include the age-grade composition of household members, food preparation techniques, wealth, and the scheduling of meal preparation. An additional complication is that cooking for large groups can be accommodated by utilizing many vessels, rather than one large vessel. Thus, the summed volumes of household cooking jars correlated more strongly with household size than the average volumes. Clearly, ceramic analysis involving the function and capacity of the pottery of a household must be refined further before it will be a useful tool for estimating household size.

Ciolek-Torrello and Reid (1974) use evidence for changes over time in average hearth size at Grasshopper Pueblo to suggest changes in average household size. A trend toward smaller cooking hearths is interpreted to indicate a trend toward smaller households. Support for this interpretation comes from additional analysis at Grasshopper, suggesting that multiroom, and presumably larger, households tend to be earlier than single-room, and presumably smaller, households (Reid and Whittlesey 1982). Hearth size contrasts, like the related vessel size contrasts, may become useful tools for demonstrating change over time in average household size.

The above examples suggest that numerical estimates of prehistoric household size are less sound than comparative estimates. Furthermore, since no single indicator of even comparative household size is unambiguous on its own, the most powerful statements about changes over time in average household size, or about contrasts in average size between contemporary households, should incorporate many lines of evidence. Finally, since we know from cross-cultural ethnographic data that a wide range of intravillage variability is normal, such variability also should be expected in prehistoric times.

Household Configuration and Descent Systems

Given the nature of archaeological data, it is easier to classify prehistoric households by function than by the configuration of individuals that occupied them. Furthermore, classifying households by function is preferable, "since it is the functions of the household that mediate between the wider socioeconomic realm and the nuts and bolts of household size and composition" (Wilk and Rathje 1982: 621). It has taken archaeologists of the Pueblo Southwest some time to retreat from a preoccupation with household configuration and the descent systems that contribute to it, and to begin looking more closely at household function.

Longacre's work at Carter Ranch typifies the earlier preoccupation with descent systems. He reasoned that "If there were a system of localized matrilineal descent groups in the village, then ceramic manufacture and decoration would be learned and passed down within the lineage frame, it being assumed that the potters were female as they are today among the Western Pueblos" (Longacre 1964: 317).

He found that certain design elements were associated with two major room blocks of the pueblo. In addition, since some room types were repeated within the room blocks, he concluded that this pattern "probably reflects household units housing an extended family or lineage segment" (Longacre 1964: 317). Furthermore, kivas and burial areas appeared to be associated with certain room blocks. On the basis of these lines of evidence, Longacre suggested that "localized matrilineages and lineage segments" were present at Carter Ranch (Longacre 1964: 318).

Hill carried out a similar analysis at Broken K Pueblo, but focused on residence, rather than descent, systems. He presented a chart of test implications suggesting what distribution patterns of male and female stylistic items should be found if various residence patterns were in effect (Hill 1970a: 39; 1970b: 63). Through factor analysis, he found that the distribution of styles of female associated items, notably ceramics and firepits, tended to be spatially localized into five units that could be collapsed into two larger units. From this pattern, he concluded that a uxorilocal residence pattern was present (Hill 1970b: 63–64). Hill stopped short of making a strong interpretation concerning descent systems. Instead, he made the important point that descent systems probably cannot be identified using archaeological evidence since "Descent systems are abstractions that exist in the minds of people..., and as such they often have no material correlates" (Hill 1970b: 107).

Even Hill's interpretation of uxorilocality on the basis of spatially discrete design similarities is open to criticism, since alternate and equally plausible hypotheses could account for areal style differences. For instance, two formerly separate villages, each with its own slightly different ways of doing things, could have come together into one village, creating a pattern of two spatially distinct style orientations. Temporal shifts, too, need to be filtered out as potential contributors to design contrasts in different areas of the pueblo. Although Hill did attempt to date rooms relative to each other (Hill 1970b: 29–34), he did not clearly eliminate possible temporal trends from his residence analysis. A glance at his maps shows, for instance, that on the basis of room floors on trash, his subgroup I C is later than subgroup I B (Hill 1970b: 30, Figs. 7 and 15). These room group style contrasts, then, may represent temporal style shifts rather than residence group style preferences.

Archaeological efforts to determine residence and descent rules are criticized by Allen and Richardson (1971). They maintain that "the analysis of kinship is best left to the ethnographer" (Allen and Richardson 1971: 51) and that, even for ethnographers, this task is difficult. They further note that residence rules are not rigid, that within the rule system of a culture is a range of acceptable choices individuals may make, and that such choices are impossible to discern prehistorically. This point is well taken. For example, even given an expressed rule of matrilocal residence, tremendous variability in historic Hopi and Zuni household configuration exists (Lowell 1987). Allen and Richardson (1971: 50) also note that ceramic styles have not been ethnographically demonstrated to follow descent lines, although there is no current evidence to discount this possibility completely.

Stephen Plog (1976) has also questioned the inferences of Longacre, Hill, and others. He points out problems with their design classification systems, statistical methods, control of time and space, understanding of site formation processes, and assumptions that ignore alternate explanations for design variability. All of these problems contribute to the difficulty of making sound social organizational inferences on the basis of design variability.

Hill developed a set of test implications to distinguish prehistoric nuclear family household units from extended family household units (Hill 1970a: 35). This set of test implications makes use of architectural characteristics that separate each unit from other similar units, attributes that define room types, and stylistic attributes that are consistent within units. Essentially the two basic household types contrast in size, as determined by numbers of rooms. The nuclear family household units are smaller (2–5 rooms), and the extended family household units are larger (15–25 rooms). The latter type may be made up of two or more units of the former type. Unfortunately, as yet, we do not have solid, quantitative ethnographic data to support these suggestions of Hill's, reasonable as they may be.

To conclude, prehistoric descent and residence rules are hard to discover, given the nature of prehistoric data. However, by studying room function and architecturally distinct units, archaeologists may have some chance of distinguishing nuclear from extended or multifamily households, along the lines suggested by Hill (see also Chang 1958: 303). Before such interpretations can be made with any confidence, we need far more cross-cultural ethnographic data on the architectural reflections of these various types of households than we have to date.

Household Function

Many archaeologists studying prehistoric Southwestern pueblos have tried to identify room function. One reason for this orientation is that, in an aggregated situation, pueblo dwellings tend to be contiguous, so that discrete dwellings often are not immediately obvious, but discrete rooms are. Therefore, in order to say anything about activities within dwellings in aggregated villages, it is first necessary to ascertain the functions of rooms and then to combine these rooms into dwellings.

One such research project was carried out by Rohn (1965), utilizing information from Mug House, a cliff dwelling at Mesa Verde. At Mug House Rohn identified three types of rooms distinguishable by size that tended to group into household units, or suites. Building sequences and movement patterns, as indicated by doors, were used to distinguish one architectural group from another. A large room with a hearth formed the nucleus of a typical suite of four to five rooms. Also, there were one or more small rooms that were probably storerooms, and sometimes an intermediate sized room, perhaps a sleeping room. Such suites of rooms always had access to an outdoor area with a hearth. Furthermore, Rohn identified three architectural units, hierarchically arranged from least to most inclusive. These three units were: first, room suites; second, courtyard units; and third, villages.

Rohn offers sensible advice about how archaeologists should conceptualize socioeconomic groups as they are perceived in archaeological data. He argues that, although it is impossible to determine the exact membership configuration or kinship relationships of household groups from prehistoric data, it is possible to find discrete socioeconomic groups. "It is in this sharing of material goods and the cooperation involved in satisfying the needs and wants of all the individuals concerned that may be reflected in archaeological remains" (Rohn 1965: 65). Rohn's archaeological conceptualization of socioeconomic groups is functional rather than configurational.

At Betatakin and Kiet Siel, late Pueblo III period cliff dwellings in Tsegi Canyon in northern Arizona, Dean (1970) identified a social arrangement similar to that of Mug House. He defined the following functional room types: living rooms, courtyards, granaries, storerooms, and grinding rooms. Also present were highly variable ceremonial structures that were probably kivas and ceremonial annexes to kivas (Dean 1970: 153–155). These rooms tended to group into clusters, perhaps similar to Rohn's suites, each with outdoor access. Sometimes two or more room clusters were associated with one courtyard. Dean terms these higher level social units "courtyard complexes" (Dean 1970: 157). He proposes that the room clusters were occupied by households. Three characteristics suggest to Dean that these were extended households. First, some clusters had more than one living room. Second, some dwellings were added to other clusters. And, third, courtyard complexes occurred (Dean 1970: 163). Since kivas could not be structurally associated with subvillage level residence units, Dean suggests that kiva membership crosscut household units and may have served to strengthen village integration (Dean 1970: 165, 169).

At Broken K Pueblo, Hill (1970b) identified three functional room types: living rooms, storage rooms, and ceremonial rooms. These he described according to a number of architectural and artifactual attributes.

Using multivariate statistical techniques to analyze room floor assemblages, Ciolek-Torrello (1978; 1985) developed an activity-oriented typology of rooms for Grasshopper Pueblo. In addition, he postulated a contrast in activity emphasis between the central zones of the Pueblo and the peripheral zones. In brief, he argued that the central zone emphasized refuse disposal, storage, and manufacturing activities, and the peripheral zone emphasized food processing and storage (Ciolek-Torrello 1978: 183). However, this interpretation may be biased by the fact that Ciolek-Torrello could use only first-story rooms in the multistoried core area, whereas he could use all rooms in the single-storied peripheral zones. This apparent dearth of identifiable habitation rooms in the central zone is the pattern one would expect if, as is the pattern reported ethnographically, habitation rooms were located in the upper stories and storage rooms in the lower ones (Adams 1983: 52).

Reid and Whittlesey (1982) have refined Ciolek-Torrello's Grasshopper room typology and identified nine functionally described room types at the pueblo. In addition, they contrast two types of households, the multiroom and the single-room household. Differences in frequency of these household types occur between the main pueblo and the outliers. The pivotal point that variability characterizes Southwestern pueblo households is stressed (Reid and Whittlesey 1982: 701). Such prehistoric variability in household form and function, whether it is within villages, across space, or over time, needs to be both identified and explained.

Control of Time

That archaeological data reflect the passage of time is at once their greatest challenge and their greatest strength. Although detailed interpretations about the synchronic structure of a prehistoric social system may be tenuous, broad interpretations about change over time in such systems may be solid.

The development of construction and abandonment sequences is essential before any reasonable interpretations can be presented concerning within-site social organization and activities in space, and any change in this organization (see Wilcox 1975: 133). Some of the techniques Southwestern archaeologists use to establish such sequences are listed below.

Construction Sequence Indicators

1. Wall bond-abut analysis (Reid and Shimada 1982; Wilcox 1975; 1982)
2. Exterior wall construction (see Martin and others 1964: 49; Reid and Shimada 1982: 14)
3. Walls in offset relationship (Wilcox 1975: 137–138)
4. Abutment against plastered walls (Wilcox 1975:138)
5. Room-to-room access through wall openings (Wilcox 1975: 144)
6. Tree-ring dates (Dean 1970; Dean and Robinson 1982; Reid and Shimada 1982)
7. Pottery dates (Hill 1970b; Rohn 1971)
8. Stratigraphic analysis of relationships (Reid and Shimada 1982: 15)
9. Trash below floors (Hill 1970b: 29–30)
10. Pollen analysis (Hill 1970b: 31–32)

Abandonment Sequence Indicators

1. Trash in room (Ciolek-Torrello 1978; Hill 1970b: 30–31; Reid 1973; Reid and Shimada 1982: 14–15; Wilcox 1975: 154–158)
2. De facto refuse on floors (Reid and Shimada 1982: 14–15; Schiffer 1985)

Because each of the above temporal indicators has drawbacks, the best approach to the development of construction and abandonment sequences is to make use of a combination of techniques. Hill (1970b), for example, used several techniques to develop a temporal sequence for Broken K Pueblo. He used pottery dates, trash below floors, and pollen analysis as indicators of relative construction sequence. In addition, he used trash in the rooms as an indicator of relative room abandonment. None of these temporal indicators can stand on its own, but when used together they support each other in providing a fair reconstruction of the sequence of pueblo construction and abandonment.

Ethnoarchaeological Approaches to Understanding Activities in Space

With a few notable exceptions (Freeman 1971; Geertz and Geertz 1975; Goody 1971; Rapoport 1969; Sahlins 1957), studies of the material correlates of social organization or of activities in space are not common research foci of ethnographers. Consequently, archaeologists have carried out ethnoarchaeological studies of living peoples to develop an understanding of the interaction between human organization and the archaeological record. A number of such studies have produced information relevant to pueblo household archaeology.

Some of this ethnoarchaeological work has been undertaken in small Near Eastern farming villages and has concentrated on discovering the material correlates of behavior at the household level. For example, Watson (1978), working in Hasanabad in the Zagros Mountains of Western Iran, found that contrasts in household wealth were reflected in the architecture of dwellings and in the features and artifacts associated with the dwellings.

Kramer (1979; 1982) studied Shahabad, a Kurdish village in Iran. She looked at how domestic architecture in this small village relates to variability in household population and wealth. Some of the most relevant findings at Shahabad are as follows.

1. The number of dwelling rooms per household compound is the best predictor of the number of nuclear families in the household (Kramer 1979:155).
2. In this village, the often postulated relationship between the number of cooking facilities and the number of nuclear families was not substantiated (Kramer 1982: 670).
3. Strong positive correlations between the area of the compound and the size and wealth of the household group were found (Kramer 1982: 669).
4. One might use "architecturally bounded spaces, patterns of circulation within and among them, and structural and perhaps artifactual redundancies within them to reconstruct the number and possible relations among the inhabitants of those spaces, which they may term households" (Kramer 1982: 673).

5. Variability characterizes the households of the village, and such variability is a useful focus for archaeologists (Kramer 1982: 674).

Another Near Eastern village study deserves mention. Horne (1982) finds that the majority of households in a small Iranian village utilize rooms that are not near the main household dwelling. Inheritance patterns contribute the most to this dispersed pattern of household rooms. The possibility that such a practice may occur prehistorically should be recognized by archaeologists, although it would be hard to document with archaeological data.

Some archaeologists interested in the pueblo Southwest have undertaken ethnoarchaeological projects. Longacre (1974; 1981) studied patterns of ceramic production and disposal among the Kalinga of the Philippines to test models of how the social organization and behavior of people might be reflected in ceramic data. During the restoration of Walpi, Adams (1983) used Hopi informants to give him data on the architectural reflections of room use and ownership. His best predictors of room use were: "room size, room story location, number of wall doors, and presence or absence of doors in exterior walls." In addition, he found that dwelling units occupied by households are characterized by connecting doors between storage and granary rooms (Adams 1983: 59). Adams' ethnoarchaeological study, with its focus on architecture, is a particularly helpful one for archaeologists studying prehistoric pueblos.

CONCLUSION

Archaeologists interested in the ways people organize to get work done have developed approaches that suit the material nature of archaeological data. Most frequently, they look for the reflections of activities in spatially bounded areas. The subdivisions of this space are interpreted to represent social units such as household units, suprahousehold units, villages, and so on. For Pueblo archaeologists, the development of functional room typologies through architectural and artifactual data, the material reflections of domestic unit boundaries, and ways to establish contemporaneity have been pivotal concerns. In addition, ethnoarchaeological studies of simple farming villages have proved useful in sharpening interpretations concerning both domestic unit boundaries and domestic activities in space.

Much archaeological research concerned with households has not progressed far beyond the basic problem of the identification and functional description of households as they are reflected in the data. Success at this primary interpretive level will provide the foundation enabling archaeologists to progress to the next level of interpretation. This higher level requires identifying the variability in prehistoric households and explaining this variability in terms of the forces, economic and otherwise, that helped produce it.

CHAPTER TWO

Turkey Creek Pueblo

Figure 2.1. Aerial view of Turkey Creek Pueblo as seen from the north.
Several of the perimeter rooms on the north and west side are being excavated.

Turkey Creek Pueblo (AZ W:9:123) is a large thirteenth-century ruin located in the Point of Pines region of the San Carlos Apache Reservation in east-central Arizona, about 60 miles east of Globe (see Fig. 1.1). It is a single-story masonry ruin of approximately 335 rooms. Features of the pueblo include three small subterranean or semisubterranean structures that may be kivas, four pit houses, a rectangular Great Kiva, two plazas, several outlier room blocks, and a circle of eight trash and burial mounds around the pueblo (Figs. 2.1, 2.2). The 27 cremations found at Turkey Creek (M. Stein 1962), as well as the adult inhumations (Robinson and Sprague 1965: 442), tend to be found in these mounds (Fig. 2.3).

EXCAVATION

Turkey Creek Pueblo was excavated during the summers of 1958, 1959, and 1960 by the University of Arizona Archaeological Field School at Point of Pines, then under the direction of Emil W. Haury and Raymond H. Thompson. The first two summers of work at the pueblo focused on the excavation of rooms and was supervised by Alfred Johnson. During the final summer the trash mounds surrounding the pueblo were trenched. In the room excavations an effort was made to open up and collect information on as many rooms as possible. Toward this end, a crew of Apache workers dug a

Figure 2.2. Pit House 1 under Room 40. The rectangular stone–lined hearth (*left center*) is built into the floor of Room 40.

row at a time, while three to four people kept records (Johnson 1964: 10). Using this system, 314 rooms were excavated or trenched (Fig. 2.4).

As each room was excavated, a standard room form was completed that provided basic information on features and artifacts and included plan view and cross-sectional floor maps. The weight of the potsherds pulled from each room was estimated, and the ceramic types were identified and listed in order from most common to least common, according to a visual estimate. Selected sherd samples were kept. Because the pueblo was occupied for a relatively short period of time, and the material appeared to be uniform through all levels, detailed stratigraphic records were not kept (Johnson 1964). Artifacts were considered floor artifacts if they were found within 10 cm of the floor (Johnson 1964: 8). However, in most room reports fill and floor artifacts are combined in the lists of material retrieved. Photographs were taken of representative room floors and special features (Johnson 1964: 11).

The materials collected from the Turkey Creek excavation are stored in the Arizona State Museum. They include whole pots, a representative collection of potsherds, collections of stone tools and other artifacts, field notes, site maps, room forms, burial forms, skeletal material, and photographs.

ASSESSMENT OF THE VALUE OF THE TURKEY CREEK PUEBLO DATA

In terms of their usefulness for improving our understanding of prehistoric households, the data from Turkey Creek Pueblo provide some advantages and some disadvantages. An extraordinary advantage of the excavation is that almost all of the rooms were excavated or trenched. Only the southernmost rooms were not at least trenched (Fig. 2.3). Such a broad excavation of a major ruin could not be carried out today, given the money and time constraints imposed by the exacting methods of modern archaeology. Yet the pueblo-wide architectural and floor feature data resulting from this excavation are uniquely suited to investigation of prehistoric pueblo dwellings. In many archaeological situations, the identification of dwellings is hampered by the fact that only a small and scattered sample of rooms is excavated.

A second strength of the Turkey Creek data is that a uniform system of reporting was used over the few seasons of excavation. The information on rooms is both broad and consistent across the pueblo and provides a large sample of rooms that can be compared on a number of critical architectural attributes.

A third advantage of Turkey Creek Pueblo for identifying activities in space is that, unlike many other large prehistoric pueblos, it had only one story. The host of interpretive problems associated with having ground floor rooms intact but upper story rooms collapsed is avoided.

A fourth strength of the Turkey Creek data is that the village had a relatively short occupation span. Room remodeling, therefore, is easier to interpret than in long-occupied, multiphase sites with many remodeling episodes.

The major weakness in the data is the lack of consistent information on floor artifacts, the kind of information that Ciolek-Torrello (1978, 1985) and Reid and Whittlesey (1982), working with Grasshopper Pueblo data, have used in identifying room function. The relative dearth of floor artifact data from Turkey Creek Pueblo is not attributable to excavation techniques alone. Contrasts in abandonment processes impact on the amount of floor material found, and the abandonment pattern of Turkey Creek apparently resulted in relatively empty floors. Fortunately, large room samples with weak floor artifact data and small room samples with strong floor artifact data are complementary. Together they can help archaeologists understand household function and change.

OTHER STUDIES THAT INCLUDE DATA FROM TURKEY CREEK PUEBLO

General information on Turkey Creek Pueblo is included in Johnson (1965) and in an unpublished manuscript by Johnson (1964) on file in the Archives of the Arizona State Museum. In addition, discussion of the burials is included in papers by Bennett (1973), Merbs (1967), Robinson and Sprague (1965), and Stein (1962). Tree-ring dates from Turkey Creek Pueblo are listed in Bannister and Robinson (1971). Cook (1961) reports on an unusual circular structure under one masonry room of Turkey Creek. Information on the White Mountain Red Ware pottery is included in Carlson (1970) and in a more recent paper by Graves (1984). Information on the environment and on agricultural features that might be associated with Turkey Creek are found in Woodbury (1961). Finally, information on mammal remains from sites in the area, including Turkey Creek Pueblo, are in Stein (1963). In spite of these contributions, the information that might be gleaned from the extensive collection of material from Turkey Creek has only begun to be realized.

ENVIRONMENT AND SUBSISTENCE

Turkey Creek Pueblo is situated in a grassy environment, on a low ridge on the south bank of Turkey Creek. The area is dominated by blue grama grassland and a forest of Western Yellow Pine. Juniper and pinyon vegetation zones also occur nearby (Wendorf 1950: 18). Woodbury (1961: 1) provides basic information on the environment and the agricultural potential of the Point of Pines region:

> Point of Pines lies at the edge of a broad, almost level plain, bordered by gently rolling land, with mountains and ridges in the distance on all sides. The plain is known as Circle Prairie...and extends north for about ten miles from the Nantanes Mountains (locally referred to as the Nantack Ridge).... The northern foot of Nantack Ridge breaks up into small, low, subsidiary ridges fingering out towards the prairie, separated from each other by small, flat valleys drained by intermittent streams. These low ridges and small open valleys provided the pre-historic population with village locations that were above the level of the prairie, close to the higher, forested slopes of the main ridge but also close to the lands used for farming.

The elevation of Circle Prairie averages 6000 feet (1829 m) and the highest point of Nantack Ridge is at 7600 feet (2316 m; Woodbury 1961: 1). Nantack Ridge is made up, in part, of tuff and basalt, the materials used in the prehistoric masonry construction of the area (Wheat 1952: 185; Wendorf 1950: 15, 25). Annual precipitation is about 18 to 19 inches (46 to 48 cm) per year, and the frost-free period is about 165 to 170 days (Wendorf 1950: 17; Woodbury 1961: 4). Frost and precipitation uncertainties combine to create agricultural possibilities that are "precarious at best...." (Woodbury 1961: 5).

Agricultural Features

Woodbury (1961: 11) looks at the agricultural features found in the Point of Pines region. These include terraces or check dams ("lines of stones across stream channels"), linear borders ("long lines of stones arranged in more or less parallel or concentric lines"), and grid borders ("lines of stones arranged as in the linear borders, but with added transverse rows of stones"). One field system is located on the north side of Turkey Creek, about a mile east of Turkey Creek Pueblo. Although dating such agricultural sites is difficult, it is possible that this system was used by occupants of the pueblo. The site consists of six or so groups of linear borders of tuff and basalt on a south-facing slope of land. If the total slope were planted, it would cover about 5 hectares (Woodbury 1961: 30–31). Also found in the Point of Pines region are field houses, boundary markers (Woodbury 1961: 11), and wells and reservoirs, the latter probably used as domestic water sources (Wheat 1952; Woodbury 1961: 15). No evidence of ditch or canal irrigation is found in the region (Woodbury 1961: 10, 38).

The crops grown in the Point of Pines area were the traditional Southwestern staples of maize, beans, and squash (Woodbury 1961: 35), but, considering the probable difficul-

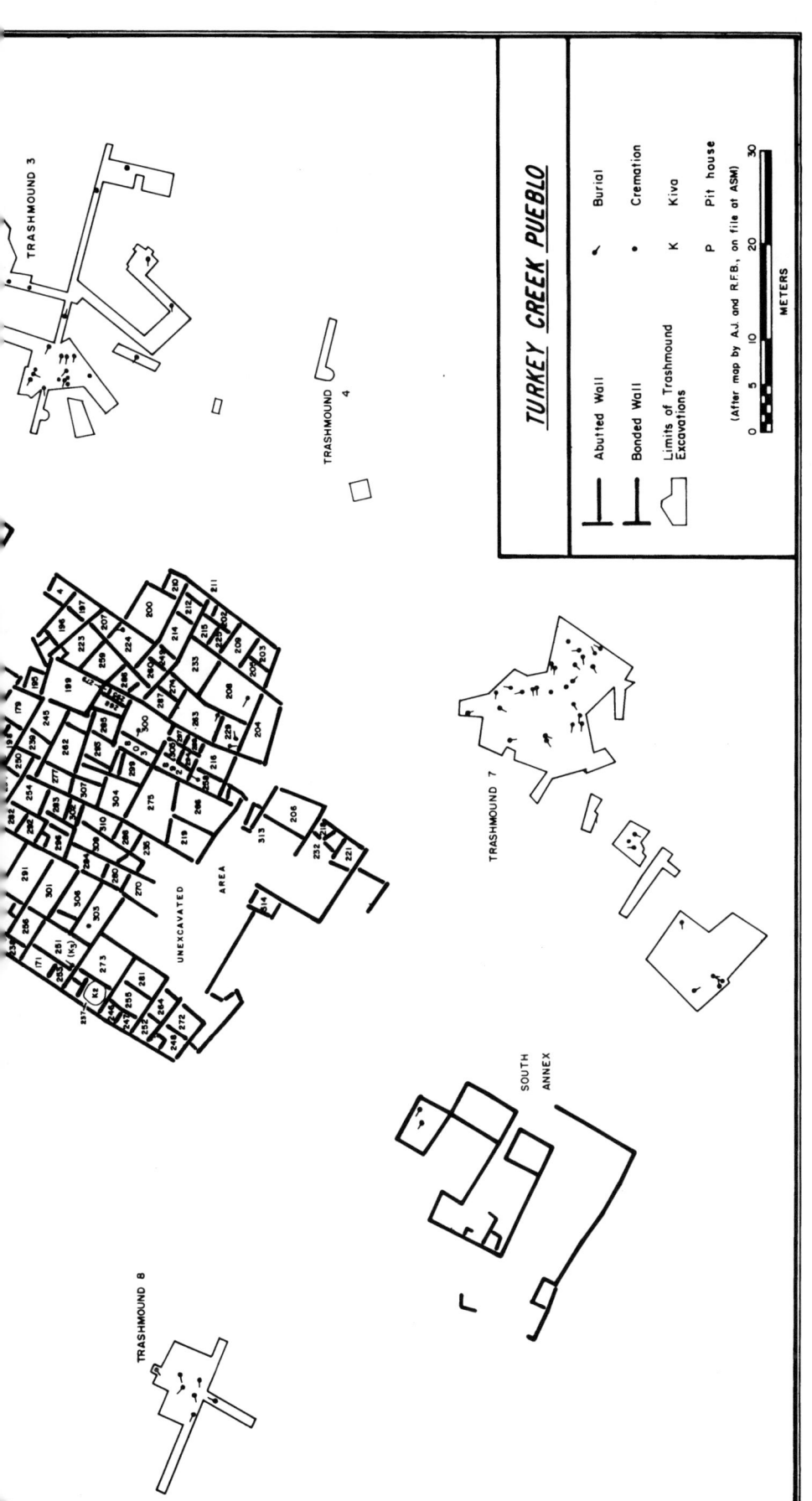

Figure 2.3. Turkey Creek Pueblo, showing the surrounding trash mounds and locations of burials.

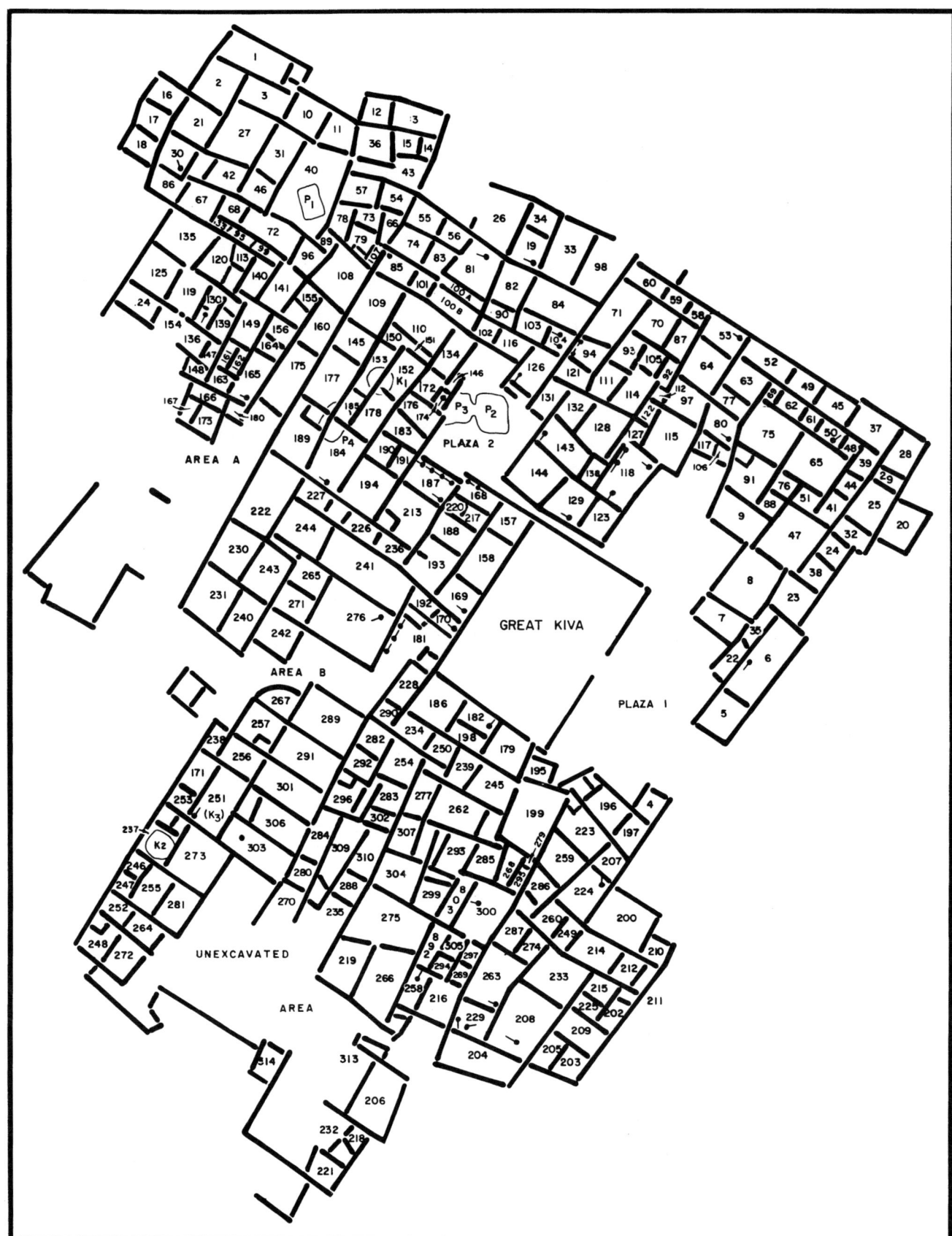

Figure 2.4. Plan of Turkey Creek Pueblo, showing room numbers.

ties with agriculture in the area, gathering wild plants was certainly important to subsistence (Woodbury 1961: 5).

Hunting

Wild animals found in the region today and probably present in prehistoric times include deer, bear, rabbits, coyotes, turkeys, and porcupines (Wendorf 1950: 19). Bones found in archaeological sites in the area are of rabbit, deer, antelope, rodent, dog, bighorn or mountain sheep, and bear (Stein 1963). Dogs appear to be domestic, since evidence of litters is indicated (Stein 1963: 215). At Turkey Creek Pueblo, turkey bones are found, but not turkey pens; these animals may have been hunted but not kept (Johnson 1965: 73). Bison bones are not present in Reserve, Tularosa, or Pinedale phase sites, but appear in the later Canyon Creek phase sites (Stein 1963). Peccary were present in the area but, because their bones are not found in prehistoric sites, they apparently were not hunted (Stein 1963: 215). In general, the environment of Turkey Creek Pueblo would appear to provide a rich fauna for hunters.

DATING TURKEY CREEK PUEBLO

Two related sources of information are available to assist in dating Turkey Creek Pueblo, tree-ring dates and ceramic dates.

Tree-ring Dates: Dating the Construction of the Pueblo

Table 2.1 gives the tree-ring dates from Turkey Creek Pueblo. These dates cluster around A.D. 1240. Bannister and Robinson (1971: 43) say the following about them: "The one structure with adequate dates, Room 115, can be placed confidently at A.D. 1242 for construction. Although other units have few dates, there is a general, and fairly convincing, agreement in placing major construction at Turkey Creek Pueblo within a few years of A.D. 1240." Four of the rooms with dated tree-ring samples, including Room 115, appear to have been burned. This finding suggests that the dates from these rooms come from structural wood (roof beams), rather than from firewood and are therefore useful dates for inferring room construction.

The Ceramic Sequence: Dating the Occupation Span of the Pueblo

Within the Point of Pines phase sequence, based on the ceramic sequence, Turkey Creek Pueblo was occupied during the Tularosa phase (Johnson 1965). Early estimates of the dating of this phase were between A.D. 1100 and 1200 (Haury 1957: 12; Johnson 1965). However, more recent information on ceramic dating, based on improved associations with tree-ring dates, indicates that these dates are too early. A current estimate for dating the Tularosa Black-on-white ceramics of the Tularosa phase suggests that they span the 1200s. The earlier Reserve Black-on-white ceramics are most frequent during

Table 2.1. Turkey Creek Pueblo Tree-ring Dates (From Bannister and Robinson 1971: 42–43)

Room	Date*	Comments
1	1238r	
151	1217vv	
184	1238vv	
267	1243v	
158	1242r	Burned
	1243r	
Great Kiva	1240vv	
8	1226v	
97	1237vv	Burned?
115	1240r	Burned?
	1241r	
	1242r	
65	1242r	Burned?

*According to Bannister and Robinson (1971: 5):
"r—less than a full section is present, but the outermost ring is continuous around available circumference
v—a subjective judgment that, although there is no direct evidence of the true outside on the specimen, the date is within a very few years of being a cutting date
vv—there is no way of estimating how far the last ring is from the true outside."

the A.D. 1100s, but continue in decreasing numbers into the 1200s, along with Tularosa Black-on-white. The later Pinedale Black-on-white ceramics appear to date between 1300 and 1350 (Tuggle and Reid 1982: 16–17).

Turkey Creek Pueblo is the earliest aggregated pueblo and the largest Tularosa phase site of the region. Nearby Point of Pines Pueblo is the dominant large pueblo of the following phases and appears to have succeeded Turkey Creek Pueblo as the major aggregated settlement of the region. The Maverick Mountain phase of Point of Pines Pueblo, dating between about A.D. 1265–1300 (Breternitz, Gifford, and Olson 1957, Fig. 1), is believed to reflect a Kayenta migration into the area (Haury 1958).

When during the Tularosa phase was Turkey Creek Pueblo occupied? Johnson (1965: 64–68) provides a listing of the ceramic types found at the site. In addition, Graves' seriation of White Mountain Red Ware design styles includes Turkey Creek Pueblo pottery. Using this seriation, Graves (1984: 9) estimates that Turkey Creek was occupied between about A.D. 1225 and 1286, a time span that fits reasonably well with the tree-ring dates and the phase sequence.

WHO LIVED AT TURKEY CREEK PUEBLO?

The knotty problem of cultural labels for prehistoric Pueblo peoples of this region of the Southwest is, fortunately, peripheral to the focus of the current research. The term "Mogollon" is generally used to designate the earlier pit house dwellers of the Point of Pines and neighboring regions. Some archaeologists are inclined to drop this designation after the shift to above-ground masonry dwellings occurred. Reed (1950) labels the prehistoric Pueblo dwellers of the mountain region "Western Pueblo" to distinguish them from the Anasazi. This cultural label is misleading since certain ethnographically known Pueblo groups, the Hopi, Zuni, Acoma, and Laguna peoples, are similarly designated (Eggan 1950).

However, since Johnson (1965: 14), following Reed, labels Turkey Creek Pueblo as prehistoric Western Pueblo, the current presentation accepts it as such. Johnson defines prehistoric Western Pueblo as the Pueblo manifestation in east-central Arizona and west-central New Mexico from about A.D. 1000 onward, and Turkey Creek fits this geographic and temporal definition. However, my use of the term implies neither specific cultural ties to historic Western Pueblo groups, nor acceptance or rejection of any of the various scenarios for cultural ties among prehistoric Southwestern groups.

CHAPTER THREE

Turkey Creek Pueblo Data Analysis

The Turkey Creek household study is designed to take the fullest possible advantage of the positive aspects of the available architectural data. Since individual rooms are discrete and easy to identify, rooms are the basic units of analysis. Site maps, room forms, and room floor maps provide the primary data. The fixed, or architectural, room variables most consistently reported are the variables included in the analysis. Selected portable artifact types form a secondary set of variables. The spatial distribution of these artifacts in the pueblo augments information gleaned from the architectural study.

THE ROOM SAMPLE

Turkey Creek Pueblo proper has about 325 to 335 rooms, depending on how one estimates the number of unexcavated rooms in the south part of the pueblo (Fig. 2.4). In all, 314 rooms were excavated or trenched, 94 to 97 percent of the total. Of these, 301 rooms (90 to 93 percent) provided enough information to be included in the data set. Just 21 (7 percent) of the 301 rooms were not completely excavated, but even these rooms yield adequate architectural information for analyses involving certain variables. Individual rooms are dropped in specific analyses whenever the variables involved are unclear.

The number of rooms used for the architectural analyses is unusual in its robustness. Rarely do archaeological data provide a collection of rooms from a large pueblo that approaches that of Turkey Creek; approximately 70 to 90 percent of the rooms are used for each architectural variable.

THE ROOM VARIABLES

The variables used in the Turkey Creek Pueblo quantitative analysis are defined below. Shortened names for the variables are given in parentheses. Appendix A provides brief definitions of each variable, and Appendix C shows the number of cases for which there is information on each variable.

Definitions of Architectural Attributes and Features

Hearth. This dichotomous variable identifies rooms with or without hearths. Rooms with hearths present might have hearths of circular, rectangular, or amorphous shape. Rooms with hearths absent have no hearth or firepit of any kind.

Circular Hearth (C. Hearth). This dichotomous variable indicates the presence or absence of a circular hearth or hearths within a room. Four subtypes of circular hearths are identified at Turkey Creek Pueblo: slab-lined, clay-lined, rock and clay-lined, and miscellaneous or poorly defined. Since preliminary analysis demonstrated that hearth shape rather than hearth construction correlated with room area, these subtypes are collapsed into one type.

Rectangular Hearth (R. Hearth). This dichotomous variable indicates the presence or absence of a rectangular or square hearth or hearths within a room. Three subtypes of rectangular hearths are slab-lined, clay-lined, and miscellaneous or poorly defined. Since preliminary analysis demonstrated that hearth shape rather than hearth construction correlated with room area, these subtypes were collapsed into one type. R. Hearth and C. Hearth do not exhibit a mutually exclusive distribution and a number of rooms at Turkey Creek contain both rectangular and circular hearths.

Hearth Class (Class). This variable distinguishes three mutually exclusive classes of rooms with hearths of either or both types.

Class 1 rooms have just a circular hearth or hearths
Class 2 rooms have just a rectangular hearth or hearths
Class 3 rooms have both a circular hearth or hearths and a rectangular hearth or hearths

Room Area (Area). The value for this variable is the product of the average (in meters) of the two long walls of a room and the average of its two short walls.

Room Size (Size). The floor area of each room is computed by averaging the measured length in meters of the two long walls and doing the same for the two short walls. These two figures are then multiplied to find the floor area in square meters for the room. To create discrete categories for cross-tabulations, several size categories were tested to find the system that best discriminated among rooms that are small and without hearths, rooms that are mid-sized with circular hearths, and rooms that are large with rectangular hearths. The resulting categories are:

Size 1: area<=6
Size 2: 6<area<=11
Size 3: 11<area<=34

Room Area Group (Areagp). This variable is used in conjunction with Room Size in statistical analyses concerning the floor area of rooms. Since Room Area Group contains nine categories and Room Size contains three, the former provides a more detailed breakdown of room area than the latter. Furthermore, Room Area Group often has an inferential advantage over Size, since examination of its many cells may show a stepped pattern of relationship that is obscured by the limited groupings of Room Size. On the other hand, Room Size provides a sounder indication of a relationship between variables than Room Area Group, because the latter creates many cells that may have low expectancy figures, calling into question the validity of the contingency table test. Therefore, Room Size and Room Area Group are used together to provide the strongest possible basis for inferences concerning the patterning of room area with other variables. The Room Area Groups are:

If area<=4.0 then areagp=1
If 4.0<area<=7.0 then areagp=2
If 7.0<area<=10.0 then areagp=3
If 10.0<area<=13.0 then areagp=4
If 13.0<area<=16.0 then areagp=5
If 16.0<area<=19.0 then areagp=6
If 19.0<area<=22.0 then areagp=7
If 22.0<area<=25.0 then areagp=8
If 25.0<area then areagp=9

Medium or Large Circular Hearth Rooms (Csize). This dichotomous variable compares medium sized rooms with circular hearths (Size 2 circular hearth rooms) with large rooms with circular hearths (Size 3 circular hearth rooms).

Medium or Large Rectangular Hearth Rooms (Rsize). This dichotomous variable compares medium sized rooms with rectangular hearths (Size 2 rectangular hearth rooms) with large rooms with rectangular hearths (Size 3 rectangular hearth rooms).

Sterile (Sterile). This dichotomous variable distinguishes rooms whose original floor is constructed on trash from those whose original floor is constructed on sterile soil. Two kinds of sterile soil, mixed native and native, are distinguished by the Turkey Creek excavators (see Heindl 1955). If either of these soil types is under the last excavated room floor, sterile is considered present. If any trash is noted under the last floor, sterile is considered absent. This variable is used for temporal inferences. Rooms whose original floors are built on sterile soil, before trash had a chance to accumulate, are considered earlier constructed than those whose original floors are built on trash.

Pounds of Sherds per Square Meters (lbs). The values for this continuous variable are computed by dividing estimates of the total pounds of sherds removed from the floor and fill of each room by its floor area.

Sherd Density Index (SDI). The sherd density index was devised as a temporal measure of comparative room abandonment. The concept behind the index is that rooms that are abandoned early in the history of the pueblo would tend to get filled with trash and exhibit a heavy sherd accumulation (high SDI), whereas rooms that stay in use up to or close to pueblo abandonment would not accumulate much trash (low SDI). The measure of sherd density for Turkey Creek corrects pounds of sherds per square meter for wall height. It is computed by dividing the pounds of sherds per square meter by the average wall height in courses. The Turkey Creek Pueblo sherd density index is, therefore, a measure of the average weight in pounds of sherds per square meter per wall course. Wall height and pounds of sherds per square meter are uncorrelated variables (Pearson's r, the Product-Moment Correlation Coefficient equals 0.067).

Sherd Density Index Group (SDIGP). This variable turns the sherd density index, a continuous variable, into a discrete variable suitable for cross-tabulations. The breakdown is:

If SDI<=.05 then SDIGP=1
If 0.5<SDI<=1.0 then SDIGP=2
If 1.0<SDI<=1.5 then SDIGP=3
If 1.5<SDI<=2.0 then SDIGP=4
If 2.0<SDI<=2.5 then SDIGP=5
If 2.5<SDI then SDIGP=6

Room Group (Group). Each room at Turkey Creek Pueblo is assigned to one of 20 groups of contiguous rooms lettered A through T (see Fig. 5.2). The initial criterion for these grouping decisions involved the nature of wall construction. Long walls, along with some bonded T- and L-shaped wall configurations, define large areas of the pueblo that are filled in with rooms (see Fig. 6.1). Wall bonding is not common at Turkey Creek, and large rectangular units with four bonded corners are absent. This lack of consistent bonding has a long history in the Point of Pines area (Olson 1959: 24, 282; Wasley 1952: 114).

The present 20 Room Groups represent a refinement of an original grouping system. The original system was revised after working with the room attributes and finding that within-group uniformity could be improved by shifting the group membership of some rooms.

Some bonded corners contradict the groupings. Because the long wall patterns at Turkey Creek are stronger than the bonding patterns, when conflict between bonded corners and long walls occurred, the criterion of long straight walls took precedence over the bonded corner. Also, since many of the walls at Turkey Creek were low, decisions concerning the structure of the corners were probably often tenuous (see Wilcox 1982: 21, for a discussion of another difficulty with interpreting bonding).

The 20 Room Groups vary broadly in the number of rooms they contain, and many can be broken down into smaller subgroups using the same criteria. Therefore, it is not assumed that these groups were occupied by comparable social units, nor assumed that they necessarily have any social, functional, or temporal significance. Instead, the groups are used as a convenient tool for making horizontal comparisons across the pueblo. However, it is argued in the text that certain of these Room Groups do have real systemic significance relating to social organization, function, or time. Such significance is inferred only after careful evaluation of the data.

Room Placement (Place). Each room is assigned to one of five locational categories.

- I = Interior Placement. Rooms do not border on the exterior of the pueblo, the kiva, or the plazas.
- E = Exterior Placement. Rooms border on the exterior of the pueblo.
- O = Plaza 1 (One) Placement. Rooms border on Plaza 1.
- T = Plaza 2 (Two) Placement. Rooms border on Plaza 2.
- K = Kiva Placement. Rooms border on the Great Kiva.

Occasionally rooms fall into two Room Placement categories. In these cases, assignments are made according to an intuitive concept of relative behavioral significance. For instance, a room bordering on both a plaza and the exterior of the pueblo would be assigned a plaza placement, following the assumption that its activity focus might be more plaza than exterior oriented.

Room Side (Side). This dichotomous variable compares the attributes of rooms in the north side of the pueblo with those of rooms in the south side. Rooms in Groups A–L are placed in the north side and those in Groups M–T are placed in the south side.

Storage Pit (Pit). This dichotomous variable indicates the presence or absence of a possible storage pit or pits in the floor of a room. It was not always clear that a floor pit was indeed a storage pit. In this analysis, all rooms with possible storage pits are coded present for Storage Pit.

Hatch (Hatch). This dichotomous variable indicates the presence or absence of a notched or unnotched slab or slabs that were interpreted as part of a collapsed hatchway structure in the roof.

Storage Bin (Bin). This dichotomous variable indicates the presence or absence of a storage bin or bins within a room.

Vent. This dichotomous variable indicates the presence or absence of any small opening or openings in the walls of a room.

Burial. This dichotomous variable identifies the presence or absence of a burial or burials within a room. Such burials are under the floors of rooms and are assumed to be associated with the room. It is possible, however, that some of these burials predate their rooms. The majority of these burials are inhumations of fetuses or infants (Johnson 1965: 63; Robinson and Sprague 1965:442). Most of the cremations and adult inhumations are located in the trash mounds around the village, so are excluded from the present analysis.

Plaster. This dichotomous variable distinguishes rooms without plaster on the walls from rooms with plaster found on one or more walls.

Multiple Plaster (Multi-plaster). Rooms at Turkey Creek Pueblo have from zero to five coats of plaster on the walls. Rooms with Multiple Plaster have more than one coat of plaster present. Since there is some spatial patterning of the presence of multiple coats of plaster at Turkey Creek, both Plaster and Multiple Plaster are retained in the analysis.

Room Shape (Shape). Room Shape is computed for each room by averaging the measured length in meters of the two long walls (average length) and doing the same for the two short walls (average width). The average length is then divided by the average width to compute an index of room shape. Rooms with indices closest to one are the most square in shape, whereas rooms with the highest indices are the least square, exhibiting the most contrast between length and width. This continuous variable is converted into a discrete variable suitable for cross-tabulations by rounding each index into Shapes 1, 2, or 3.

Wall Height (Height). The values for this variable are computed by averaging the counts of wall courses for the walls of each room. Since the number of courses for each wall was more consistently recorded than wall height in meters, this measure is considered more useful for comparative purposes than a meter measure. The values for each room are rounded off to whole numbers to create a discrete variable.

Basalt-based Walls (Basalt). The wall construction descriptions on the Turkey Creek Pueblo room reports fall into two general types. The first type, called here basalt-based, is constructed with a footing of basalt boulders. The remaining courses are of tuff. The second wall type is constructed of tuff courses with no basalt base. In both types basalt is occasionally mixed in with the tuff. Rooms with one or more walls based with basalt are assigned to the basalt-based wall category.

Posthole (Post). This dichotomous variable identifies the presence or absence of a hole or holes that might have been postholes. In this analysis all rooms with possible, if uncertain, postholes are coded present for Posthole.

Door. This dichotomous variable identifies the presence or absence of a door or doors in the walls of a room. Such doors may be open or sealed. Note that a door between any two rooms is automatically counted twice in the computer analysis.

Definitions of Portable Artifacts

Trough Metate (Trough). Three types of metates are found at Turkey Creek Pueblo: trough metates, slab metates, and basin metates. Because of their low frequencies, slab and basin metates are not included in the present analysis. The within-room provenience of each trough metate is recorded as on the floor, or in the fill, or is unspecified. Preliminary computer analysis attempted to deal with all of these aspects of metate provenience. Coping with the unspecified proveniences was problematic, as were the small samples created by breaking down the proveniences. Therefore, complete computer tests were run on simply the presence or absence of trough metates within a room, regardless of provenience. Both whole trough metates and metate fragments are included. Trough metates are the only portable artifacts used in the study that are not necessarily in floor contact.

Vessel. This dichotomous variable identifies the presence or absence of any reconstructible ceramic vessels (jars or bowls) listed in association with a room floor.

Jar. This dichotomous variable identifies the presence or absence of any reconstructible jars listed in association with the floor of each room.

Bowl. This dichotomous variable identifies the presence or absence of any reconstructible bowls listed in association with the floor of each room.

Individual Artifacts. Because of ambiguities involved with interpreting floor versus fill proveniences of portable artifacts at Turkey Creek Pueblo, only a limited study of individual floor artifacts other than vessels was undertaken. Just eight individual artifact types that are frequently noted, and that may be used to make reasonably sound inferences regarding behavior, are included in the study.

1. Shaft Straightener (SS)
2. Axe
3. Antler Flaker (Ant. Flak.)
4. Awl
5. Hoe
6. Knife
7. Drill
8. Projectile Point (PP)

Each individual artifact is recorded as present or absent on a room floor. All apparent trends related to individual floor artifacts are essentially hypotheses and should be treated with caution.

These eight artifact types are treated in one of two ways in the analyses. The Limited Room Sample (L.R.S.) operates under the assumption that floor artifact information is not available for most rooms. It involves comparisons among only those rooms in which artifacts of any of the eight individual types are explicitly listed in association with the floor. In contrast, the Total Room Sample (T.R.S.) operates under the assumption that floor artifacts are always recorded separately from fill artifacts. It involves comparisons within a larger sample of rooms.

Floor Artifacts (Artifact). This dichotomous variable identifies the presence or absence of an individual artifact or artifacts listed in association with the floor. In all analyses, floor artifacts exclude metates and vessels but include all eight individual artifact types listed above. This variable does not specify what type or types of individual artifacts may be present.

COMPUTER PROCEDURES

Because most of the variables recorded for the Turkey Creek Pueblo rooms are nominal, this analysis makes extensive use of contingency tables. For continuous variables Pearson's r, the Produce-Moment Correlation Coefficient, is used. Continuous variables are converted to nominal variables for use in contingency table tests with nominal variables. Initially, computer-generated maps were used to highlight the pueblo-wide areal patterns of important variables. In this presentation these crude maps are replaced with hand-drafted maps that show spatial patterning more clearly. The Statistical Analysis System was employed for carrying out all of the computer procedures.

The inferences from the contingency table analysis require comment. The arbitrary 0.05 level, as determined by the Likelihood Ratio Chi Square (Feinberg 1977: 36), is used as the cut-off figure for rejection of the null hypothesis of no relationship between variables. Since the room sample from Turkey Creek is not a random sample of a population, the assumptions on which the significance tests rest are not strictly satisfied and must be interpreted cautiously. The Likelihood Ratio Chi Square test is used here mainly as a consistent and impartial criterion to assist in decisions about whether or not the relationship of the variables in individual contingency tables is considered noteworthy. Strength of association tests are not used in this analysis, since they present additional inferential difficulties.

In some tests the expected cell frequencies are low, yielding uncertain results. This problem occurs with many of the tests involving individual floor artifacts and the total room sample (see Appendix D). It also occurs with the few architectural variables that have many possible attribute states. In order to make a stronger case for the relationships involving two critical variables, the attribute states were collapsed. Room Area Group with nine attribute states was collapsed into Room Size with three. Similarly, Room Group with 20 states was collapsed into Room Side with two. Although the Sherd Density Index Group and Wall Height variables were not collapsed, the results of problematic tests were not taken at face value. Instead, the large tables were individually scrutinized. Strong patterning is suggested by the stepwise increasing or decreasing relationships in the cells.

This heuristic approach to contingency table analysis assisted in the discovery of patterns in the data that otherwise would have remained obscure. The conclusions of this analysis are based on the observation of consistent patterning in the data that is supported by multiple lines of evidence. In no case is a strong conclusion based on a single statistical test.

In the discussions that follow, information on ethnographically known Hopi and Zuni households is frequently cited. This use of ethnographic data is not meant to suggest that the Turkey Creek inhabitants were ancestral to the historic Hopi or Zuni. Instead, I am utilizing some of the results of a previous analysis of Hopi and Zuni households (Lowell 1987) to help assess the reasonableness of certain inferences drawn from the archaeological data at Turkey Creek Pueblo.

ORGANIZATION OF THE ANALYSIS

It is essential to distinguish conceptually the three dimensions that might influence the patterning of room attributes.

1. Room function, the set of activities that take place within a room
2. Temporal change, change over time in room attributes
3. Spatial contrasts, areal contrasts in function or time

I made an effort to sort out the interactions of these dimensions of influence on the room attribute data. Toward this end, the presentation of the analysis is organized into a hierarchy of increasingly inclusive spatial units. Within each level of the hierarchy, the dimensions of function and time are addressed. This order of presentation lays the foundation for higher level inferences concerning the organization of activities in space as carried out by an inferred hierarchy of social units at Turkey Creek Pueblo. The household is the primary and least inclusive social unit of the inferred social hierarchy. This unit is reflected in the archaeological record by physical spaces termed dwellings. The total village unit is the highest level of social inclusiveness. The presence of this social unit is reflected in the complete and discrete set of pueblo rooms. Between these two social levels are two less obvious ones: suprahousehold units and dual division units. These intermediate level units are also reflected architecturally.

The order of presentation of the data analysis progresses from the least inclusive to the most inclusive levels of the inferred social hierarchy, as this hierarchy is reflected in architectural space.

In Chapter 4 a functional room typology is developed so that rooms may be combined hypothetically into dwellings. The patterning of room attributes within room types is examined in detail. In addition, the patterning of those variables that provide information on access to and communication within dwellings is discussed.

Temporal considerations are reviewed in Chapter 5. Three measures of relative time provide the foundation for understanding the impact of temporal change on room attributes. First, the sterile-trash dichotomy is used to establish a relative construction sequence. Other variables are then studied as they relate to relative room construction. Second, room floor remodelings are investigated to elucidate functional change within rooms. Third, the Sherd Density Index is used to establish a relative abandonment sequence. Other variables are then discussed as they relate to relative room abandonment.

Variability in room attributes among the 20 Room Groups is examined in Chapter 6. It is argued that both time and function contribute to the areal variability observed. The impact of postabandonment formation processes on the patterning of room attributes is assessed through the analysis of room placement. In addition, both structural indicators and quantitative analysis of room attributes point toward a dual division at Turkey Creek. Possible functional, temporal, and stylistic influences on the apparent contrasts between the North side and South side room attributes are suggested.

The final chapter presents a model for the organization of activities in space by a four-level hierarchy of social units at Turkey Creek Pueblo.

CHAPTER FOUR

Toward the Identification of Dwellings

To approach questions on household organization and function in archaeological situations it is first necessary to identify houses or dwellings. Dwellings are the physical structures associated with the social units termed households. Unfortunately, archaeologists seeking to identify dwellings in masonry pueblos are faced with a major problem. Rather than building discrete dwellings, spatially distinct from those of their neighbors, aggregated pueblo households share walls with other households such that their dwellings are contiguous and not easily distinguished from each other. Although individual rooms are easy to identify, the ways in which these rooms are organized into dwellings for use by individual household units are not. For this reason, the development of functional typologies of rooms is a first step toward understanding dwellings and the households that occupy dwellings.

A FUNCTIONAL ROOM TYPOLOGY FOR TURKEY CREEK PUEBLO

At Grasshopper Pueblo and elsewhere, both room size (Adams 1983; Ciolek-Torrello 1978: 185; Hill 1970b) and hearth type (Ciolek-Torrello 1978: 119; Reid and Whittlesey 1982: 692–693) have been found to relate to room function. These findings are not surprising. Since contrasting activities are likely to need contrasting amounts of space, it is reasonable to expect that room area and room function are related. Fire facilities, too, should vary according to at least some of the major activities or functions related to a room. Some activities, such as storage, may require no fire whereas others, such as sleeping, may require a simple heat-producing fireplace. Cooking may require specialized fire facilities.

At Turkey Creek Pueblo rooms were divided into three classes based on the hearth category: rooms without hearths, rooms with circular hearths, and rooms with rectangular hearths (Fig. 4.1). Mean areas contrast sharply for these three preliminary room types by hearth category. On the average, rooms without hearths tend to be small, rooms with circular hearths tend to be mid-sized, and rooms with rectangular hearths tend to be large. The figures are given in Table 4.1.

The breakdown by number and percent of rooms in the three hearth categories, by Room Sizes 1, 2, and 3, is shown in Table 4.2.

Table 4.1. Average Room Area by Hearth Category

	Area in Square Meters	Standard Deviation	Min.	Max.
Whole Pueblo	8.13	5.38	1.19	32.77
No Hearth	5.50	4.16	1.19	23.97
Circ. Hearth	9.33	4.18	2.66	25.12
Rect. Hearth	12.22	5.61	5.28	32.77

Table 4.2. Numbers and Percentages of Rooms by Hearth Category and Room Size

	No Hearth	Circular Hearth	Rectangular Hearth
Size 1 area<=6	98 (74%)	14 (16%)	3 (5%)
Size 2 6<area<=11	22 (17%)	51 (58%)	25 (42%)
Size 3 11<area<=34	12 (9%)	23 (26%)	31 (53%)
Total	132 (100%)	88 (100%)	59 (100%)

Some rooms occur in two hearth categories, since rooms containing both circular and rectangular hearths (N = 12) are counted as both circular and rectangular hearth rooms. Rooms with amorphous fire facilities are included as hearth present in all hearth-no hearth analyses, as circular hearth absent in all circular hearth analyses, and as rectangular hearth absent in all rectangular hearth analyses.

Although there is a strong tendency for rooms with no hearth to be small, rooms with circular hearths to be mid-sized, and rooms with rectangular hearths to be mid-sized and large, too much overlap exists for the creation of a room typology combining the size and hearth attributes of rooms. To do so would eliminate many rooms from analysis and create a rigid archaeological typology that is not sustainable in the systemic context. Instead, hearth category and room size are treated separately, as the two most basic functional room attributes. These two basic variables pattern similarly with respect to most secondary variables (see Table 4.9).

Identification of Dwellings 23

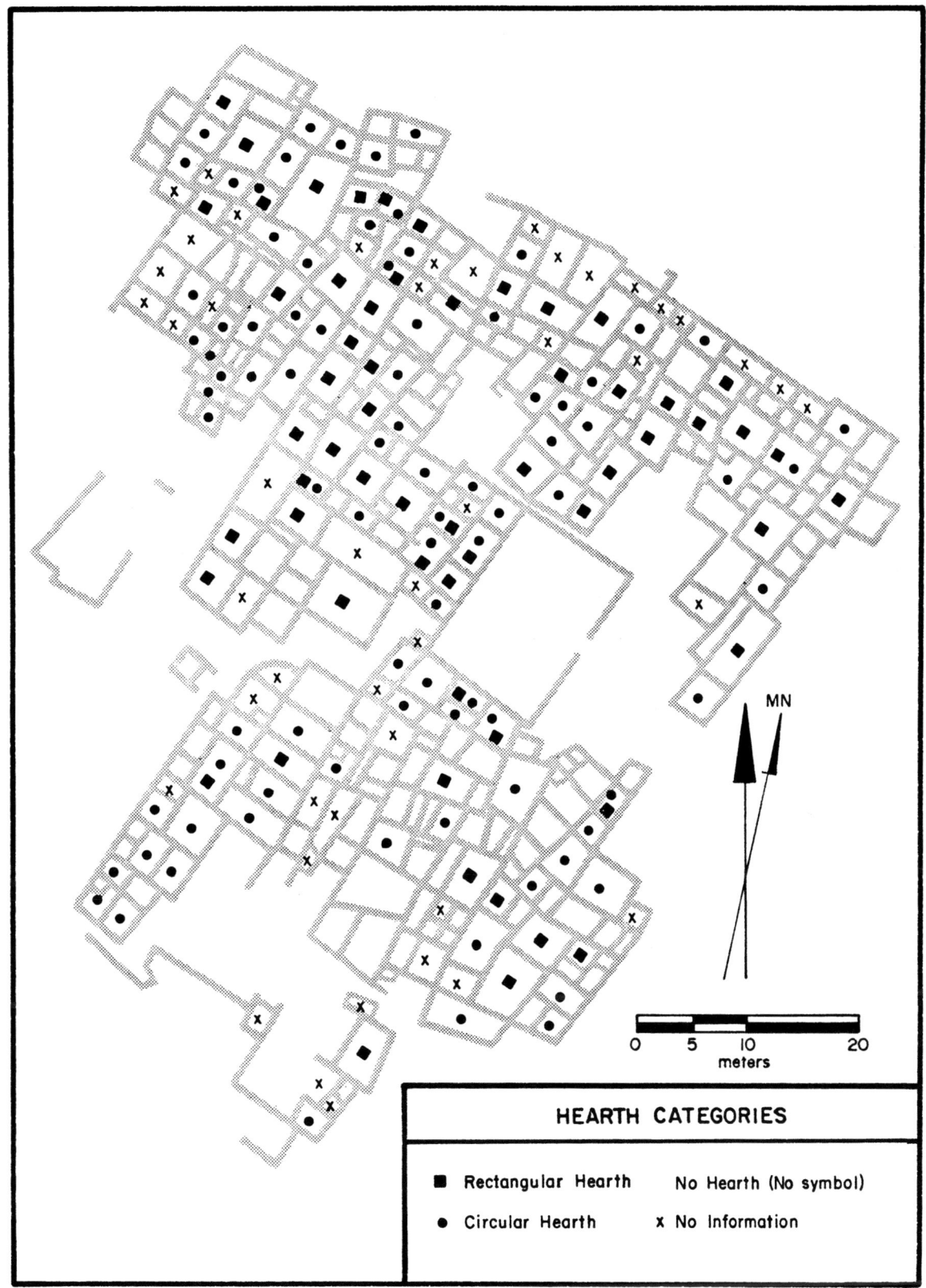

Figure 4.1. Hearth category of rooms.

The following sections discuss the results of cross-tabulations involving the three room types by hearth category. Working labels suggesting function are provided for each category.

1. Storage rooms: rooms without hearths (N = 132)
2. Miscellaneous activity rooms: rooms with circular hearths (N = 88)
3. Habitation rooms: rooms with rectangular hearths (N = 59)

Rooms without Hearths (Storage Rooms)

Tables 4.3 and 4.4 list the characteristics of rooms without hearths. Among archaeologists of the Southwest, the functional interpretation of pueblo rooms without hearths is that they were used for the storage of food and other items (see Adams 1983; Hill 1970b; Jorgensen 1975; Rohn 1965). This interpretation makes sense intuitively and fits well with what is known about historic Hopi and Zuni room function. In both archaeological and ethnographic reports (Forde 1934: 231; Powell 1972: 18) these rooms tend to be small in size.

At Turkey Creek Pueblo rooms without hearths have no temporal patterning as indicated by sherd density and construction on sterile soil. They are, then, important room types throughout the occupation of the pueblo.

Although these rooms do not vary by Room Location, they do vary by Room Group. This finding suggests that there is some areal clustering of functional room types at Turkey Creek. Certain room groups appear to specialize in storage space whereas others seem to lack it.

Rooms without hearths are best characterized by the architectural attributes they do not have rather than by those they do have. The comparative lack of hatches and vents in these rooms probably relates directly to the lack of a hearth and less need for a ventilation system. The lack of vents in such rooms is in line with ethnographic findings on storage rooms (Forde 1934: 231, 241; V. Mindeleff 1891: 208). The relative lack of posts probably relates to room size. Smaller rooms are less likely to need posts to assist in roof support, since their roof beams do not span long distances. That wall plaster is not a feature of storage rooms is consistent with findings among the Hopi (V. Mindeleff 1891: 143).

There are fewer portable artifacts of all kinds in association with these rooms than expected. Of the portable artifacts that tend to be absent in storage rooms, vessels, especially jars, are the most interesting. It is suggested that at Turkey Creek Pueblo,

Table 4.4. Rooms with No Hearth and Nominal Variables

Nominal variables	Rooms with No Hearth More than expected with	Rooms with No Hearth Fewer than expected with	Varies by	No Relationship with
Size 1 (small)	*			
Room Group			*	
Room Location				*
Sterile				*
SDIGP				*
Hatch		*		
Vent		*		
Burial		*		
Plaster		*		
Multi-plaster		*		
Post		*		
Pit				*
Bin				*
Shape				*
Height				*
Basalt				*
Door				*
Vessel		*		
Bowl		*		
Jar		*		
Trough		*		
Artifact		*		
Ant. Flak.		*		
Awl		*		
Knife		*		
Proj. Point		*		

storage in jars is associated with rooms with hearths rather than with storage rooms.

In spite of their lack of attributes, storage rooms are obviously of high importance. About 46.8 percent of the rooms at Turkey Creek Pueblo are in this category. Furthermore, some of the unnumbered bins within rooms are probably no different in structure, and perhaps function, than some of the numbered small rooms without hearths. The bin areas combined with the numbered rooms without hearths comprise about 32 percent of the enclosed floor area of the pueblo. If the storage function of these spaces is correct, an impressive amount of space is devoted to the storage of food and other items. Furthermore, the temporal pattern suggests that storage space maintains its importance throughout the history of the pueblo.

Rooms with Circular Hearths (Miscellaneous Activity Rooms)

Tables 4.5 and 4.6 provide a listing of the characteristics of rooms with circular hearths. Rooms with circular hearths tend to be mid-sized; their average size is slightly larger than the pueblo average. They vary by both Room Group and Room Placement (Table 6.3), suggesting some spatial patterning. Although scattered throughout the pueblo, their concentration in certain groups and locations has implications for household

Table 4.3. Rooms with No Hearth and Continuous Variables

	% of Total Rooms	Mean Room Area (sq.m)	Mean Sherd Density Index	Mean Wall Height Index	Mean Room Shape Index
No Hearth rooms	46.8	5.50	1.44	4.11	1.53
Pueblo average		8.13	1.39	4.04	1.47

Table 4.5. Rooms with Circular Hearths and Continuous Variables

	% of Total Rooms	Mean Room Area (sq.m)	Mean Sherd Density Index	Mean Wall Height Index	Mean Room Shape Index
Circular Hearth rooms	31.3	9.33	1.41	4.05	1.45
Pueblo average		8.13	1.39	4.04	1.47

use of space, as discussed below. Briefly, rooms with circular hearths occur more frequently than expected directly bordering the Great Kiva and in the Room Groups that border the Great Kiva, Groups K and P (Fig. 5.2). Furthermore, Room Groups K and P have a multiplicity of circular hearths in some of their rooms, and the Great Kiva itself has a circular firepit (Johnson 1965: 62). This pattern suggests that circular hearths are used in ceremonial contexts. On the other hand, the broad, pueblo-wide distribution of circular hearths and the nature of the other attributes that covary with them, suggest that they are used in domestic contexts as well.

Rooms with circular hearths show a tendency to be more frequently constructed on sterile soil and less frequently on trash than expected. This occurrence suggests that these rooms tend to be constructed early. An analysis of room remodeling (Chapter 5) supports the above pattern. Circular hearth rooms appear to decrease through time in relation to rooms with no hearths and rooms with rectangular hearths.

Is this temporal shift away from circular hearth construction functional or stylistic? Although later sites in the area show a decrease in proportion of circular hearths, the within-pueblo analysis does not support the hypothesis of a simple style shift from circular to rectangular hearths. First, at Turkey Creek Pueblo there are six cases of circular hearths on the same floor as rectangular hearths, suggesting a functional rather than stylistic contrast between the two hearth types. Second, there are ten cases in which rooms with circular hearths are refloored with a new circular hearth on the late floor. Finally, there are three instances in which rectangular hearth rooms are remodeled and turned into circular hearth rooms. The subtle temporal shift away from circular hearth construction is most likely functional rather than stylistic. Whatever their function or functions, rooms with circular hearths become rarer as the pueblo becomes filled in with rooms. Apparently rooms without hearths and rooms with rectangular hearths are more essential than rooms with circular hearths.

The features that tend to co-occur with circular hearths are hatches, posts, and, perhaps, burials. Hatches tend to occur with firepits of either type and appear to serve both chimney and entry functions. The co-occurrence of posts and circular hearths probably reflects the relative difficulty of roof support in Room Sizes 2 and 3. Burials tend to be found in rooms with hearths of either type. Most of these within-room burials are infants and fetuses. One possible explanation for this pattern is the belief, documented ethnographically among some Pueblo groups, that deceased infants may be reincarnated into the mother (Parsons 1939: 71).

Rooms with circular hearths co-occur with most of the items used in the study of portable artifacts. The presence of trough metates suggests that grinding was an activity in circular hearth rooms or on their roofs. Both jars and bowls are found more often than expected in rooms with circular hearths, suggesting that storage, cooking, or serving of food and water are possible activities in these rooms.

The presence of floor artifacts is more frequent than expected. Awls, drills, knives, and particularly projectile points tend to be found (Table D.6). These artifacts suggest that some manufacturing activities occurred in rooms with circular hearths. Shaft straighteners tend not to be found in these rooms (Table D.6), and antler flakers, axes, and hoes show no relationship with them. All patterns involving these eight individual

Table 4.6. Rooms with Circular Hearths and Nominal Variables

	Rooms with Circular Hearths			
Nominal variables	More than expected with	Fewer than expected with	Varies by	No relationship with
Size 2 (Mid-sized)	*			
Room Group			*	
Room Location			*	
Interior		*		
Exterior	*			
Kiva	*			
Plaza 1		*		
Sterile	*			
SDIGP				*
Hatch	*			
Post	*			
Burial?	*1			
Pit				*
Bin				*
Vent				*
Basalt				*
Plaster				*
Multi-plaster				*
Shape				*
Door				*
Height				*
Trough	*			
Vessel	*			
Bowl	*			
Jar	*			
Artifact	*			
Awl	*			
Drill	*			
Proj. Point	*			
Knife?	*2			
Shaft Straight.			*	

1. $p = 0.052$
2. $p = 0.057$

artifact types are regarded as tentative. I am more confident that artifacts in general tend to be found on the floors of these rooms. Furthermore, the presence of any of these floor artifacts is more frequent in large circular hearth rooms than in middle-sized ones. This can be reasonably explained by the observation that larger rooms in general are more likely to have artifacts on the floor than smaller rooms.

In summary, a variety of domestic activities, including grinding, cooking, serving, and food storage, and some manufacturing appear to occur in rooms with circular hearths. In addition, the spatial distribution of rooms with circular hearths suggests a ceremonial connection for at least some of them. At Grasshopper Pueblo circular hearths occur in rooms associated with ritual, manufacturing, and food processing activities (Ciolek-Torrello 1978: 198; Reid and Whittlesey 1982: 693). These hearths may be used primarily for room warmth rather than for cooking.

Rooms with Rectangular Hearths (Habitation Rooms)

Tables 4.7 and 4.8 (see also Table 4.9) list the characteristics of rooms with rectangular hearths. They have a variety of characteristics and tend to be the largest rooms in the pueblo. Most rectangular hearth rooms are in the Size 2 or Size 3 category and their average area (12.22 square meters) is much larger than the pueblo average (8.13 square meters). In addition, the room remodeling analysis (Chapter 5) suggests that there is a minimal area required before a rectangular hearth is constructed in a room. Presumably the activities taking place in these rooms require a relatively large amount of space.

Rectangular hearth rooms vary by room group, which suggests that there is a spatial contrast in function across the pueblo. Unlike rooms with circular hearths, rooms with rectangular hearths do not vary by room location (Table 6.3).

Rooms with rectangular hearths show no temporal trends; they are clearly an important room type from the beginning to the end of the occupation of Turkey Creek Pueblo. This consistent importance is underscored in the room remodeling analysis.

Fixed attributes that tend to covary with rectangular hearths are hatches, burials, plaster, multiple plaster, posts, and a slight tendency to be more square than other room types. Hatches suggest roof entry and function as chimneys in all rooms with hearths. Burials, like hatches, tend to be found more frequently

Table 4.7. Rooms with Rectangular Hearths and Continuous Variables

	% of Total Rooms	Mean Room Area (sq.m)	Mean Sherd Density Index	Mean Wall Height Index	Mean Room Shape Index
Rectangular Hearth rooms	21.0	12.22	1.24	4.26	1.36
Pueblo average		8.13	1.39	4.04	1.47

Table 4.8. Rooms with Rectangular Hearths and Nominal Variables

| Nominal variables | Rooms with Rectangular Hearths | | | |
	More than expected with	Fewer than expected with	Varies by	No relationship with
Size 2	*			
Size 3	*			
Room Group			*	
Room Location				*
Sterile				*
SDIGP				*
Hatch	*			
Burial?	*1			
Plaster	*			
Multi-plaster	*			
Shape?			*2	
Post	*			
Basalt		*		
Pit				*
Bin				*
Vent				*
Height				*
Door				*
Trough	*			
Vessel	*			
Bowl	*			
Jar	*			
Artifact	*			
Ant. Flak.	*			
Awl	*			
Proj. Point	*			
Shaft. Str.	*			
Axe				*
Drill				*
Knife				*
Hoe				*

1. $p = 0.055$
2. $p = 0.056$ (more square)

than expected in rooms with hearths of either type. The presence of postholes is consistent with the large size of rectangular hearth rooms and perhaps with their squareness. That large rooms and square rooms show a tendency to have postholes suggests that postholes indicate roof supports. Both relatively large and relatively square rooms would be spanned by long beams that might require post support. In general, rectangular hearth rooms, with their large size, tendency to be plastered, and squarish shape, appear to be more formal and finished than other room types.

Rooms with rectangular hearths tend not to have basalt-based walls. Room function may contribute to this trend. The pattern suggests that rooms with basalt-based walls are storage or miscellaneous activity rooms rather than habitation rooms. Pits, bins, vents, wall height, and doors show no trends related to rectangular hearth rooms.

The results of the portable artifact tests with rectangular hearth rooms suggest that these rooms were centers for activities of many kinds. Rectangular hearths tend to occur with trough metates and vessels on the floor (both bowls and jars). At Turkey Creek, jars but not bowls tend to be found with trough metates (Table D.3). Jars may be used primarily for storage of food and water and for cooking, whereas bowls may be used primarily for serving (Hill 1970b: 49–50).

Floor artifacts tend to occur in rectangular hearth rooms. Of the eight individual artifact types used in this analysis, antler flakers, awls, projectile points, and shaft straighteners are more likely than expected to occur with rectangular hearths. The total pattern suggests that domestic activities, such as grinding, food and water storage, cooking, and serving, and some manufacturing took place in these rooms.

Possible bimodality in habitation room size was explored using the variable Rsize (Tables D.1, D.2). The only notable trends are that Size 3 habitation rooms are more likely than Size 2 habitation rooms to have vessels on the floor and, perhaps, to have hatches (p = 0.056). There appears to be little functional differentiation between the two sizes of habitation rooms.

Because of their artifact associations in other prehistoric pueblo ruins, rectangular hearths are generally interpreted as cooking hearths, and large rooms with rectangular hearths as habitation rooms (Ciolek-Torrello 1985; Ciolek-Torrello and Reid 1974; Hill 1970b: 39; Jorgensen 1975: 158; Reid and Whittlesey 1982: 692; Rohn 1965: 65). Since the Turkey Creek data are consistent with this inference, rectangular hearth rooms at Turkey Creek are interpreted as habitation rooms.

Comparisons between Habitation Rooms and Miscellaneous Activity Rooms

Any functional contrasts between rectangular and circular hearths are obscure both in the archaeological and in the ethnographic literature of the Pueblo Southwest. However, it is clear that different firepit types have different uses (Adams 1983: 49; Ciolek-Torrello 1978: 119; Hill 1970b: 46–47; Morgan 1881: 146).

Ethnographic and Archaeological Patterns

Ethnographic Hopi and Zuni information underscores the variability likely to occur both in types of cooking facilities and in the locations of such facilities. Cooking of various kinds, with various types of fireplaces, occurs on roofs (Cushing 1979: 18; V. Mindeleff 1891: 104), in living rooms (Cushing 1979: 62; James 1919: 39), in Hopi Piki rooms (Hough 1915: 23), in specialized Zuni cooking rooms (Cushing 1979: 284), and in outdoor areas (Cushing 1920: 219; Cushing 1979: 318; Hough 1915: 23; V. Mindeleff 1891: 163; Stephen 1936: 135, 481; Stevenson 1904: 365). In addition, special fireplace forms may be associated with kivas (Stevenson 1904: 62). Because Pueblo fire facilities were greatly influenced by contact with the West, it is difficult to draw inferences about prehistoric forms from what is known about ethnographic forms.

At many prehistoric pueblo sites, rectangular hearths, particularly rectangular slab-lined hearths, occur in habitation room contexts and appear to be most closely related to cooking, and circular hearths occur, at least some of the time, in ceremonial contexts such as kivas for light, heat, and noncooking activities (Ciolek-Torrello 1978, 1985; Ciolek-Torrello and Reid 1974; Hill 1970b: 41; Reid and Whittlesey 1982: 692–693; Shafer 1982: 26).

In the Point of Pines area, an interesting late development in rectangular slab-lined firepit styles involves notches in the slabs that may have facilitated holding cooking pots in place with sticks (Wasley 1952: 39; Wendorf 1950: 28–30). If this inference for the function of these notches is correct, it supports the interpretation that rectangular slab-lined hearths were cooking hearths.

In the Point of Pines region, circular hearths are found in kivas, including the Great Kiva at Turkey Creek, although they are also found in many rooms that apparently are not ceremonial. In addition, circular hearths as a style appear to have some temporal importance. Earlier kivas in the area tend to have circular firepits (Johnson 1965: 62; Olson 1959), and later kivas tend to have rectangular firepits (Smiley 1952). During the early Reserve phase in the region, both hearth types occur, but rectangular hearths turn up slightly later than circular hearths (Olson 1959: 484). Also, Reserve phase pit houses have circular hearths (Olson 1959: 482). Tularosa phase sites in the area, like Turkey Creek, have both rectangular and circular hearths (Olson 1959: 497). Circular hearths decrease in occurrence during the latest pueblo phase of the area, the Point of Pines phase, when rectangular slab-lined hearths predominate (Wendorf 1950; Wasley 1952).

The pattern of rooms being remodeled from circular hearth to rectangular hearth rooms has been noted in other sites in the region (Morris 1957: 76). This shift may reflect a room function change rather than a hearth style shift. It might, for instance, relate to changes in the household developmental cycle, such that as a community matures habitation rooms become more prevalent than miscellaneous activity rooms.

In summary, in the Point of Pines region the contrast between circular and rectangular hearths has temporal significance. Circular hearths tend to be earlier, and rectangular hearths tend to be later. However, they also show functional contrasts, which are most apparent during the middle phases when both types of hearths are used in slightly different contexts in rooms of different sizes.

Comparisons at Turkey Creek Pueblo

At Turkey Creek Pueblo habitation rooms with their rectangular hearths and miscellaneous activity rooms with their circular hearths are architecturally similar and together contrast sharply with storage rooms. Although circular hearth rooms, on the average, are smaller than rectangular hearth rooms, both can be medium (Size 2) to large (Size 3). They share

Table 4.9. Contingency Table Summary of Room Type Variables by Room Size and Hearth Category

	Storage Rooms		Miscellaneous Activity Rooms		Habitation Rooms	
	No Hearth	Size 1 (small)	Circ. Hearth	Size 2 (medium)	Rect. Hearth	Size 3 (large)
No Hearth	–	M	–	F	–	F
Circ. Hearth	–	F	–	M	–	A
Rect. Hearth	–	F	–	M	–	M
Sterile	X	X	M	X	X	X
SDIGP	X	X	X	X	X	X
Shape	X	X	X	X	more square?	X
Group	R	R	R	R	R	R
Place	X	X	R	X	X	X
Height	X	X	X	X	X	X
Basalt	X	M	X	F	F	F
Plaster	F	F	X	M	M	M
Door	X	F	X	A	X	M
Post	F	F	M	M	M	M
Hatch	F	F	M	M	M	M
Bin	X	F	X	A	X	M
Vent	F	F	X	M	X	M
Burial	F	F	M	M	M	M
Pit	X	X	X	X	X	X
Trough	F	F	M	M	M	M
Vessel	F	F	M	A	M	M
Jar	F	F	M	A	M	A
Bowl	F	X	M	X	M	X
Artifacts	F	F	M	A	M	M
Side	X	X	X	X	more north	X

M = More than expected. F = Fewer than expected.
A = As expected. X = No apparent relationship between variables.
R = Relationship exists between variables.

tendencies to have hatchways, subfloor infant and child burials, and postholes. Neither alone shows a relationship with vents, but combined they tend to have vents, whereas rooms without hearths do not. In their portable artifact assemblages both rectangular and circular hearth rooms show more evidence of domestic and manufacturing activity than storage rooms. They tend to have trough metates, which may originate either on the floor or on the roofs, and vessels and other portable artifacts on the floor.

No inferences related to the archaeological concept of tool kits can be drawn from the study of individual artifacts at Turkey Creek Pueblo. Although the analyses comparing individual artifact types and using the limited room sample (Table D.5) show almost no patterning, the analyses using the total room sample (Table D.4) produce many positive relationships among tool types. However, the cells in these tables with low expected counts are questionable, and the artifact types with relatively large samples tend to demonstrate more positive correlations than those with relatively small samples. This observation suggests that the positive correlations imply only that when one artifact is found or noted on the floor of a particular room, other artifacts are likely to be found or noted as well.

If any credence can be given to patterns relating individual artifact types to particular room types at Turkey Creek, miscellaneous activity rooms show evidence of more drills and knives than habitation rooms, and habitation rooms show evidence of more antler flakers and shaft straighteners than miscellaneous activity rooms (Tables D.6, D.7). Detailed analysis of all floor artifacts would be required before these slim trends could be supported or refuted.

ROOM SIZE

The most important variables relating to room function at Turkey Creek are hearth category and room area. Room size relates closely to room function among the Hopi and Zuni (Beaglehole 1937: 59; Forde 1934: 231, 241; V. Mindeleff 1891: 104; Powell 1972: 18; Stevenson 1904: 173, 179) and in most archaeological studies of room function (Adams 1983; Dean 1970; Hill 1970b; Jorgensen 1975; Reid and Whittlesey

1982; Sullivan 1974). A contrasting view comes from Ciolek-Torrello (1985: 46–47), who does not find room size at Grasshopper Pueblo to be as closely related to room function as in other pueblos.

Table 4.9 demonstrates that, in general, room size and hearth category pattern similarly with regard to the other variables; Size 1 rooms and rooms without hearths have similar characteristics and Sizes 2 and 3 rooms and rooms with circular and rectangular hearths have similar characteristics.

The co-occurrence of other attributes can usually be explained by their common occurrence within room types defined by room size or hearth category. For example, postholes tend to occur with hatches (Table D.1). These two attributes probably covary because both tend to be found in large rooms and in rooms with firepits (Table 4.9). Since the covariance of so many attributes is explainable by their parallel occurrence within room types, it is argued that room size and hearth category are the pivotal functional variables at Turkey Creek Pueblo. Table 4.9 clarifies the following discussion.

Spatially, room size varies by room group, as do all hearth categories, but room size does not vary by room placement. Of the room type variables, only circular hearth rooms vary by room placement.

Temporally, room size shows no relationship to room construction; all sizes of rooms are constructed throughout the Turkey Creek occupation. Again, only the circular hearth rooms do not fall into place here, since they tend to be constructed early. The room abandonment analysis shows interesting patterning. Although the overall contingency table test suggests no relationship between SDIGP and room size, the individual cells indicate that medium-sized rooms tend to be early-abandoned. This trend accords with the importance of size in remodeling behavior and the early construction tendency for circular hearth rooms. Both mid-sized and circular hearth rooms appear to have been somewhat expendable.

Room Sizes 2 and 3 have more hatches, vents, burials, plaster, and posts than expected. Multiple plaster and doors are especially frequent in Size 3 rooms. Room size appears to be more important than hearth category in determining the presence or absence of doors, bins, and, perhaps, vents. Rooms with basalt-based walls tend to be Size 1 rooms.

Bins tend to be found more frequently than expected in Size 3 rooms, since there is more space for a bin in a large room than in a small one. The only portable artifact that co-occurs with bins are trough metates (Table D.2). It is possible that the bins in these large rooms provide short-term storage for corn that is soon to be processed by grinding.

Room size and hearth category show the expected parallel patterning regarding trough metates, vessels, and artifacts on the floor. Trough metates are found more frequently than expected in Room Sizes 2 and 3, and artifacts and vessels on the floor are especially likely to be found in Size 3 rooms. Jars are absent completely in Size 1 rooms and are rare (2 cases) in rooms without hearths. Bowls show no significant patterning with room size, although they are found more often than expected in rooms with hearths.

In summary, the most important variables relating to room function at Turkey Creek are hearth category and room size. In general, more features and artifacts co-occur with larger rooms with hearths than in smaller rooms without hearths. It is in the relatively large rooms with hearths of either type that most human activity apparently occurs.

INFERENCES REGARDING THE NATURE OF DWELLINGS AT TURKEY CREEK PUEBLO

Two aspects of the analysis are helpful in defining dwellings at Turkey Creek Pueblo. These involve, first, the room types and, second, the variables relating to access into and within dwellings.

Inferences about Dwellings from Room Types

The size contrast between circular hearth and rectangular hearth rooms suggests several things. One is that the activities that take place in habitation rooms require more space than those that take place in miscellaneous activity rooms. Another is that more people use each habitation room than use each miscellaneous activity room. The latter suggestion is supported by the frequencies of the two room types. There are 88 rooms with circular hearths and 59 rooms with rectangular hearths, or about half again as many circular hearth rooms as rectangular hearth rooms. These figures are somewhat inaccurate because of room conversions and the presence of both kinds of hearths on some floors. A more precise breakdown is shown in Table 4.10.

Let us assume that each of the three basic room types is somewhat different in domestic function. Each household would need access to at least one rectangular hearth, one circular hearth, and storage space. We can now put these room types together into a hypothetical dwelling. For simplicity we exclude, for the moment, the rooms with amorphous or inadequately reported hearth types and the Class 3 rooms, and work with only the 76 Class 1 rooms, the 47 Class 2 rooms, and the 132 storage rooms. Therefore, 255 rooms are in this working sample. If the above assumptions are valid, then 18 percent of all domestic rooms are habitation rooms, 30 percent are miscellaneous activity rooms, and 52 percent are storage rooms.

Table 4.10. Number and Percent of Rooms with Hearths by Class

Class	Definition	Frequency	Percent
1	Circular hearth only	76	56
2	Rectangular hearth only	47	35
3	Both circular and rectangular hearth	12	9
	Total	135	100

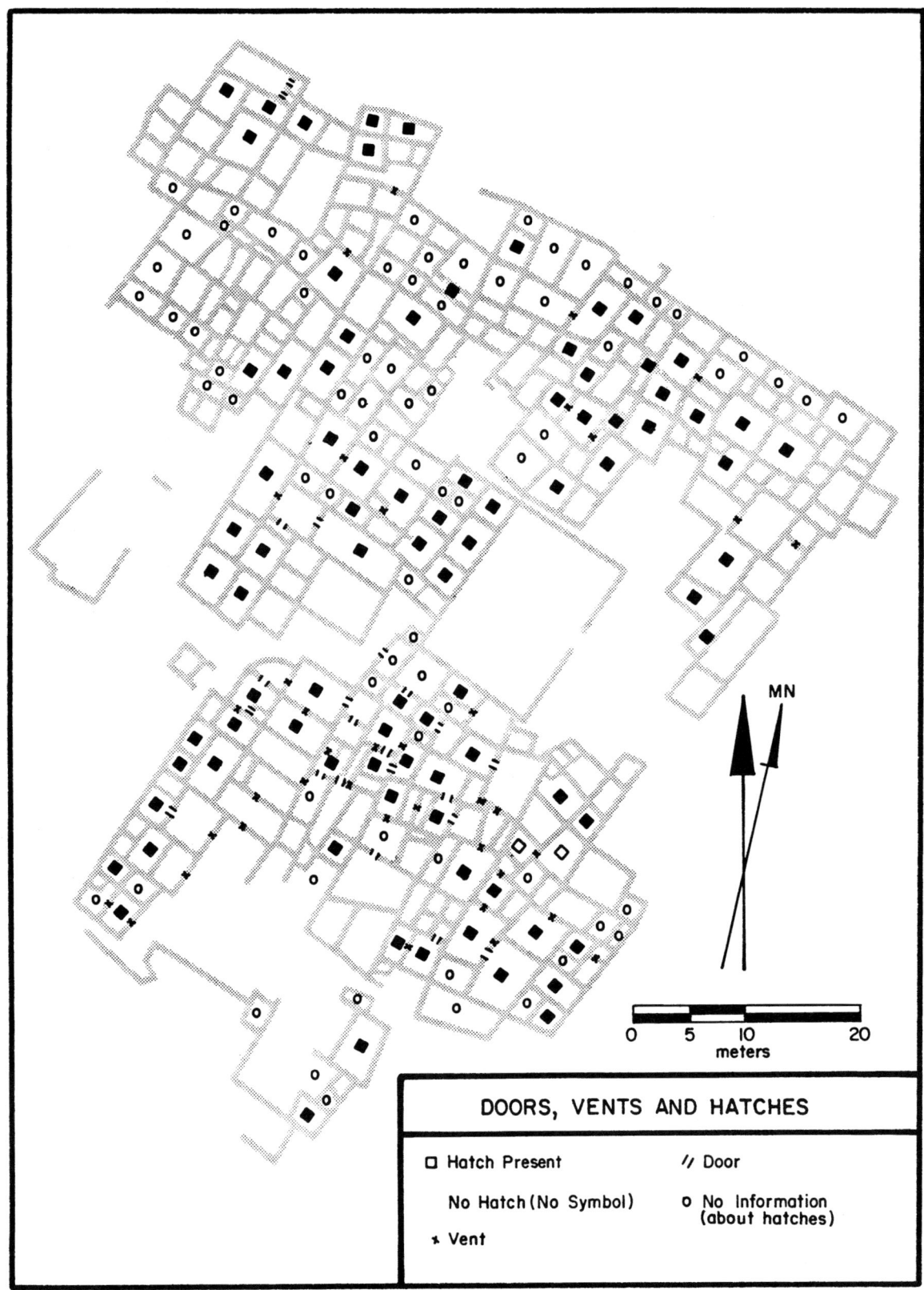

Figure 4.2. Doors, vents, and hatches.

Very roughly, then, a typical dwelling might have one habitation room, one or two miscellaneous activity rooms, and two or three storage rooms.

Their large size and relative scarcity suggest that rectangular hearth rooms are in some sense the most central rooms for domestic activity in dwellings. Other trends contrasting rectangular and circular hearth rooms support this inference. Rooms with circular hearths are more expendable than rooms with rectangular hearths. Circular hearth rooms tend to be constructed early rather than late and, in the room remodeling analysis (Chapter 5), tend to be converted to either rectangular hearth or no hearth rooms. Rectangular hearth rooms, on the other hand, are constructed throughout the life of the pueblo and are frequent end products of room conversions. In addition, they appear to be more formal or finished in appearance than circular hearth rooms. They are plastered more frequently and are somewhat more square. Finally, unlike circular hearth rooms, they are rarely of basalt-based construction, a finding with unclear but perhaps both functional and temporal implications.

All three room types vary by room group. These patterns suggest areal contrasts in the organization of domestic space. There are broad contrasts, also, between the north groups and the south groups regarding room types. Rectangular hearths occur in a higher proportion in the north than in the south (Fig. 4.1). Variability in the arrangement of rooms into dwellings at Turkey Creek Pueblo is clearly the rule.

Access to and Communication within Dwellings: Hatches, Doors, and Vents

Hatches serve as openings for smoke, light, and people. Their positive association with vents and with hearths of either kind underscores that they function, in part, to help draw smoke from rooms. That they tend to be absent in small rooms and in rooms without hearths suggests that they do not usually provide access into the storage rooms of dwellings. The covariance of hatch slabs with metates, vessels, and artifacts on the floor indicates hatch entry occurs in rooms where domestic activities take place.

Hatches show no patterning with doors. Although logically both doors and hatches can be used for access into rooms, they are not mutually exclusive in function. Doors show no relationship with hearth category and are absent in exterior and plaza walls. This patterning suggests that hatches provide the initial access into a dwelling (Olson 1959: 300; Shafer 1982: 23) and doors provide access between its rooms (see Adams 1983). Because dwelling access is apparently into the rooms in which household activity is centered, some protection for the stored goods of dwellings is provided.

Vents never occur in exterior walls nor in plaza walls (Fig. 4.2). Instead, they invariably connect two rooms. It is possible, then, that vents do not simply assist air flow, but also provide a communication channel between the rooms of dwellings.

CONCLUSION: TURKEY CREEK PUEBLO DWELLINGS

Since dwellings are not clearly bounded architectural units at Turkey Creek Pueblo, one cannot identify specific groups of rooms as dwellings. Nevertheless, one can say something about the function and organization of dwellings by devising a typology of domestic rooms and putting them together into hypothetical dwellings. I hypothesize that the typical dwelling at Turkey Creek consists of one large habitation room, one or two mid-sized miscellaneous activity rooms, and two to three small storage rooms. However, spatial contrasts in the proportions of rooms by type suggest that wide variability characterizes Turkey Creek dwellings. In terms of function, the full range of domestic and manufacturing activities apparently occurs in dwellings. Finally, the patterning of hatches and doors suggests that hatches provide initial entry into dwellings through the active, nonstorage rooms, and doors provide access between the rooms of individual dwellings.

CHAPTER FIVE

Temporal Considerations

What evidence is there at Turkey Creek for change over time? Some tree-ring dates were retrieved from the pueblo (Table 2.1), but they are not helpful for an intrapueblo temporal analysis. First, since the dates cluster around A.D. 1240, inadequate time depth information is available. Second, tree-ring dates are absent for the southern portion of the pueblo, the area that looks more recent by other criteria. Unlike tree-ring dating, ceramic analysis offers some hope for yielding intrapueblo temporal information. However, such an analysis is beyond the scope of the current study. Consequently, in the absence of these dating techniques, three less traditional ordinal measures of time are utilized.

1. The sterile-trash dichotomy (see Appendix A), for development of a relative room construction sequence and analysis of attributes associated with relative construction.
2. Room floor remodeling, for analysis of within-room change.
3. The sherd density index (see Appendix A), for development of a relative room abandonment sequence and analysis of attributes associated with abandonment.

Both the sterile-trash dichotomy and the sherd density index present some inferential difficulties. The sterile-trash dichotomy may be influenced by construction methods. When some later rooms were built, trash may have been removed before the floor was constructed, giving the appearance of early construction on sterile soil. The sherd density of an excavated room might be influenced by room function and roof function as well as by time. In particular, the presence of many pots on the roof or floor of a room at abandonment might increase the sherd density of that room relative to a room without many associated pots but abandoned at the same time. However, in the contingency table tests for Turkey Creek Pueblo, the patterning of vessels and that of sherd density operate independently, suggesting that density of sherd fill is a good indicator of relative abandonment.

The three temporal indicators offer interpretive possibilities on three different aspects of the passage of time at Turkey Creek. First, the sterile-trash dichotomy indicates earlier versus later room construction. Second, the sherd density index indicates earlier versus later room abandonment. And, third, analysis of the multiple floors of rooms indicates earlier versus later room functions within individual rooms. Logically, all three of these measures may operate independently.

THE STERILE-TRASH DICHOTOMY: A MEASURE OF RELATIVE ROOM CONSTRUCTION

At Turkey Creek Pueblo, 29.8 percent of the rooms (N = 75) are constructed on sterile soil and 70.2 percent (N = 177) are constructed on trash. If the sterile-trash dichotomy is an accurate reflection of early or late construction, then Turkey Creek more than tripled its size from the time of establishment to the time of abandonment. Considering the evidence for a rather short occupancy, much of this growth must be a reflection of aggregation instead of intrapueblo growth through reproduction.

Sequence of Construction

Figure 5.1 shows the distribution of the sterile-trash dichotomy by room and Table 5.1 lists the room groups in descending order from groups with a high proportion of room floors on sterile to groups with a low proportion. Figure 5.2 shows the locations of the room groups, Figure 2.4 indicates room numbers, and Figure 2.3 may be consulted for the locations of Area B, the pit houses, and the small kivas.

The northwest area of the pueblo (Room Groups A, B, and I) has the heaviest overall proportion of early-constructed room floors. Within these groups, room floors on sterile cluster together, as do room floors on trash. Some of the room clusters on sterile may reflect the founding dwellings of the village. Later rooms may have been added, in part, as households grew, budded off, or both. For example, Rooms 1, 2, 16, 21, 17, 30, 18, and 36 form a discrete group on sterile that may represent one large early dwelling, or perhaps several dwellings, inhabited by related households. That this group of early rooms forms a discrete unit is supported by their construction of basalt-based walls (see Fig. 6.2), contrasting with the nonbasalt-based walls of Rooms 27 and 42 to the east. Rooms 3 and 10 are also of basalt-based wall construction, but it is unknown whether their floors are on trash or on sterile. These rooms may have been built with the earliest rooms or added later.

Groups K and P are also early groups. Since the north and west walls of the Great Kiva define Room Group K in part,

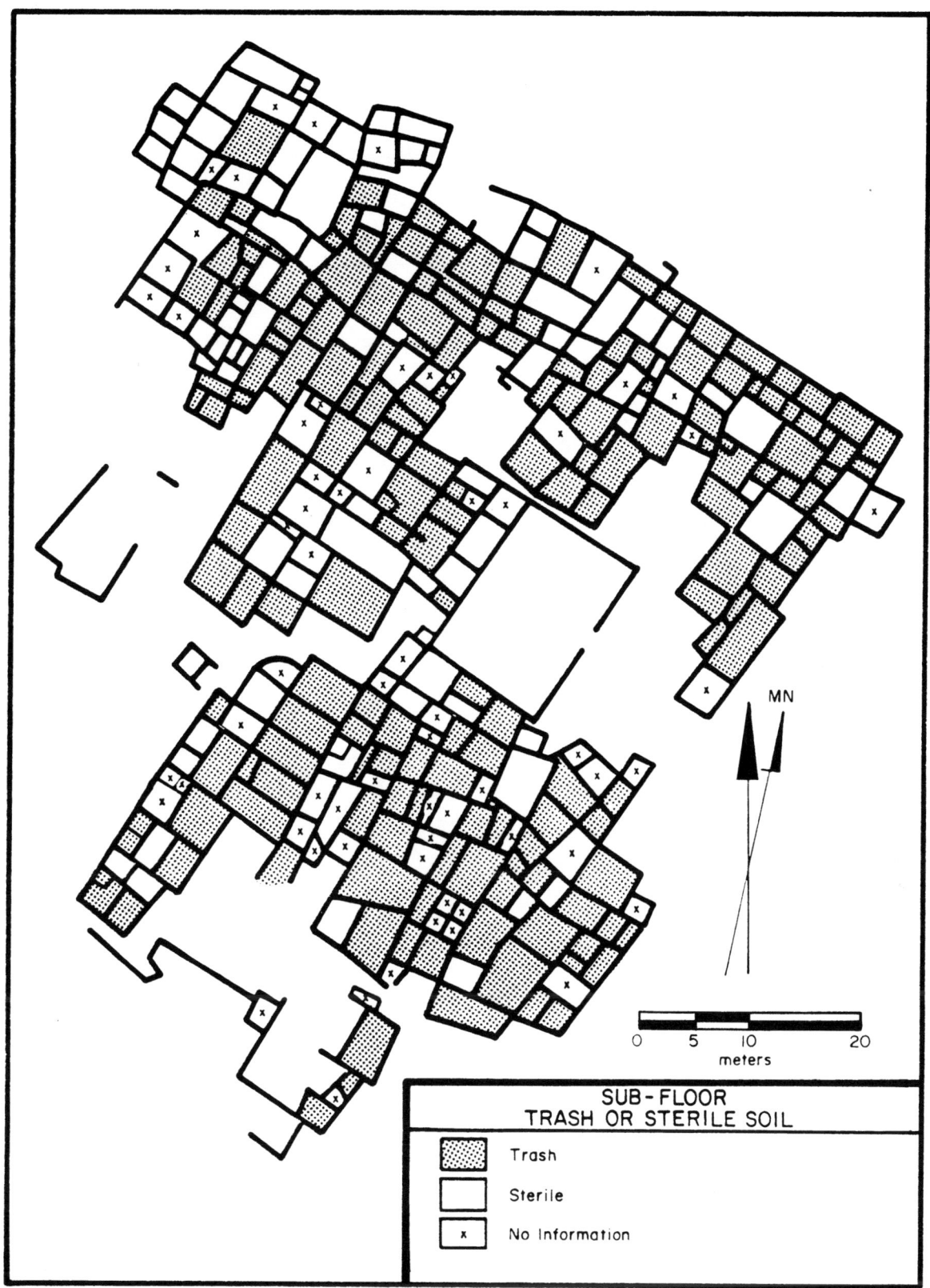

Figure 5.1. The sterile-trash dichotomy.

34 *Chapter 5*

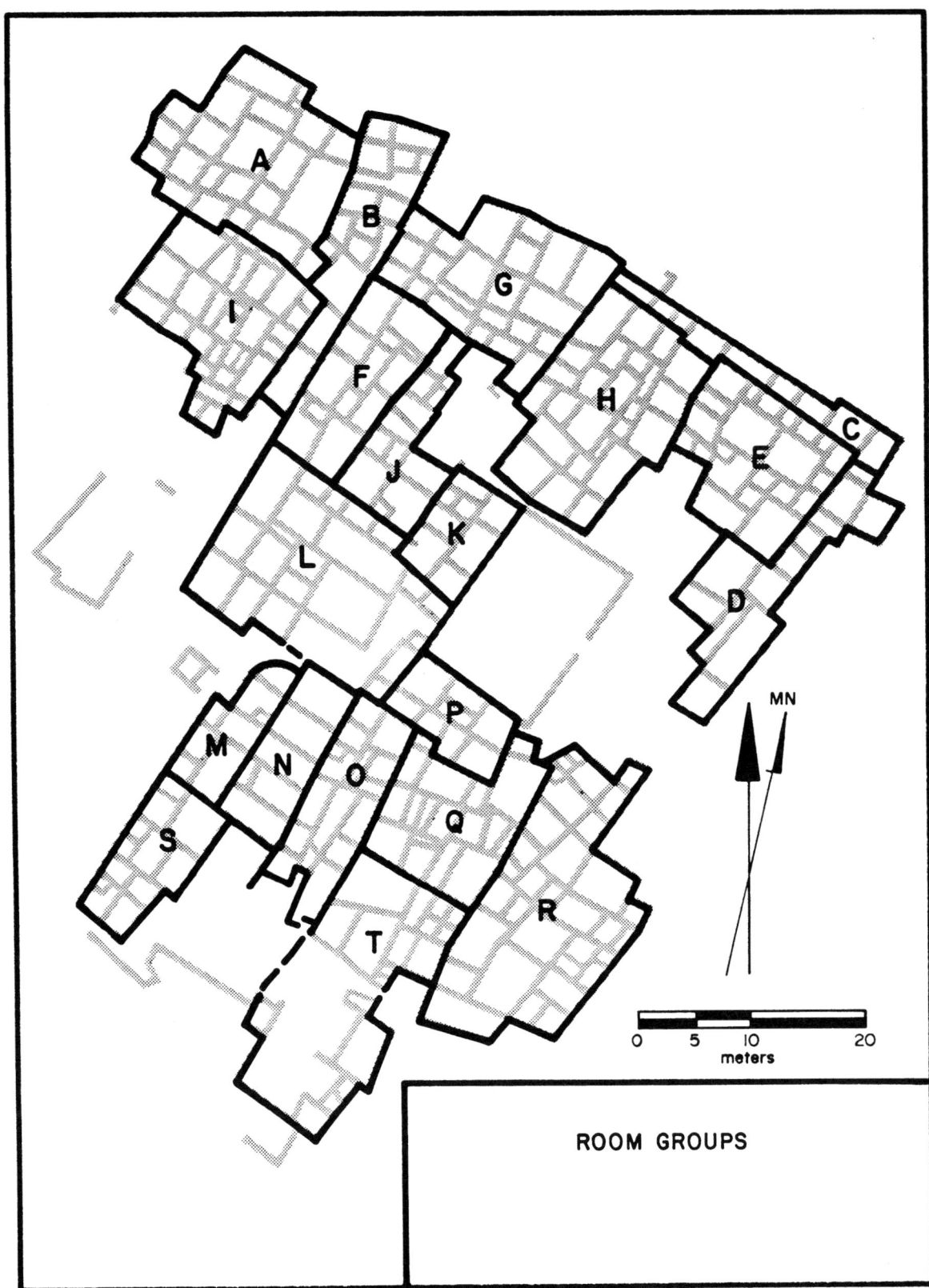

Figure 5.2. Room groups.

Table 5.1. Relative Construction Sequence by Room Group

Room Group	Percent of floors on sterile	Room Group	Percent of floors on sterile
A	82	E	21
M	60	F	20
K	50	Q	20
P	43	O	14
L	42	R	13
B	40	T	11
I	37	D	9
G	35	C	0
S	33	J	0
H	32	N	0

and the south and west walls of the Great Kiva define Room Group P in part (see Fig. 6.5), it is argued that the Great Kiva was constructed fairly early in the history of the pueblo, along with Groups K and P. Groups M and S contain small, discrete clusters of rooms on sterile soil that may reflect small early houses toward the southwest end of the pueblo. Groups L and G show some early activity, as does the north part of Group H and some rooms in Group E. Because only scattered room floors are on sterile in the eastern and southern areas of the pueblo, these areas appear to be constructed late.

Plaza 2 may be an early outdoor activity area. This plaza was originally large, but rooms eventually encroached on its space as Groups F and J were constructed. One particularly large room, Room 40 in Group A, originally may have formed part of Plaza 2, but was later cut off from it by room construction. Room 40 perhaps remained an open unroofed mini-plaza. Plaza 1 is defined later in the life of the pueblo. At an unknown time, it is separated from Plaza 2 when the southern rooms of Group H are constructed. Also at an unknown time, Plaza 1 is defined on the east by the on-trash south rooms of Group D and the north rooms of Group R. Early in the history of the pueblo, the space covered by Group N, Area B, and Rooms 276 and 181 constituted a plaza area to the southwest of the Great Kiva, paralleling the early Plaza 2 to the north and northwest of it.

Groups Q, O, and T reflect late construction to the south. Group R is most likely a late addition to the pueblo. It has many room floors on trash and a consistent long wall defining its western boundary. Group C is a late addition of storage rooms on the northeast border of the pueblo. And, finally, Group N may reflect a late use of what had been the open, plazalike area separating Groups M and O.

Pit Houses 1 through 4 and Kiva 1 appear to be contemporary with the early above-ground masonry rooms of the pueblo. Pit Houses 2, 3, and 4, and Kiva 1 are all inside the original Plaza 2, and Pit House 1 is under Room 40. Four arguments support the possibility that these nonmasonry structures are contemporary with the earliest above-ground masonry structures at Turkey Creek. First, if the nonmasonry structures were earlier than the masonry rooms and were occupied for any length of time, trash would have been generated in the northwest area such that the masonry rooms in the northwest would be constructed on trash. Instead, the opposite pattern occurs; the northwest area of the pueblo has a particularly high proportion of room floors constructed on sterile. Second, these nonmasonry rooms are positioned nicely within the original bounds of Plaza 2 and Room 40, suggesting that they were avoided by the earliest above-ground buildings. Third, other pueblos in the Point of Pines area (Olson 1959; Wendorf 1950) and elsewhere (Cordell 1984: 230) appear to have pit house structures occupied at the same time as masonry rooms, indicating that such a pattern is not unusual. Fourth, the pottery types listed in the Turkey Creek pit house reports are all present in masonry rooms of the pueblo as well. If the above inferences are correct, there is no reason to assume that any nonmasonry structures at Turkey Creek are necessarily earlier than the first masonry rooms. Therefore, Kivas 2 and 3 to the southwest and the circle of postholes under Room 222 (see Cook 1961, for an alternate view) in Group L may also represent structures contemporary with the earliest masonry structures.

In summary, the sterile-trash dichotomy forms the basis of a relative construction sequence at Turkey Creek Pueblo. The earliest constructed area of the pueblo included the northwest rooms. These are separated from the eastern parts of the pueblo by a long north-south wall. Room Groups K and P and the Great Kiva to which they are attached, Plaza 2, and a number of subterranean structures may have been part of the earliest construction as well. Growth progressed east and south. The north and west areas were filled in and the final definition of the plazas was established. The latest construction occurred to the south and southeast of the Great Kiva. Some or all of the non-masonry rooms probably ceased to function as they were gradually covered by masonry rooms later in the history of the pueblo.

Relationship between the Turkey Creek Pueblo Construction Sequence and its Tree-ring Dates

The tree-ring dates (Table 2.1) neither confirm nor contradict the construction sequence as worked out using the sterile-trash dichotomy. A contradiction, however, appears between Room 158, on sterile, and Rooms 115 and 65, both on trash, all of which yield dates from A.D. 1240 to 1243. The dates from Room 158 are not earlier than those from Rooms 115 and 65, as one would expect from the sterile-trash data. This lack of agreement might reflect difficulties with the sterile-trash dichotomy as an indicator of relative room construction. Alternatively, it is possible that stockpiling of beams began around A.D. 1240, and that these beams were used to construct later rooms as well as earlier rooms. Stockpiling wood by

Table 5.2. Transitions Between Floor Levels

Transitions			
Early room type	Late room type	Number of cases	Average room area (sq. m)
Storage	Storage	22	9.0
Misc. Activ.	Misc. Activ.	10	8.3
Habitation	Habitation	2	10.8
Storage	Misc. Activ.	3	15.3
Storage	Habitation	10	11.5
Misc. Activ.	Storage	9	8.9
Misc. Activ.	Habitation	5	10.1
Habitation	Storage	3	10.2
Habitation	Misc. Activ.	3	7.0
Total transitions		67	

prehistoric Pueblo groups is documented at other sites (Dean 1970; Graves 1983; Graves and others 1982) and for historically known Pueblo people by a Spanish observer (Schroeder 1979: 433).

Room 1, on sterile and with a reasonably good date of A.D. 1238, suggests that the earliest Turkey Creek rooms were built about this time. There are no other dates for the early northwest section of the pueblo. The latest southern areas of the pueblo yield no tree-ring dates at all and probably date later than any of the known dates would suggest.

Temporal Changes in Room Construction

The sterile-trash dichotomy suggests that there is some shift over time in the construction of rooms by hearth category (Table 4.9). Rooms with circular hearths are more likely than expected to be constructed early. On the other hand, rooms with no hearths and rooms with rectangular hearths show no such temporal shift. According to the sterile-trash distinction each of these room types is constructed both early and late in the history of the pueblo.

The tendency for the construction of rooms with circular hearths to be early is supported by the analysis of rooms with multiple floors (Tables 5.2, 5.3, and Fig. 5.3). In the process of room remodeling, rooms with circular hearths suffer a net loss over time.

Although several explanations are reasonable for this decrease in the construction of rooms with circular hearths, inferences are hampered by the lack of clear information on the functions of circular hearths. Although circular hearth rooms share many attributes with rectangular hearth rooms (Table 4.9), there are some indications that the functions of the former are more general than the functions of the latter. The rooms with circular hearths, or miscellaneous activity rooms, may be used, in part, as general habitation rooms, ceremonial rooms, sleeping rooms, and, perhaps, manufacturing rooms. It is possible that the shift away from circular hearth room construction over time relates in some way to pueblo crowding or to the developmental cycle of households, or both.

The sterile-trash dichotomy indicates that several other architectural attributes tend to shift over time (Table D.1). Notably, rooms with basalt-based walls tend to be built early. This trend may reflect a style shift or a functional shift. In the Point of Pines region, basalt-based wall construction tends to be an early attribute, common during the Reserve and Tularosa phases (Morris 1957; Olson 1959; 1960).

Storage pits show a possible tendency to be constructed early ($p = 0.062$). Pits are rare features at Turkey Creek Pueblo (N = 13), and their function is not clear. If they do reflect a system of storage, it tends to be early and probably never important.

Architectural shifts through time are not dramatic at Turkey Creek Pueblo. The general impression is one of continuity of construction techniques accompanied by several subtle shifts in emphasis over time. The most important shifts appear to involve a de-emphasis on construction of rooms with circular hearths and rooms with basalt-based walls.

TEMPORAL IMPLICATIONS OF ROOMS WITH MULTIPLE FLOORS: A STUDY IN REMODELING

Rooms with multiple floors are examined to evaluate changes in room function. About one-half of the 67 room floor transitions exhibit room type continuity between floor levels, and another one-half exhibit room type discontinuity, or change (see Tables 5.2, 5.3, and Fig. 5.3).

Conversions Involving Storage Rooms

Rooms without hearths, interpreted as storage rooms, are generally small, averaging only 5.5 square meters in floor space. Of the three basic room types, the storage rooms stand out as maintaining the most continuity between floor levels. In fact, 71 percent of the instances of functional continuity between levels involve storage rooms. Also, nearly every instance of a storage room converting to a nonstorage room (13 cases), is compensated by a nonstorage room converting to a storage room (12 cases). This consistency in storage rooms, coupled with the fact that 46.8 percent of the rooms at the pueblo are storage rooms, supports an inference that provision of ample storage space is critical throughout the occupation of the pueblo.

Table 5.3. Summary of Room Floor Transitions*

Room types	Transitions	
	From	To
Storage	35	34
Misc. Activity	24	16
Habitation	8	17

*Transitions involving miscellaneous hearths are excluded.

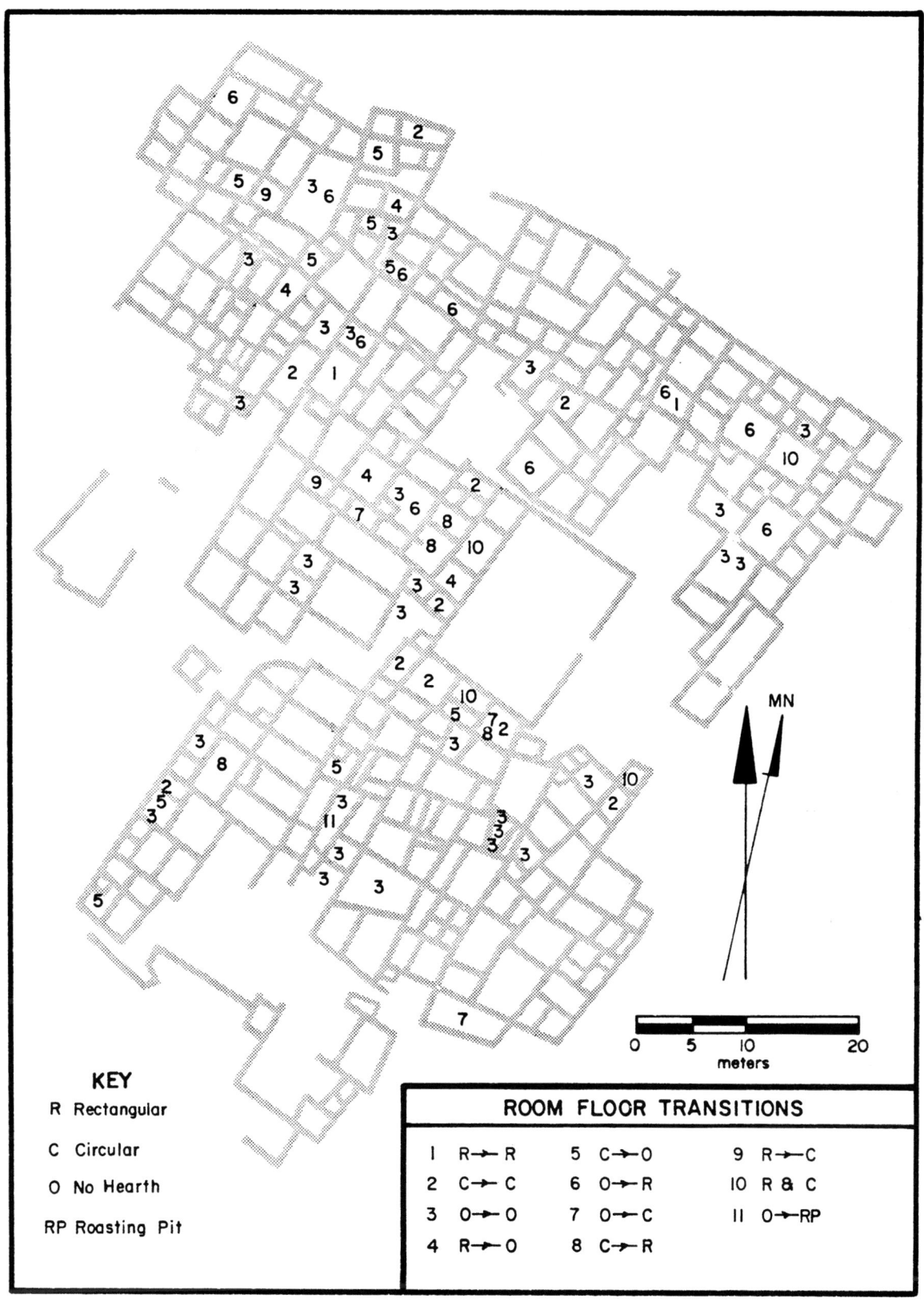

Figure 5.3. Room floor transitions.

38   Chapter 5

Table 5.4. Frequencies and Percentages of Rooms in each SDIGP

SDIGP	Frequency	Percent	Cumulative Percent
1	78	29.3	29.3
2	67	25.2	54.5
3	38	14.3	68.8
4	34	12.8	81.6
5	17	6.4	88.0
6	32	12.0	100.0

When storage rooms do change function, they are rarely remodeled into miscellaneous activity rooms (rooms with circular hearths). Instead, they tend to convert to habitation rooms (rooms with rectangular hearths). In these transitions, the important relationship between room area and room function is underscored. Only unusually large storage rooms, averaging 11.5 square meters, are so remodeled.

Conversions Involving Miscellaneous Activity Rooms

Rooms with circular hearths, the miscellaneous activity rooms, tend to be middle-sized, averaging 9.3 square meters, and they may have been used for a variety of ritual, manufacturing, and domestic activities. As might be predicted from their intermediate size, miscellaneous activity rooms exhibit the most variability between floor levels (Table 5.2). These rooms are readily remodeled into rooms with other functions or are refloored and used again as miscellaneous activity rooms. Like storage rooms, when they are transformed into habitation rooms, these rooms tend to be large for their class, averaging 10.2 square meters. It seems that habitation rooms, in particular, require a certain minimal area. Although miscellaneous activity rooms are frequently remodeled into other types of rooms, the reverse occurs rarely. Storage and habitation rooms are seldom converted into miscellaneous activity rooms. As discussed above, the tendency for miscellaneous activity rooms to be most prevalent somewhat early in the life of the pueblo is supported by the tendency for these rooms to be built on sterile soil.

Conversions Involving Habitation Rooms

Rooms with rectangular hearths have the largest average area, 12.2 square meters. These habitation rooms are stable in character (Table 5.2). Whereas miscellaneous activity and storage rooms, if large enough, are sometimes converted into habitation rooms, habitation rooms are rarely remodeled. Habitation space may be added to a dwelling by remodeling another type of room into an additional habitation room.

In summary, an analysis of transitions between room floors has uncovered several trends at Turkey Creek Pueblo. First, room area and room types are shown to be closely related. Only large storage and miscellaneous activity rooms are converted into habitation rooms. Second, a hierarchy of importance in room types is reflected in the room floor remodelings. Most expendable are the miscellaneous activity rooms, whose numbers suffer a net loss; less expendable are the storage rooms, whose numbers remain stable; and most critical are the habitation rooms, whose numbers achieve a net gain through remodeling behavior (Table 5.3). This pattern may reflect expansion within households.

THE SHERD DENSITY INDEX: A MEASURE OF RELATIVE ROOM ABANDONMENT

The Sherd Density Index is a measure of relative room abandonment. It is inferred that a room with a high SDI is relatively early-abandoned and one with a low SDI is relatively late-abandoned. The categories of sherd density (SDIGP), as used in the contingency tables, are given in Appendix A. Table 5.4 gives the frequencies of each SDIGP, from the lowest density of sherds (SDIGP 1) to the highest (SDIGP 6).

Sequence of Abandonment

For development of the Turkey Creek Pueblo abandonment sequence, the rooms are grouped into 20 Room Groups (Fig. 5.2). This grouping makes it easier to visualize the overall abandonment pattern (Fig. 5.4). The SDIGP by room group contingency table appears to be patterned ($p = 0.002$). However, since so many cells are generated, producing many low expectancy cells, the result is tentative. Nevertheless, the deviations from the expected figures in many of the cells are large enough to appear meaningful. Furthermore, the average sherd density index varies considerably among the room groups.

In Table 5.5 the room groups are ranked by average room sherd density index into three phases that demonstrate early, middle, and late abandonment trends. A few rooms with extremely high sherd density indexes are deleted from the group averages, since they skew the averages upward, presenting an inaccurate picture of the mean group sherd density.

A comparison of the abandonment sequence (Table 5.5) with the construction sequence (Table 5.1) shows that early-abandoned rooms tend to group to the north with the early-constructed rooms. The average sherd density index for all of the north rooms is 1.62, and that for the south rooms is 1.14. Wholesale abandonment of the north rooms is not suggested by the pattern, since low sherd density rooms are scattered throughout the north groups. Nor are the south rooms all late-abandoned, since high sherd density rooms are scattered throughout the south groups, as well. SDIGP and room placement show no significant relationship.

The contingency table test concerning the relationship between the sterile-trash dichotomy (room construction) and SDIGP (room abandonment) shows no clear relationship.

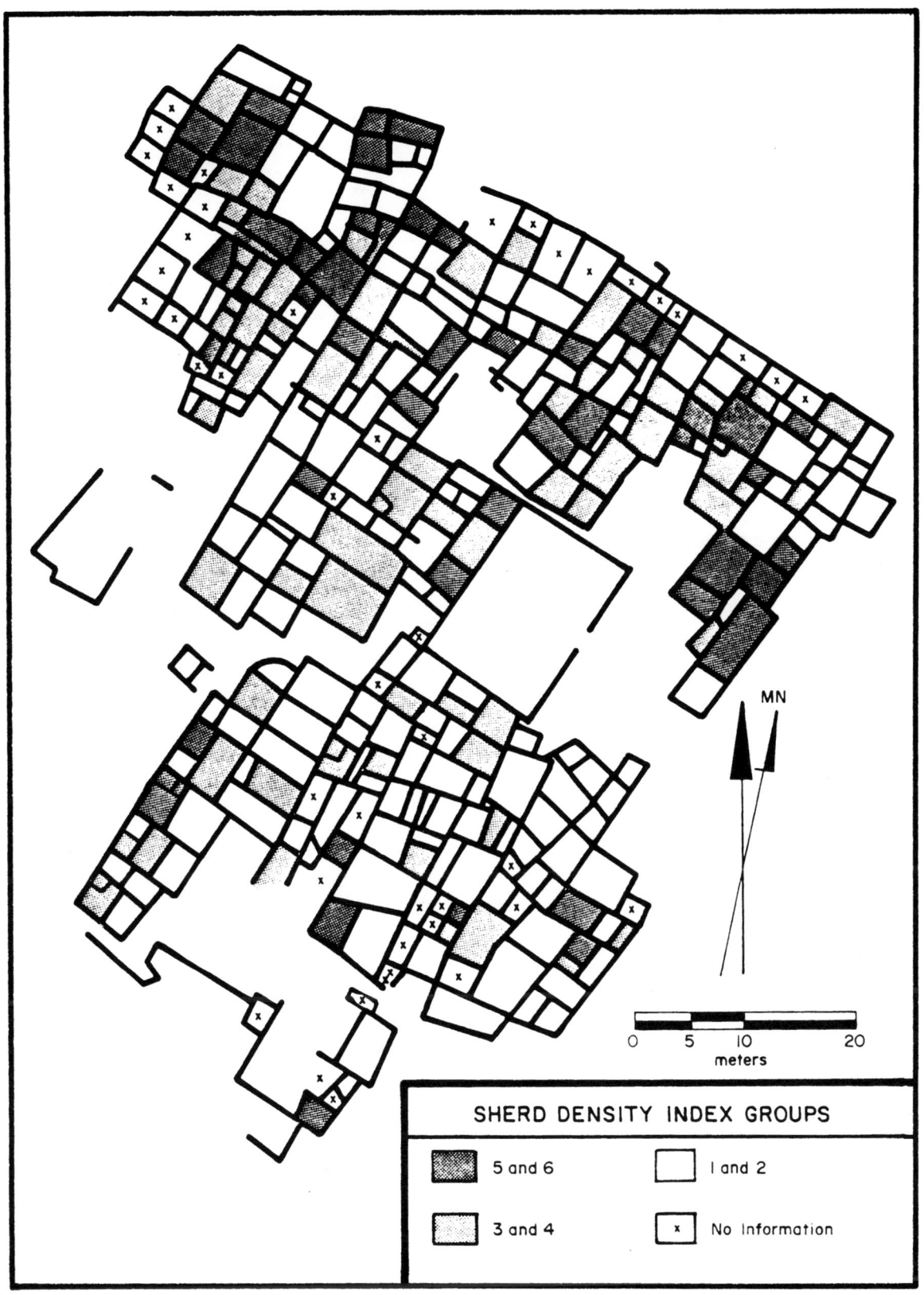

Figure 5.4. Sherd density index groups.

Table 5.5. Relative Abandonment Sequence by Room Group and
Location in the North (N) or South (S) Sides of the Pueblo

Early-abandoned			Middle-abandoned			Late-abandoned		
Room Group	Av. SDI	North-South	Room Group	Av. SDI	North-South	Room Group	Av. SDI	North-South
A	1.97	N	M	1.35	S	P	1.03	S
T	1.91	S	I	1.32	N	O	0.98	S
D	1.90	N	H	1.24	N	L	0.92	N
B	1.65	N	J	1.23	N	R	0.82	S
K	1.64	N	F	1.19	N	C	0.81	N
E	1.59	N	G	1.17	N	Q	0.61	S
			S	1.12	S	N	0.48	S

However, individual cells suggest that there is a slight tendency for more rooms than expected in SDIGP 6, and fewer than expected in SDIGP 1, to be constructed on sterile. There is, therefore, a weak tendency for individual early-constructed rooms to be early-abandoned, as well.

Relationships between the SDI and other Variables

The ways in which sherd density interacts with other variables (Appendix D) is pivotal in terms of inferences concerning both site formation processes and systemic behavior.

Wall height shows little correlation with sherd density (Pearson's correlation coefficient for Height with pounds of sherds per square meter = +0.067). This lack of correlation rules out the possibility that wall stones were habitually internally scavenged after room abandonment to build later rooms within the pueblo. The Turkey Creek Pueblo occupants apparently dumped trash into abandoned rooms, but did not usually dismantle these rooms to reuse construction materials. On the other hand, the lack of correlation between wall height and pounds of sherds does not rule out the possibility of wall stone scavenging after the entire pueblo was abandoned by people constructing later nearby masonry pueblos.

The lack of a strong negative correlation between wall height and sherd density eliminates the worrisome possibility that the sherd density index is influenced by the deflation of room fill after the walls of a room were lowered by scavenging or tumbling.

Rooms with basalt-based walls demonstrate a relationship to SDIGP as follows:

1. SDIGPs 5–6: More basalt-based walls than expected
2. SDIGP 2: Fewer than expected
3. SDIGPs 1, 3, 4: As many as expected

This pattern suggests that rooms with basalt-based walls tend to be early-abandoned as well as early-constructed. However, apparently many of these rooms are still in use at abandonment.

Rooms with bins are most common in SDIGPs 2 and 3 (Table D.1). It is possible that bins were particularly important features during the peak of population at the pueblo. Storage space for food might have been at a premium during this time. In the Point of Pines region, in general, bins are absent during the Reserve phase (Olson 1959: 287) and common in the Tularosa phase (Olson 1959: 23, 497). They sometimes occur during the late Point of Pines phase, as well (Morris 1957: 76; Wasley 1952: 116; Wendorf 1950: 31–32). However, one completely excavated small Point of Pines phase site had no bins (Wasley 1952: 36).

Vents tend to occur in both late-constructed and late-abandoned rooms (Table D.1). It is possible that as the pueblo became filled with contiguous rooms, adequate ventilation became more difficult than previously and vents helped to cope with this difficulty.

Sherd Density, Portable Artifacts, and Patterns of Abandonment

Both vessels on the floor and artifacts on the floor tend to be frequent in early-abandoned rooms and rare in late-abandoned rooms (Table D.2 and Fig. 5.5). It is argued that this finding reflects a pattern in which the floors of early-abandoned rooms were sometimes left with artifact assemblages intact, but that the floors of late-abandoned rooms were cleared.

Vessels tend to be common in rooms with a high sherd density index and rare in rooms with a low index. Several possibilities might account for this pattern. First, rooms may have been abandoned at the death of an adult occupant, left intact, but used for dumping trash. Second, burned rooms may have been abandoned and filled with trash. Eleven of the rooms with vessels on the floor were burned (Fig. 6.6). A third possibility is that some households moved away from the pueblo before its final abandonment and left vessels behind. Leaving vessels and other de facto refuse on the floors of abandoned rooms was customary at the end of the Point of Pines phase, the last phase of Pueblo occupation in the Point of Pines region. One of the latest sites had only 21 rooms, but 116 vessels had been left on

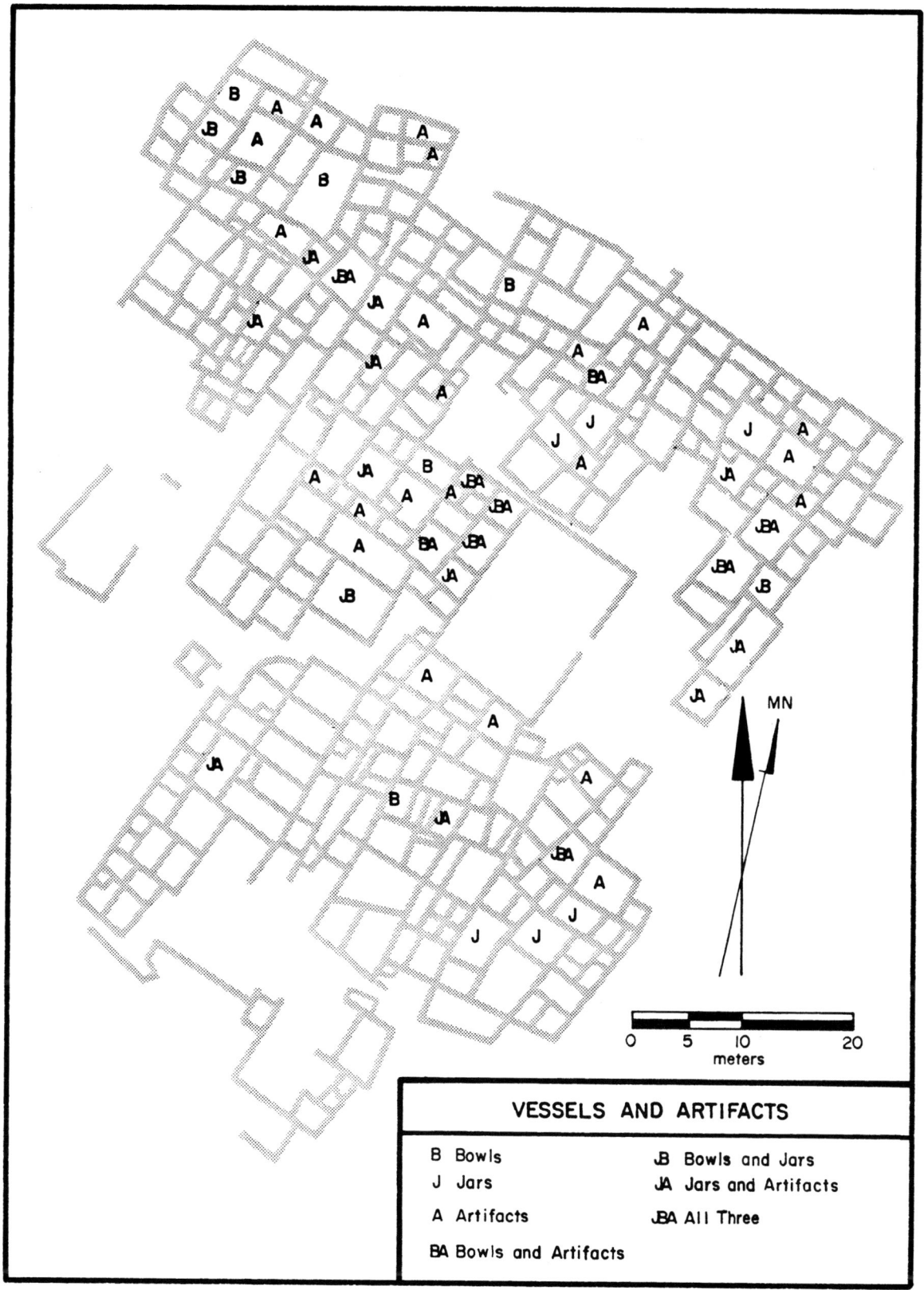

Figure 5.5. Jars, bowls, and artifacts on room floors.

the floors (Wendorf 1950: 35), and another had 12 rooms with 49 vessels on the floors (Wasley 1952: 46). Leaving functional jars and bowls behind suggests that the people who left moved so far away that they were unable to take their vessels with them. In contrast, the last occupants of Turkey Creek apparently took their vessels with them when they left. Perhaps these people moved close by and were able to carry their possessions with them.

Another explanation for the patterning of high sherd density with vessels on the floor must be considered. This is the possibility that high sherd density results largely from the heavy use of vessels inside rooms and on the roofs of rooms, rather than from trash fill in abandoned rooms. If this were the case, then the sherd density index would be a measure of vessel use rather than of room abandonment. However, the evidence supports the proposition that sherd density primarily reflects relative room abandonment rather than relative vessel use inside and on the roofs of rooms. If high sherd density measures vessel use rather than abandonment, then it should vary according to the major functional attributes, hearth category and room size. The sherd density index does not vary with any of the three room types by hearth category (Table 4.9), nor does it vary significantly by room size (Pearson's Correlation Coefficient Test, -0.031). Sherd density, then, operates independently of room function and reflects relative room abandonment.

Like vessels, other floor artifacts tend to be present in rooms with heavy sherd density and absent in rooms with light sherd density (Table D.2). This finding suggests that artifacts in floor contact, at least in part, might simply reflect the beginnings of trash fill in early-abandoned rooms rather than behaviorally meaningful floor artifacts (see Schiffer 1985). Alternatively, artifacts on the floor might be de facto refuse left in early-abandoned rooms that were later filled with trash. If so, these artifacts were not retrieved by their owners or scavenged. Eleven rooms with artifacts on the floor were burned and probably represent good in situ floor assemblages.

If artifacts on the floor are simply trash, then high sherd density and floor artifacts should behave similarly with regard to other attributes. However, the patterning of the sherd density index and the presence or absence of floor artifacts in relationship to other variables is not parallel (see Appendix D and Table 4.9). SDIGP and floor artifacts are similar in pattern regarding 6 variables, contrast in pattern regarding 11 variables, and are indeterminate in pattern regarding 2 variables. Most importantly, SDIGP and floor artifacts relate in different ways to the primary functional attributes: room size and hearth category (Table 4.9). High sherd density shows no relationship to room size, but floor artifacts show a significant tendency to occur in large rooms. Similarly, sherd density shows no relationship to hearth category, but artifacts on the floor are more likely to be found in rooms with hearths of either kind than in rooms without hearths.

In summary, whereas some of the cases of artifacts listed on room floors may reflect the beginnings of trash fill, most cases probably have at least some functional significance related to room types. Notably, floor artifacts are more likely to occur in large rooms and in rooms with hearths than in small rooms and rooms without hearths.

Furthermore, this evidence supports the hypothesis that some early-abandoned rooms were abandoned with vessels and other artifacts left on the floor. At the last occupied sites in the region, many rooms were left this way, with heavy primary refuse of all kinds on their floors (Wasley 1952: 143; Wendorf 1950). The Turkey Creek patterning suggests that late-abandoned rooms here tended to be cleared of vessels and other portable artifacts, presumably because these last occupants moved close by and, unlike both the early-abandoners of Turkey Creek and the late-abandoners of the total region, they could easily carry away their belongings when they moved. It is possible that they moved to nearby Point of Pines Pueblo, the largest village of the region after the abandonment of Turkey Creek Pueblo.

CHAPTER SIX

Variability Across Space at Turkey Creek Pueblo and the Dual Division

The Room Group and Room Placement analyses provide an assessment of spatial variability at Turkey Creek Pueblo. Areal contrasts in function, time, style, and site formation processes contribute to this variability.

THE ROOM GROUP ANALYSIS

Twenty room groups (Fig. 5.2), defined primarily by long wall configurations (Fig. 6.1), are identified. Table 6.1 gives the numbers of rooms in each group. These groups vary greatly in the numbers of rooms included in each, and, in some cases, alternative boundary decisions between groups are as plausible as those used in this analysis. Furthermore, many of the groups can be broken down into subgroups using the long wall criterion.

The present discussion of the spatial variability of Turkey Creek Pueblo uses room groups simply as an initial tool to partition the pueblo into manageable units of contiguous rooms. It is then possible to identify functional, temporal, and stylistic dimensions of spatial variability above the dwelling level. In Chapter 7 I argue that groups of rooms separated by long walls reflect a suprahousehold level of social organization at Turkey Creek Pueblo. However, the precise boundaries between these supradwellings are probably impossible to determine.

In the contingency tables using the room group variable, the 20 groups tend to create many cells with low expected frequencies. Nevertheless, many individual cells demonstrate impressive contrasts between expected and actual frequencies. The following discussion focuses on the cells that show these high contrasts and some of the groups are combined to highlight their similarities and differences.

Groups A, I, and B: The Early Basalt Groups

These three contiguous groups form a distinct northwest appendage to the otherwise roughly rectangular outline of Turkey Creek Pueblo (Fig. 5.2). They are visually separated from the room groups to the east by a particularly long wall running north to south (Fig. 6.1). The northwest portion of the pueblo has a high proportion of room floors built on sterile, and thus forms part of the early-construction phase of the pueblo (see Fig. 5.1). Room 40 (Figs. 2.2, 2.4), with a pit house in the middle, may be an unroofed outdoor activity area serving this part of the pueblo.

This area also has a relatively high proportion of rooms with basalt-based walls (Fig. 6.2). At Turkey Creek Pueblo as a whole, rooms with basalt-based walls stand out in several ways (see Table 4.9 and Appendix D). First, they tend to be constructed early in the history of the pueblo. Second, they tend to be storage or miscellaneous activity rooms, rather than habitation rooms. Third, they tend to have low walls. Fourth, they tend to be located in exterior positions (see Table 6.3), a vulnerable situation that might be partly responsible for their low walls. Fifth, they are more common in the north than in the south division. Sixth, they are rarely plastered (Fig. 6.2) and never multiplastered. It is possible that at least some rooms with basalt-based walls were not full masonry structures but instead had a superstructure of jacal or brush (see Breternitz 1959: 55, 59; Olson 1960: 194).

Group A

Room Group A has the highest percentage of rooms on sterile (Fig. 5.1), so apparently is an early-constructed group (Table 5.1). It also has the highest average Sherd Density Index (Table 5.5), suggesting that its rooms tend to be early-abandoned as well as early-constructed. However, a number of rooms around and including Room 40 appear to be late-abandoned rooms (Fig. 5.4).

Functionally this group is unusual for its low proportion of rooms with no hearth and rooms of small size (Size 1). It appears, in other words, to be lacking in storage rooms.

The basalt-based rooms of the group tend to cluster and to correspond somewhat with the rooms built on sterile (compare Figs. 5.1 and 6.2). This pattern suggests that the earliest wall construction in Group A is basalt-based.

Table 6.1. Number of Rooms in Each Room Group

Group	Number of Rooms	Group	Number of Rooms
A	20	K	8
B	17	L	18
C	9	M	7
D	13	N	5
E	21	O	11
F	12	P	8
G	21	Q	15
H	25	R	28
I	30	S	10
J	11	T	12
		Total	301

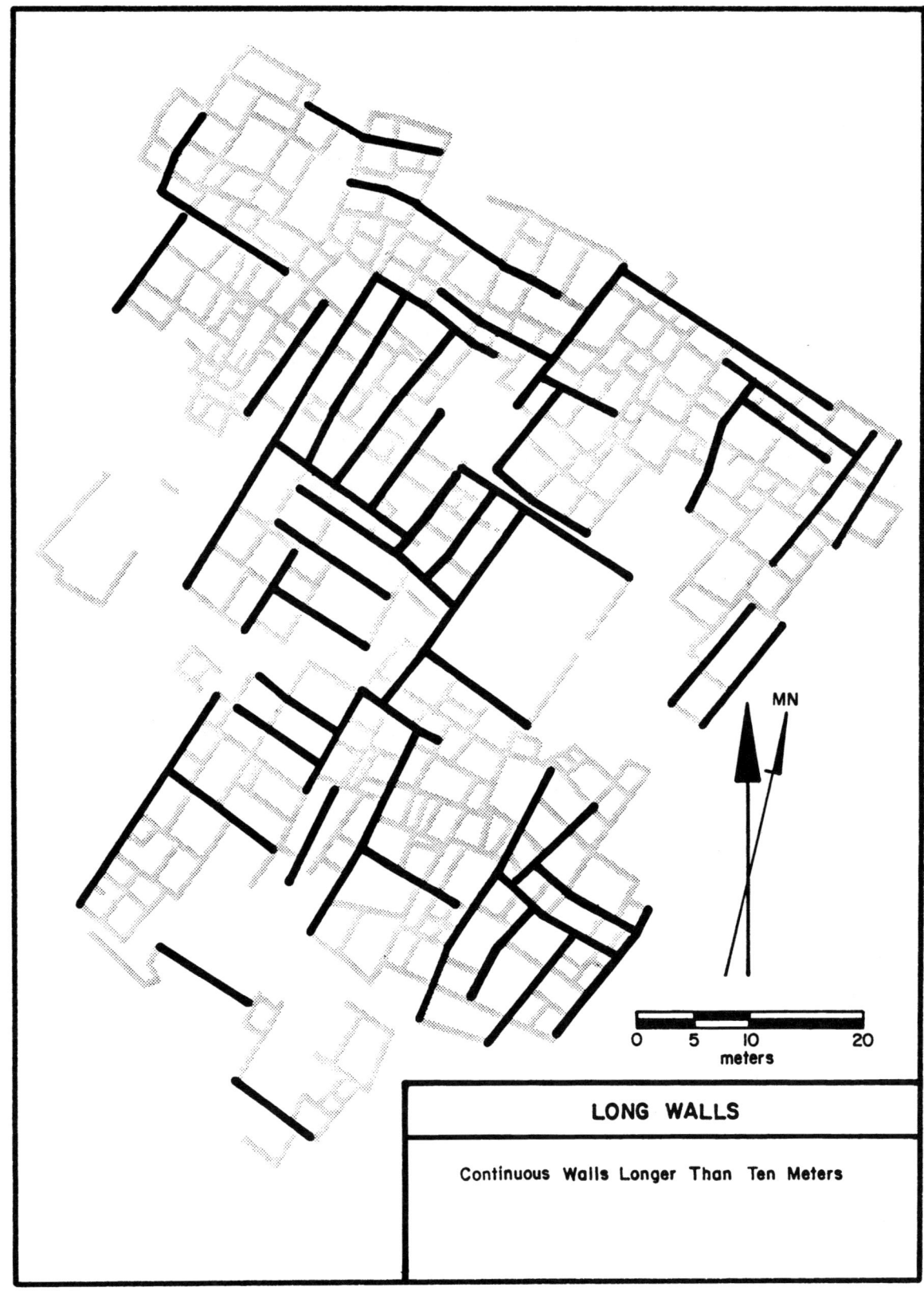

Figure 6.1. Long walls in the pueblo.

Figure 6.2. Plastered and basalt-based walls.

This group also stands out as having more posts (Fig. 6.3) and pits than expected. Posts and pits, along with basalt-based walls, may be early traits. Alternatively, the high proportion of rooms with posts might reflect the lack of small rooms, which tend not to need posts.

Group A is unusual in having many rooms with artifacts on the floor (Fig. 5.5). Vessels and axes are frequent finds. This pattern fits the observation that early-abandoned rooms tend to be left with artifacts on the floor, and that late-abandoned rooms tend to be cleared of floor artifacts. Trough metates are also common (Fig. 6.4).

Group I

Many rooms in this group were only partly excavated. However, it, like Group A, has a subcluster of rooms on sterile that appear to be early-constructed (see Fig. 5.5). According to the Sherd Density Index, Group I fits with the middle-abandoned groups (Table 5.5), suggesting that more of its rooms continued to be used later in the pueblo's occupation than those of Group A.

Functionally, Group I stands out as having fewer rooms with rectangular hearths (just one) than expected. It has as many circular hearth rooms as expected, far more Size 1 rooms than expected, fewer Size 2 rooms, and no Size 3 rooms. Group I, then, shows a lack of habitation rooms and a multitude of storage rooms (Fig. 4.1).

It is possible that Group I, so oddly lacking in habitation rooms but containing miscellaneous activity and storage rooms, served as a kind of storage and miscellaneous activity annex to Group A, which has few small rooms and few rooms without hearths. If this is true, then Groups A and I together exhibit a different use of space than most other areas of the pueblo, where rooms with no hearth, rooms with circular hearths, rooms with rectangular hearths, and all three sizes of rooms are mixed together. In contrast, Groups A and I appear to separate activities into spatially distinct room groups, one with a focus on habitation room activities and the other with a focus on storage and miscellaneous room activities.

Group I, like Group A, has a high proportion of rooms with basalt-based walls (Fig. 6.2). Its modal wall height is four courses and this low wall height may account for the absence of visible doors and vents (Fig. 6.5). Group I also shows a dearth of hatches, which would correlate with the small sizes of most of its rooms. Finally, Group I rooms tend to lack plaster, correlating with storage rooms and rooms with basalt-based walls, both of which are typically unplastered.

Unlike Group A, Group I has fewer rooms than expected with vessels and other artifacts on the floor. This, again, follows the pattern of storage rooms, in general. However, the group has as many rooms as expected with trough metates. These are most likely associated with the circular hearth rooms in the group.

Group B

Many of the north rooms of Group B appear to be early (Fig. 5.1), but its southern rooms are on trash and probably reflect the filling in of what had been open space between the early rooms of the northwest groups and the long wall that separates these groups from the rest of the pueblo. Some of the northern rooms are basalt-based, whereas the southern rooms are not (Fig. 6.2), underscoring the early nature of basalt-based wall construction. Like Group A, Group B tends to be early-abandoned.

Unlike Groups A and I, Group B has a typical mix of rooms by hearth type and room size. Its modal wall height is a low three to four courses. This tendency probably accounts for the lack of doors and plaster. Group B is not noteworthy regarding portable artifacts, but it does yield more trough metates than expected, a characteristic it shares with Group A.

Groups G and H: Expansion Eastward in the Northern Rooms

Both Groups G and H show early-construction subgroups and subgroups constructed later, as the pueblo expanded eastward and encroached on Plaza 2 (Fig. 5.1).

Group G

The north rooms and some of the east rooms of Group G are its earliest and tend to be of basalt-based wall construction (Figs. 5.1 and 6.2). The later rooms in the southwest part of the group are of full tuff construction. The rooms of Group G tend to be middle-abandoned (Table 5.5).

Functionally, Group G does not stand out as different from the pueblo as a whole. Its rooms are in the expected range in size and in presence or absence of hearths. The storage rooms in Group G tend to cluster on Plaza 2.

The walls of Group G are low (modal number of courses is three) and are partly missing in some of the north rooms, so there is a dearth of doors, vents, and plaster. The group has more posts than expected. This is both an early trait and a north trait. It may reflect either building style or deteriorating structures that needed to be supported. Group G has fewer hatches than expected and more burials (see Fig. 2.4). No nonceramic floor artifacts are listed and only one room has a vessel on the floor.

Group H

Like Group G, Group H has an early-constructed subgroup of rooms in the north. However, unlike those of Group B, the north rooms of Group H are not of basalt (compare Figs. 5.1 and 6.2). The south and central rooms of Group H are built on trash. When the southernmost rooms of Group H were constructed, they cut off Plaza 2 from Plaza 1, forming two plazas. Only a small corridor was left connecting the two. Group

Variability and the Dual Division 47

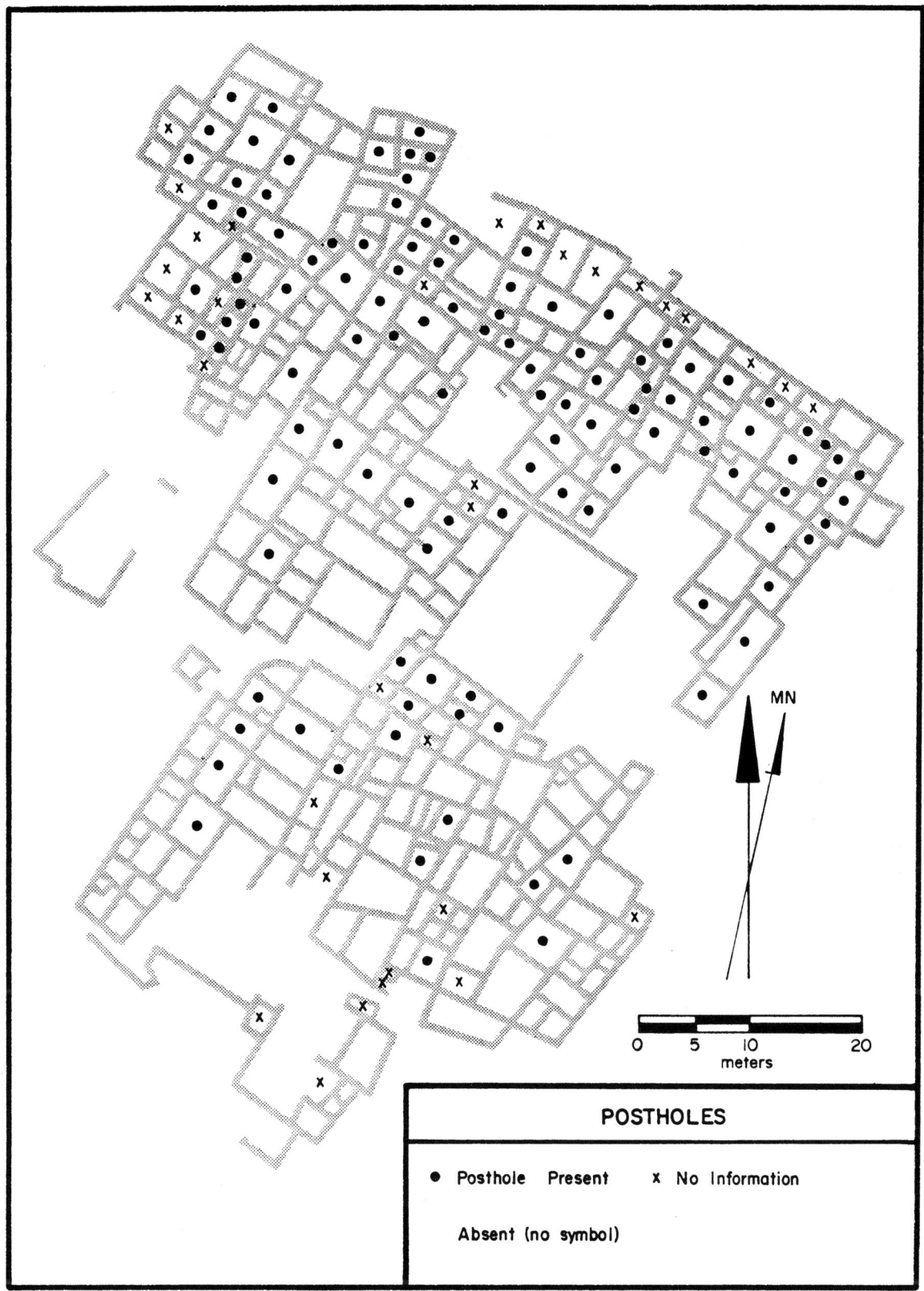

Figure 6.3. Posthole locations.

48   Chapter 6

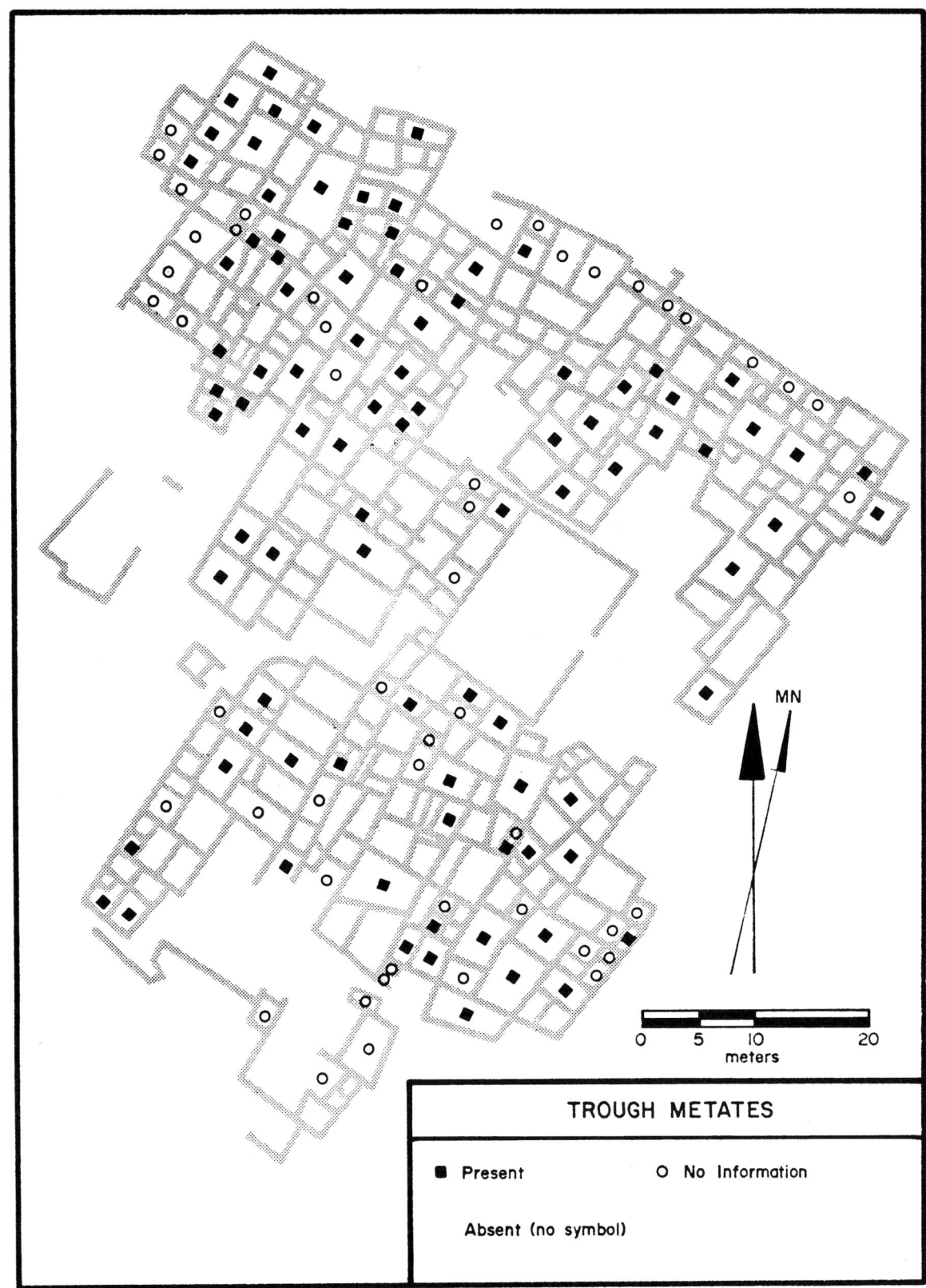

Figure 6.4. Rooms with trough metates.

Variability and the Dual Division 49

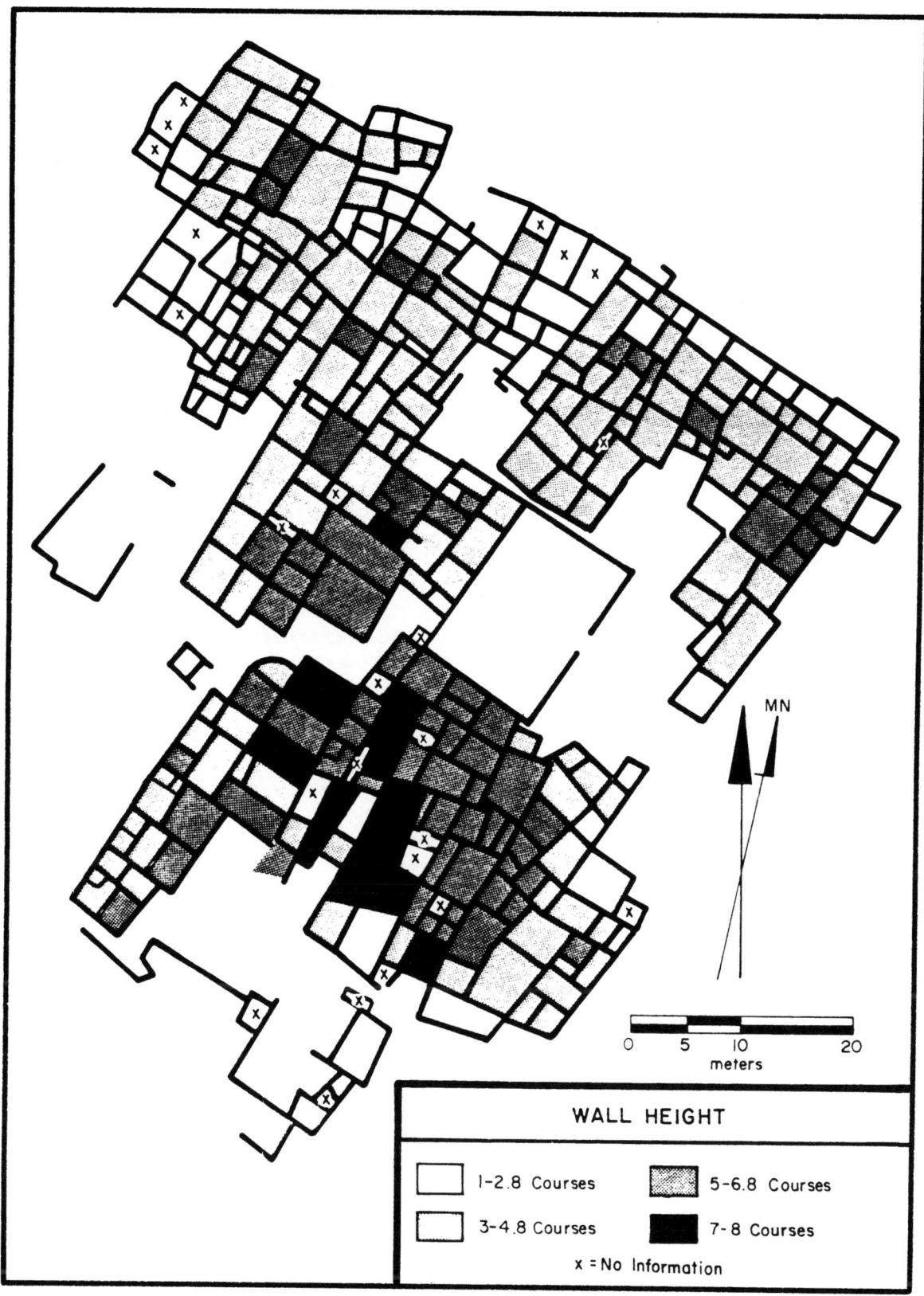

Figure 6.5. Height of pueblo walls.

H, like Group G, tends to be middle-abandoned (Table 5.5).

Group H has the usual mix of room types by size and hearth category. Storage rooms are fairly well scattered throughout the group.

The modal wall height for Group H is four courses. It has fewer doors and vents than expected, but about as much plastering as expected. It has many rooms with postholes and more hatches than expected. It has vessels and other artifacts on the floors of several of its rooms.

Groups E, D, and C: Late Construction to the Northeast

These groups reflect the eastward growth of the north rooms.

Group E

Since Group E has four rooms built on sterile, there may be some early construction in this area of the pueblo. A number of its rooms were early-abandoned, notably the large and early-built Room 75. However, other rooms are somewhat late-abandoned.

This room group is distinctive in several ways. Notably, its rooms are arranged in a more orderly fashion than those of most other groups. It has four Size 3 rooms with an especially large number of Size 1 rooms (14) arranged neatly around them. It has fewer Size 2 rooms than expected. Paralleling the size trends, it has more rooms without hearths and fewer with circular hearths than expected. Group E, then, shows a scarcity of miscellaneous activity rooms and a normal number of habitation rooms. The latter are surrounded by a multitude of storage rooms.

Another unusual characteristic of these rooms is that they tend to be more square than the rooms of other groups. The cell for Group E showed 12.4 expected Shape 1 rooms with 17 the actual number. This tendency toward squareness contributes to the visual impression of uniformity.

Group E has few rooms with basalt-based walls. It has wall heights focusing on the three-to-five course range. No doors and just one vent are recorded. There are about as many plastered rooms as expected, and three of these are multiplastered. It has more rooms with postholes than expected.

A number of rooms in Group E were abandoned with vessels and other artifacts left on their floors. Three rooms had antler flakers. Only Group K, attached to the Great Kiva and with five rooms yielding antler flakers, showed a similar possible emphasis on chipped stone tool manufacture.

Group D

This group tends to be late-constructed. The southern rooms of the group define part of the east boundary of Plaza 1. A gap between Group D and Group R to its south provides entry into Plaza 1 from the eastern exterior of the pueblo. Generally, the southern rooms of Group D tend to be early-abandoned and its northern rooms tend to be late-abandoned.

The rooms in this group, particularly its southern rooms, fall into the large Size 3 category more often than expected. There are a normal number of Size 1 rooms and fewer Size 2 rooms than expected. In this last tendency, Group D resembles Group E. It has a normal number of both rectangular and no-hearth rooms.

Since Group D, a late room group, has many rooms constructed with basalt-based walls, it is clear that although basalt-based walls tend to be early-constructed, this wall style was not completely eclipsed by full tuff construction. Modal wall height is a low three courses, typical of basalt-based construction. Doors are not in evidence here and plastered walls are rare. Group D rooms tend to have more postholes and somewhat fewer hatches than expected. It has a number of rooms with vessels and other artifacts on the floor.

Group C

Group C is a line of rooms tacked onto the north rooms of the west side of the pueblo. Most of these rooms were not completely excavated, but were trenched enough to establish that they were built on trash. Since the two hearths found were circular, and since most rooms were in the Size 2 category, one might postulate that most of these rooms were miscellaneous activity and storage rooms.

Groups F and J: The Constriction of Plaza 2

The construction of the rooms in Groups F and J constricted Plaza 2 and partially covered up the pit structures located in the original plaza area. Both have rooms that tend to fall into the middle-abandonment period.

Group F

This group has an unusually high proportion of rooms with rectangular hearths and is somewhat lacking in rooms with circular hearths. It has just three rooms without hearths. There are more Size 3 and fewer Size 1 rooms than expected. It appears, then, to focus on habitation rooms.

The rooms in Group F tend not to have basalt-based walls, and its walls are fairly high (mode is five courses). Its rooms tend to be plastered and two of these are multiplastered. It has two rooms with jars and three with other artifacts on the floor.

Group J

The room types by room size and hearth category in Group J occur about as frequently as expected. A cluster of five storage rooms occurs to the north, on Plaza 2.

Like the rooms of Group F, those of Group J tend to have full tuff walls. The modal wall height of three courses for Group J is lower than that for Group F. Because many Group J rooms are on the plaza, they may have been more susceptible to the elements and to scavengers than the more protected Group F rooms. The walls of Group J tend to be unplastered. This group has one room with vessels on the floor and three with other floor artifacts.

Group L: Constriction of an Early Plaza

Since Room Group L has five rooms built on sterile, it

shows evidence for some early construction. Its rooms tend to be late-abandoned.

Group L is structurally complex. Its east portion was originally a plaza that consisted of "Room" 181, Area B, and Room 276 (Fig. 2.4), a late room whose south and east walls were constructed on thick trash. Room 181 was probably never a room but was, instead, an unroofed remnant of the original plaza. No south wall was found during excavation of this space.

Group L has about as many of each room type by hearth category as expected. Its rooms tend to be large.

Room 222 is of basalt-based wall construction. This room has an unusual structure beneath it, consisting of a circle of postholes (see Cook 1961). The walls of Group L rooms tend to be high, with a mode of five courses. It has about as many doors and vents as expected. Its walls are generally covered with one coat of plaster. Group L has one room with vessels on the floor and four with other floor artifacts.

Groups M and S: Early Groups to the Southwest

Groups M and S have three rooms each built on sterile, suggesting that some early construction occurred in this portion of Turkey Creek Pueblo. Their rooms fit in the middle-abandonment period (Table 5.5), although the full range of abandonment is reflected in the individual rooms. Kiva 3 is located under Room 251 in Group M and Kiva 2 is located under Room 237 in Group S. Neither group has rooms with basalt-based walls.

Group M

This group has a normal mix of room types by hearth category. It has as many Size 1 and 2 rooms as expected, but just a single Size 3 room. It is possible that all or some of the large rooms to the east in Group N are associated with Group M rooms.

Group M rooms have a fairly high modal wall height of five courses. Two rooms have doors and one or two have vents. A high proportion of rooms have possible hatch entries. Five rooms have plaster but none have multiple coats of plaster. One room has a jar on the floor and one has other floor artifacts.

Group S

This group has a normal number of rooms with and without hearths, but all of the hearths are circular. Rectangular hearths tend to occur less frequently in the southern part of the pueblo than in the northern part. However, there may be additional rectangular hearths in the unexcavated south-central portion of the pueblo. It is possible that Group S is functionally specialized for a mixture of storage and miscellaneous activity room functions, as proposed for Group I in the northwest portion of the pueblo. All room sizes in Group S are represented about as frequently as expected.

Modal wall height for the rooms in Group S is four to five courses. The group has one door and more vents than expected, most opening into the unknown rooms to the east and suggesting connections in that direction. It has more hatches than expected. All but one room is plastered, most with a single coat. No vessels or other artifacts were noted on the floors of Group S rooms.

Group N: Some Fill-in Rooms

Five rooms were grouped together because of the straight north-south walls that form the west and east boundaries (Fig. 6.1). All five are large and similarly shaped rooms, constructed late. Four of the five fall into SDIGP 1, so are late-abandoned as well as late-constructed rooms. The Group N rooms appear to reflect a late filling in of an earlier open area between Groups M and O. On the other hand, several walls extending east-west are mapped as continuous and may connect the rooms of Group N to those of Group M (Fig. 2.4). The wall pattern, then, is ambiguous. It is possible that Groups M and N should be considered a single structural unit.

All but the northernmost room in Group N have hearths, three of which are circular and one is rectangular. It has no Size 1 rooms.

Group N has no rooms with basalt-based walls. Its walls tend to be in the five-to-seven course range. One room has a door, and all of the rooms have one or more vents and one coat of plaster. There are no vessels or artifacts on the floors. This pattern fits the observation that the last rooms occupied at Turkey Creek were cleared of artifacts when they were abandoned.

Groups O, Q, and T: The Late South-Central Groups

The room groups in the south-central area of Turkey Creek Pueblo share a number of characteristics. All three groups tend to be late-constructed. Groups Q and O tend to be late-abandoned as well. Group T, in contrast, has a high average Sherd Density Index (Table 5.5), although its individual rooms cover a broad range of sherd densities, suggesting they were abandoned during all periods of occupation.

All of these groups show a heavy emphasis on no-hearth rooms, with fewer circular and rectangular hearth rooms than expected. Group O and the northern part of Group T, in particular, appear to be almost exclusively devoid of hearths. It is possible that this inner core of the pueblo lacked adequate air and light for habitation room activities, so was used mostly for storage. Room sizes for these groups are generally as expected, covering the full range of sizes.

Walls based in basalt are rare in these groups. Walls tend to be high, except for the southern walls of Group T. Doors and vents are plentiful in Groups O and Q and occur about as expected in Group T, but only in the north rooms with higher walls. The walls in Groups O and Q and in the north part of Group T tend to have one coat of plaster. Postholes are rare in all three groups, and hatches occur about as frequently as expected.

Although several rooms in Group Q had items on the floor, no vessels or other floor artifacts are recorded for Groups O and T. Perhaps the rooms of groups O and T were cleared out at abandonment, or, alternatively, were stacked with corn or other goods that do not preserve well.

Group R: The Late Southeast Section

Group R is defined by a long north-south wall along its west side. It was subdivided by an east-west wall at its midsection (Fig. 6.1). Since all but three room floors are constructed on trash, it tends to be a late-constructed area of the pueblo. Its light sherd density suggests that it also tends to be late-abandoned.

Group R shows a normal mix of rooms by hearth type and room size. In general, the rooms in this group appear to be used for the full range of domestic functions.

Group R has some basalt-based walls. These tend to occur toward the exterior, in keeping with the pueblo-wide trend. Room 4 of Group R and Room 5 of Group D frame the entryway into Plaza 1. Each of these rooms has some walls consisting of just one course of basalt. It is possible that these gate rooms had superstructures of brush or jacal.

The modal wall height for Group R is four to five courses. It has fewer doors but more vents than expected. It has about as many hatches and as much plastering, mostly with one coat, as expected. Postholes are rare in Group R. Finally, the group has four rooms with vessels on the floor and three with floor artifacts.

Groups K and P: The Kiva Room Groups

Groups K and P are architecturally tied to the Great Kiva, such that two defining walls of each group are either kiva walls or extensions of kiva walls, as illustrated in Figures 5.2 and 6.1.

The rooms of Groups K and P are similarly arranged (Fig. 5.2). Group K is a group of eight rooms divided by a single wall into two rows. Group P, although less uniform, is also essentially an eight-room group divided into two rows by a single wall. Four rooms placed in Group L are probably associated with the Kiva Room Groups. Rooms 228 and 290 are attached to Group P and Rooms 192 and 170 are similarly attached to Group K (Fig. 2.4). The two rooms closest to the Great Kiva, Rooms 228 and 170, have two circular hearths in each, suggesting that they might have ritual functions.

Their structural ties to the Great Kiva indicate that Room Groups P and K were built, at least in part, at the same time, along with the Kiva. Each group has at least three rooms constructed on sterile (Fig. 5.1). This finding suggests that the Great Kiva and its two connected room groups were constructed fairly early in the pueblo's history. Two tree-ring dates come from Room 158 in Group K, a room that borders the Kiva (Table 2.1). Its room floor is on sterile and its dates, coded R, are A.D. 1242 and 1243. They indicate a construction date for Groups K and P and the Great Kiva of 1242 or 1243.

In many ways the Kiva Room Groups K and P tend to be both similar to each other and different from other Turkey Creek room groups. Their similarities suggest that the Great Kiva was constructed with a dual division in mind. Groups K and P share the following characteristics:

1. A higher percentage of rooms with circular hearths than expected.
2. A high percentage of rooms with multiple circular hearths. The pueblo average is 4.99 percent multiple circular hearth rooms. In contrast, 28.57 percent of the rooms in Group K and 35.50 percent of those in Group P have multiple circular hearths. Furthermore, each of these two groups has one room with a particularly large number of circular hearths: Room 188 in Group K has five on two floors and Room 234 in Group P has four on one floor.
3. Fewer Class 2 rooms (rectangular hearth only) and more Class 3 rooms (both types of hearths present) than expected by chance.
4. More Size 2 (mid-sized) rooms than expected. The room area averages for these groups are close to the pueblo average of 8.13 square meters. Average room area for Group K is 7.7 square meters, and for Group P is 7.79 square meters.
5. No rooms with basalt-based walls.
6. A higher percentage of rooms with hatches than expected.
7. A higher percentage of rooms with one coat of plaster, usually described as thick, than expected. No rooms in these groups have multiple plaster and just one in Group P is unplastered.
8. A higher percentage of rooms with multiple floors than the pueblo average of 22 percent. In Group K, 71 percent of the rooms have multiple floors and in Group P, 50 percent.
9. A significantly higher percentage of rooms with projectile points on the floor than expected. In fact, of only 14 rooms in which projectile points were found on the floor, 7 are in Groups K (5) and P (2).

Groups K and P significantly differ from each other in the following characteristics.

1. Sherd Density Index: Group K rooms average 1.64 and Group P rooms average 1.03. Group K rooms, therefore, tend to be early-abandoned and Group P rooms tend to be late-abandoned.
2. Wall height: For Group K the mode is four courses and for Group P, six courses.
3. Doors: Group K has no doors and Group P has five doors.
4. Group K has more floor vessels, both jars and bowls, than expected, whereas Group P has no floor vessels.
5. Group K has more rooms with artifacts on the floor than expected, whereas Group P, with just two rooms yielding floor artifacts (projectile points), has fewer.

The artifacts that turn up more frequently than expected in Group K include projectile points, knives, awls, axes, and antler flakers.

The emphasis on circular hearths in Room Groups K and P, together with the architectural ties of each group to the Great Kiva, suggest that rituals, or activities preparatory to rituals, may have occurred in these rooms. In addition, ethnographic analogy suggests that the apparent focus on ritual and on projectile points reflects male activities. Both small rooms, generally associated with food storage, and large rooms, with habitation room activities, are uncommon. Female related domestic activities, then, appear to be de-emphasized. However, it is not inferred that only ritual or only male activities took place here. On the contrary, the presence of rectangular hearths and metates suggests that food preparation occurred as well. It is possible that some of these rooms functioned as domestic rooms when ceremonies were not in progress or in preparation, on the model of the fraternity rooms among the Zuni (Parsons 1917: 191; Stevenson 1904: 227, 292). This hypothesized double domestic and ceremonial function for some or all of the rooms in Groups K and P is supported by the finding that both of these groups have several rooms that contain both circular hearths and rectangular hearths (Class 3 rooms), whereas rooms with rectangular hearths alone are rare (only one in Group K).

Although the similarities between Groups K and P appear to be functional, their differences may be temporal. The rooms in Group K tend to be abandoned earlier than those in Group P. Four rooms in Group K were burned (Fig. 6.6). Whether this fire was accidental is impossible to say, but clearly the rooms in Group P continued to function after the fire, whereas only four of the back rooms in Group K apparently continued to be used. Two of the burned rooms, 157 and 169, have high sherd densities, so were probably used for trash dumping after the fire.

The wall height contrast between Groups K and P may reflect the fire damage to Group K, within-pueblo scavenging of wall stones from the fire-damaged rooms, or both. The lack of doors in Group K most likely reflects their disappearance in the archaeological record, as some of the walls were partly dismantled or had collapsed.

That many rooms in Group K had vessels and other artifacts on floors indicates that these artifacts were not retrieved from the burned rooms after the fire. They might represent good cases of in situ floor artifacts. The items found appear to reflect a variety of activities, including food preparation, food storage, food serving, chopping fire wood, tool manufacturing, and textile manufacturing.

Aside from the presence of projectile points, Group P shows the lack of floor artifacts generally found in late-abandoned rooms at Turkey Creek. The last occupants apparently cleared out these rooms and took their belongings with them.

The unusual characteristics of Kiva Room Groups K and P, particularly their structural ties to the Great Kiva, suggest that Turkey Creek Pueblo was organized into a moiety system. This inference is discussed in Chapter 7.

ROOM PLACEMENT

Room placement contributes much to the variability observed in the above analysis of room groups. The frequencies of rooms located in or bordering on the five different placement situations are given in Table 6.2, and the contingency tests involving room placement are summarized in Table 6.3.

Room Placement and the Postabandonment Deterioration of Walls

Exterior and interior rooms contrast in a number of ways. Most striking is the tendency for exterior walls to be low and interior walls to be high. Figure 6.5 shows an almost stepwise patterning of lower to higher walls as one looks from exterior to interior walls. This pattern is what one would predict from the natural postabandonment deterioration of a contiguous-walled structure: the exterior walls would be more exposed to the elements and would tend to collapse more easily than the more protected interior walls. The higher inner walls might, in turn, retain more evidence of vents and plaster, as the room placement results for these variables suggest.

The rooms bordering on the plazas, in partially protected positions, would be expected to have neither extremely low nor extremely high walls, and this appears to be the case as well. Both plazas tend to have rooms without vents, perhaps relating to less difficulty with air circulation in rooms on the plaza than in interior rooms or, alternatively, to wall height.

The external-internal patterning in wall height probably reflects human activity as well as natural forces. If people scavenged Turkey Creek wall stones to build later pueblos, exterior walls would be more accessible than interior walls. In contrast, the lack of strong correlation between wall height and sherd density (Table D.1) suggests that scavenging of the wall stones of abandoned rooms while the pueblo was still occupied was infrequent.

That stone from early pueblos was quarried for use in later pueblos is supported by the comments of excavators of sites in the Point of Pines region. They note that early sites have meager surface wall stone debris and late sites have heavy debris, and they suggest that the wall stones from early-abandoned pueblos were scavenged for use in constructing nearby later pueblos (Olson 1959: 6; Wasley 1952: 23; Wendorf 1950: 19,

Table 6.2. Frequency and Percent of Rooms in the Room Placement Categories

Place	Frequency	Percent
Exterior	78	25.9
Interior	189	62.8
Great Kiva	8	2.7
Plaza 1	13	4.3
Plaza 2	13	4.3

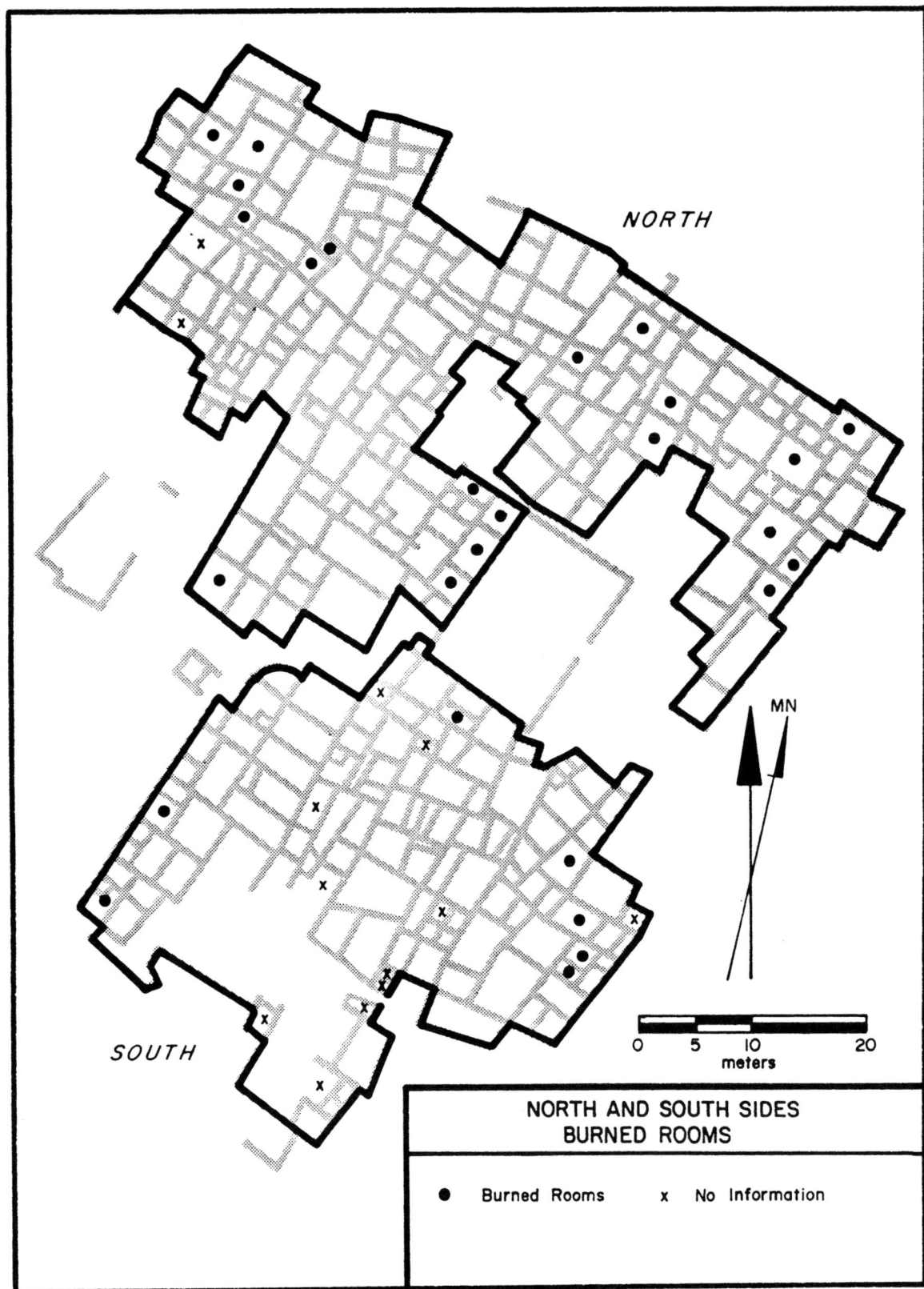

Figure 6.6. The North-South pueblo division and the locations of burned rooms.

Table 6.3. Contingency Table Summary for Room Placement*

	Placement				
	Exterior	Interior	Great Kiva	Plaza 1	Plaza 2
Miscellaneous Activ. Room	M	F	M	F	A
Vent	A	M	A	F	F
Burial	F	A	M	U	M
Plaster (1 coat)	F	M	M	A	F
Height	Low	High	Mid?	U	Mid?
Basalt	M	F	A	A	F
Artifact	F	A	M	M	A
Proj. Point	F	F	M	A	A
Ant. Flaker	F	A	M	A	A

* Only those contingency table results that indicate a relationship between the variables are included.
M = More than expected. F = Fewer than expected. A = As expected.
U = Unclear relationship between variables.

25; Woodbury 1961: 16). Hatch slabs as well as wall stones were part of this postabandonment scavenging process. A late kiva in the region sports a flagstone floor of recycled, notched, hatch slabs (Smiley 1952: 27).

Room Placement and Function

Since rooms with basalt-based walls and rooms with circular hearths tend to be more common in exterior than in interior positions and burials and floor artifacts tend to be less common, it is inferred that room function has some influence on exterior and interior room placement. Floor artifacts, however, may be less common in exterior rooms simply because they are more easily scavenged from there than from interior rooms.

The small number of rooms bordering the Great Kiva, most of which are in Kiva Room Groups K and P, contributes strongly to the patterning of several of these contingency tables. Kiva-bordering rooms tend to have more circular hearths, burials, plaster (single coat), and artifacts on the floor than expected. That several of these rooms burned contributes to the relative abundance of floor artifacts found in them.

Both projectile points and antler flakers occur more frequently than expected in kiva-bordering rooms. Projectile points are hunting tools, and hunting is traditionally a male activity. Antler flakers are used in chipped stone tool manufacture, also a male activity and one that sometimes takes place in kivas among ethnographically known Pueblo peoples (Cushing and others 1922: 256; Mindeleff 1891: 130).

The expected and actual frequencies of these artifacts in Kiva-bordering rooms and in the Kiva Room Groups K and P are given in Table 6.4.

The cases with projectile points are particularly notable from a spatial perspective. Of only 14 Turkey Creek Pueblo rooms in which projectile points are listed on the floor, 7 are in Room Groups K and P. Five out of a total of 13 cases with antler flakers present are in Group K, although none are in Group P. The spatial patterning of both of these tool types supports the inference that male-focused activities took place in the rooms and room groups bordering the Great Kiva.

Room Group and Room Placement Analysis: Conclusion

The room group analysis indicates tremendous variability in the areal dimension at Turkey Creek Pueblo. Some of the variability relates to function. The Kiva Room Groups K and P, for example, appear to have housed ritual activity. Variability across the pueblo in the organization of domestic space by functional room type is also impressive. In some areas of the pueblo, room types are intermixed and in other areas similar room types cluster together.

Temporal contrasts also contribute to variability. The rooms in some room groups tend to be built or abandoned earlier or later than those in other groups.

Some contrasts between room groups suggest subtle style preferences. Basalt-based wall structure may have some stylistic import. Likewise, the tidy square rooms of Group E are stylistically distinct.

The long wall patterns that define the room groups, in conjunction with the observed variability among these groups, suggest that a suprahousehold level of social organization exists at Turkey Creek Pueblo. This suggestion is developed in Chapter 7.

Finally, room placement contrasts contribute to areal variability. In particular, the differential impact of postabandonment processes in relatively exterior rooms, as opposed to relatively interior ones, creates wall height variability that, in turn, influences variability in other room attributes.

Table 6.4. Presence of Projectile Points and Antler Flakers in Kiva Placement Rooms and in Kiva Room Groups K and P

Artifact	N	Kiva Placement	Group K	Group P
Proj. Point	14	Expect: 1.6 Actual: 5.0	Expect: 1.9 Actual: 5.0	Expect: 0.6 Actual: 2.0
Ant. Flaker	13	Expect: 0.3 Actual: 2.0	Expect: 1.7 Actual: 5.0	Expect: 0.6 Actual: 0.0

N = total number of rooms with that artifact present on the floor.

THE DUAL DIVISION

Several lines of evidence indicate that Turkey Creek Pueblo was arranged along a principle of dual organization. There are both structural indications of duality and room attribute contrasts between the north and south rooms.

Structural Indicators of Duality

First, as discussed above, two unusual groups of rooms, Room Groups K and P, are attached to the Great Kiva (Figs. 5.2, 6.1). Together they stand out as similar to each other but different from other room groups. These two groups probably functioned in parallel ceremonial capacities related to the Great Kiva.

Second, there were two plazas at Turkey Creek Pueblo, although their locations shifted over time. The earliest two plazas were the spaces labeled Plaza 2 and Area B, both originally larger than in their final forms. The Area B plaza included Room 276, Room 181, and the rooms of Group N (Fig. 2.4). These two early plaza areas were located to the north and northwest of Kiva Room Group K and the Great Kiva, and to the west and southwest of Kiva Room Group P. Each of these plazas had a row of burials that perhaps related to them. One was in Room 187 off Plaza 2, and the other was in Room 181 off Area B. In the final configuration of the pueblo there were also two plazas, Plaza 1 and Plaza 2 (Fig. 2.4). Plaza 1 was a late outgrowth of Plaza 2 and was separated from it by the construction of the south rooms of Group H.

Finally, the rooms on the north side of the pueblo and those on the south side are segregated spatially. Figure 6.6 shows that the north and south domestic rooms share no contiguous walls. In the final configuration of the pueblo, the domestic rooms of the two sides are separated by Area B, the Great Kiva, Plaza 1, and the west entry into the pueblo. Their only architectural connection is through the Great Kiva itself, which is connected to the north rooms through Kiva Room Group K and to the south rooms through Kiva Room Group P. The Great Kiva both separates and connects the two sides of the pueblo through the two kiva room groups.

North-South Room Attribute Contrasts

The rooms in Groups A through L are considered north rooms, and those in Groups M through T are considered south rooms. Group L, in an intermediate position, was placed with the north rooms after initial analysis suggested that many of its characteristics were more like those of the north than of the south. Rooms 228 and 290 of Group L, however, belong with the south rooms.

The south side of the pueblo has 88 excavated rooms, and the north side has 178. The unexcavated portion of the south side would perhaps add 15 to 20 rooms to that side. If these unexcavated rooms are unusual in any way, they might change the results of some of the north-south contingency table trends. For the purposes of this analysis, it is assumed that these unopened rooms are similar to the other south rooms.

The results of the contingency tests for north side versus south side rooms are in Tables 4.9, D.1, D.2, and D.6. In the following discussion, the appropriate maps showing the distributions of individual attributes should be consulted.

North-South Temporal Contrasts

According to the subfloor trash patterns, there are more early-constructed rooms to the north and fewer to the south than expected (Fig. 5.1). This pattern suggests that the early construction emphasis was in the north and the later construction emphasis was in the south.

In addition, the sherd density patterns suggest contrasts in relative abandonment. There are fewer north and more south rooms in SDIGP 1 and more north and fewer south rooms in SDIGPs 5 and 6, than expected. In the mid-range abandonment groups (SDIGPs 2–4), the two sides are represented about as frequently as expected. Although north rooms were more likely to be abandoned early and south rooms were more likely to be abandoned late, there is no indication at all of wholesale abandonment of the north rooms while the pueblo was still occupied (Fig. 5.4).

One interpretation of this pattern is that the older rooms to the north became less desirable over time than the newer rooms to the south, so that late in the history of the pueblo, people preferred to live in the newer southern rooms. Perhaps the south section tended to be occupied by the offspring of older people in the north section, and older rooms in the north were gradually abandoned as the older people died. However, if this were the case, rooms built on sterile should tend to have high sherd densities and rooms built on trash should tend to have low sherd

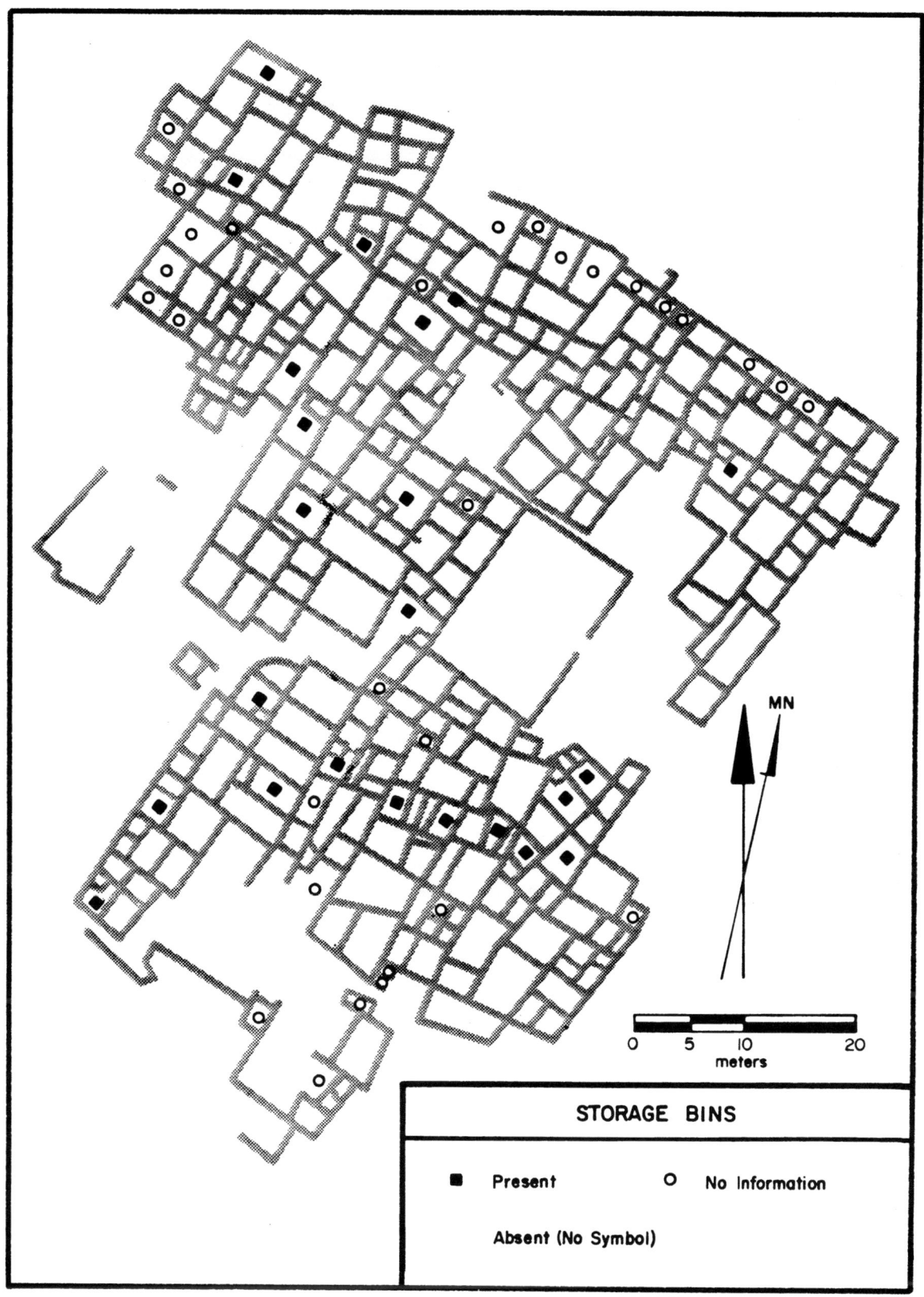

Figure 6.7. Rooms with storage bins.

densities. Although the trend is in that direction, it is not significant.

Something else must be contributing to the north-south contrast in abandonment. One possibility is that the north people as a group were in some way different from the south people. If so, then the north people tended to move to Turkey Creek Pueblo somewhat earlier than the south people and to leave it somewhat earlier, as well. The difference between the two hypothesized groups might be that they originally came from different villages, or different groups of villages, when aggregation at Turkey Creek began. They also may represent two distinguishable kin groups, the exact nature of which would be difficult to ascertain from archaeological data alone.

North-South Functional Contrasts

The north and south rooms do not contrast in their frequencies of rooms with no hearths, nor in their frequencies of rooms with circular hearths. However, they do contrast in their frequencies of rooms with rectangular hearths (Table 4.9 and Fig. 4.1). There are more rectangular hearth rooms to the north and fewer to the south than expected. It appears, then, that there is some contrast between the north and the south in the way domestic space is organized. On the other hand, the unexcavated cluster of rooms in the south might contain many rooms with rectangular hearths. Room size does not vary significantly between the north and south rooms.

North-South Postabandonment Processes

Wall height contrasts sharply between the north and south rooms (Table D.1 and Fig. 6.5). There are more north rooms with wall heights of one to four courses, and more south rooms with wall heights of five to eight courses, than expected. This contrast might be explainable in terms of the slope of the land and the location of Turkey Creek, which runs to the north of the site. It is likely that the north portion of the pueblo is more susceptible to erosion and flood damage than the south portion, and this might account for the contrast in wall height between north and south rooms.

Several other north-south room contrasts probably relate directly to the wall height contrast. South rooms tend to have more doors, vents (Fig. 4.2), and wall plaster (Fig. 6.2) than expected, and north rooms tend to have less. The survival of doors in the archaeological record is especially influenced by wall height. Doors are located only in walls of four or more courses and most are in walls of five or more courses.

Other North-South Architectural Contrasts

Rooms with basalt-based walls (Fig. 6.2), postholes (Fig. 6.3), and storage pits occur more frequently than expected in north rooms and less frequently in south rooms (Table D.1). Basalt-based walls tend to be early. However, since a number of rooms of this type of construction are built late in north room Group D, basalt-based walls may reflect a northern style preference, rather than a simple temporal style shift. Pits also tend to be early features and are uncommon, even in the north. According to the contingency table test, posts are not significantly early, although the trend is in that direction. It is possible that some posts were added to support old, sagging roofs some years after initial room construction. Hatches are found more frequently than expected to the south than to the north (Fig. 4.2), although they are common on both sides of the pueblo. Bins (Fig. 6.7) also occur more frequently than expected to the south, although the contingency table test did not quite reach the 0.05 level ($p = 0.059$).

In general, the architectural differences between the north and the south rooms are hard to distinguish from temporal contrasts. Nevertheless, the total impression is that subtle style contrasts may distinguish the two sides of the pueblo.

Portable Artifact Contrasts between North and South Rooms

Several of the contingency tests for portable artifacts show possible contrasts between the north and the south (Table D.2). These contrasts probably relate to abandonment patterns rather than to room function. There are proportionally fewer rooms with artifacts present on the floor in the south rooms and more in the north rooms (Fig. 5.5). Within the individual floor artifact types, there are more antler flakers, awls, and hoes than expected in the north, and fewer in the south. However, that so few rooms to the south have artifacts on the floor at all calls into question the validity of the patterning for individual artifacts. There are more bowls than expected on the north floors than on the south floors.

Although the contrasts related to portable artifacts are not strong, they do support the inference that the people who left Turkey Creek first tended to leave artifacts on their floors, whereas those who left last tended to clear off the floors, presumably because they took most of their belongings with them. There is a slight suggestion, then, that the north people tended to leave earlier and move farther away than the south people. It should be emphasized that the north people clearly did not leave as a group, but appeared to drift away earlier than the south people.

North-South Analysis: Conclusion

The pueblo at Turkey Creek has a dual character. Its north and south sides are architecturally divided by plazas and united by the Great Kiva. Kiva Room Group K connects the kiva to the north rooms, and Kiva Room Group P connects it to the south rooms.

The contingency table contrasts between rooms in the two sides of the pueblo reflect a variety of influences, including temporal contrasts in construction; contrasts in the functional organization of dwellings; differential erosion and other postabandonment influences on wall height; possible building style contrasts; and contrasts in the timing of, and perhaps even destination at, abandonment.

CHAPTER SEVEN

The Household at Turkey Creek Pueblo: Synthesis and Conclusions

Architectural information suggests that Turkey Creek Pueblo was organized into four levels of social units. The least inclusive unit type was the household. Households were the basic building blocks that were grouped into more inclusive social units. In the archaeological record households are reflected in hypothetical dwellings formed by combinations of rooms by type (Chapter 4). The second level of social organization was the suprahousehold. This level is reflected in subdivisions defined by long unbroken walls (Chapter 6). The third level was a dual division. The dual units are reflected as two discrete sets of domestic rooms (Chapter 6). The most inclusive unit was the total village. The village is reflected in the discrete aggregation of rooms united architecturally by the single Great Kiva. The inferred social groups associated with each type of architectural unit at Turkey Creek are summarized in Table 7.1. The following discussion addresses each level in turn and suggests possibilities concerning the nature of the social units and their functions.

DWELLINGS AT TURKEY CREEK PUEBLO: INFERENCES ABOUT HOUSEHOLDS

Because dwellings are the material reflections of households (Laslett 1972: 28), archaeologists investigate dwellings to make inferences about households. In prehistoric Pueblo villages, with their contiguous walled dwellings complicated by remodeling, dwellings are difficult to identify. However, by working with rooms as discrete physical units one can develop a room typology and then infer how rooms may be arranged into dwellings.

In Chapter 4 three kinds of domestic rooms are identified for Turkey Creek Pueblo: storage rooms (that tend to be small with no hearth), miscellaneous activity rooms (that tend to be middle sized with circular hearths), and habitation rooms (that tend to be middle sized to large, with rectangular hearths). The evidence presented in Chapter 4 further suggests that entry into individual dwellings is through hatches into miscellaneous activity or habitation rooms and that, within dwellings, doors provide access to rooms.

Variability among Households

Assuming that each household needs access to both types of hearth and to storage space, a typical dwelling comprises one habitation room, one to two miscellaneous activity rooms, and two to three storage rooms. The typical Turkey Creek dwelling thus had from four to six rooms, similar to the "average" Zuni dwelling (Stevenson 1904: 292). Variability in dwelling size, from one to eight rooms, is the norm among the Hopi and Zuni villages (Hough 1915: 100; V. Mindeleff 1891: 101; Stevenson 1904: 292; Titiev 1944: 197). Since it is impossible to arrange all of the rooms of Turkey Creek Pueblo into contiguous sets of four to six rooms with the appropriate balance of room types (see Fig. 4.1), variability in dwelling size is inferred for this village as well.

By combining information on room types and continuous and bond-abut wall structure, one can start to put together some combinations of rooms that approximate dwellings. For example, using these criteria, Rooms 5, 6, 22, and 35 of Group D (Figs. 2.4 and 5.2) comprise a four-room dwelling. However,

Table 7.1. Summary of Archaeological Evidence for a Four-level Hierarchy of Social Groups at Turkey Creek Pueblo

Level	Archaeological unit and evidence	Inferred social unit
1	Dwellings: a. room typology (3 types) b. access patterns reflected in doors, hatches, and vents	Household
2	Supradwelling Divisions: a. large groups of rooms divided by long walls b. contrasts in room attributes among room groups	Suprahousehold
3	North-South Divisions: a. two Kiva Room Groups (K and P) b. two Plazas c. no shared walls between North and South domestic rooms d. North-South contrasts in room attributes	Dual Division (moiety?)
4	Village a. architecturally discrete aggregation of rooms b. single Great Kiva	Village

contradictions and ambiguities soon turn the exercise of dwelling identification into a creative, rather than scientific, endeavor. Since dwellings share walls no clear guidelines indicate where one dwelling begins and another ends. The situation is complicated further by the large number of room remodelings (Fig. 5.3). For instance, when a miscellaneous activity room is converted to a habitation room, are there now two dwellings? In addition, there are areas of the pueblo in which certain room types are nearly absent. Some households may utilize storage or miscellaneous activity rooms that are not contiguous to their habitation rooms. Horne (1982) found this situation in a Near Eastern farming village. It is possible that the abundance of habitation rooms in Group A and the abundance of storage rooms in Group I reflect such a pattern at Turkey Creek Pueblo. Alternatively, some clusterings of like room types might signal cooperation at the suprahousehold level. Certain activities or functions such as food storage and ritual may be shared among two or more households. Another possibility is that, in some dwellings, all basic domestic activities took place in a single habitation room.

The general picture, then, is of variability in dwellings. This variability probably reflects variability in the size and structure of households. Some households perhaps occupy just a single room with a rectangular cooking hearth. These may be small, nuclear family households. Following cross-cultural data (Berkner 1972; Brown 1977; Laslett 1968; Lofgren 1974; Netting 1982; Wheaton 1975), such small households may be poorer than the larger households occupying more rooms. Turkey Creek dwellings occupied by small nuclear family households might include Rooms 189 and 184 in Group F (Figs. 2.4, 4.1, 5.2). Each of these rooms is a large habitation room with no miscellaneous activity or storage room connected to it.

Large household dwellings might be exemplified by some of the rooms of Group E, particularly Rooms 65 and 75, and perhaps 91, along with their circle of storage rooms. This group of rooms may constitute a single dwelling occupied by a multifamily household that shares an unusually large amount of storage space. This configuration also suggests that some wealth differences might be present at Turkey Creek.

One might look for evidence of multifamily households in the duplication of certain household activities within a set of rooms. If Rooms 65, 75, and 91 are indeed connected, the presence of two rectangular hearths and two circular hearths suggests that some domestic activities are duplicated. Room 75 reflects a room conversion from a large storage room to a habitation room. The late construction of a rectangular cooking hearth in this room perhaps signals the establishment of a new nuclear family within a multifamily household. A new household such as this might carry out some independent food preparation, but still share other facilities, like storage space and circular hearths, with the rest of the household.

In summary, the households of Turkey Creek Pueblo are characterized by variability. Large and small dwellings probably reflect large and small households and, perhaps, richer and poorer ones. Some households may be nuclear in configuration, and others may be multifamily or extended. Finally, there is variability in the use of space and in the arrangement of rooms by type across the pueblo. Such intracommunity variability in household organization and function is consonant with the findings of household patterns in other societies.

The Developmental Cycle of Households and Architectural Constraints

Milestones in the developmental cycle of households might show up in the archaeological record as additions to dwellings, room divisions, and room remodelings (E. Beaglehole 1937: 58; Hough 1915: 100; Kroeber 1917: 104; V. Mindeleff 1891: 102; Titiev 1944: 47). Several aspects of the Turkey Creek data are interesting from the perspective of the developmental cycle of households. One is the tendency for miscellaneous activity rooms to be built early rather than late and to be converted to storage and habitation rooms. Another is the tendency for habitation rooms to be the result of room conversions involving large rooms. It is possible that the conversions to habitation rooms reflect the establishment of new nuclear family households with their own cooking facilities. However, there is no concomitant increase in storage space. Occupants of these new habitation rooms, then, may not be completely fissioned, but instead may share storage facilities with their household of origin. A proliferation of rectangular hearths is particularly noticeable in the north part of the pueblo (Figs. 4.1, 5.3).

We may be seeing some evidence of simple crowding as the pueblo grew within the space defined by its outer walls. After a certain point in its construction, the tendency was to build inward, filling up the original plaza areas, rather than adding onto exterior walls, although the latter strategy is occasionally used as well (for example, Room 20, Group D). The construction of the Annex to the south might also reflect an attempt to cope with architectural constraints.

Mortality and Fertility

The general household literature indicates that mortality and fertility patterns have a tremendous impact on household configuration. For instance, Wheaton (1975: 606) argues that the infant mortality rate is the single most crucial factor influencing mean household size. Berkner (1972) suggests that when life expectancy rates are low and reproduction begins late, the three generation household, with both grandparents and grandchildren residing in it, cannot be achieved frequently. Short life expectancy would result in a short developmental cycle, in which an extended family household would be short-lived or truncated completely due to death in the oldest generation (Hammel 1972: 360–361; Wheaton 1975: 614–615). The three-generation extended family would be represented by just a small proportion of such a population at any one time.

Stein (1962) looks at the human skeletal material from Turkey Creek Pueblo and finds high infant mortality. However, infant mortality relative to adult mortality is probably exaggerated in the Turkey Creek burial collection. Infants are usually buried under room floors and adults in trash mounds. Since the majority of the pueblo rooms were excavated below floor and the mounds were simply trenched, the infant burial population is more complete than the adult burial population.

Bennett (1973: 9) found a high proportion of young adult females buried in the Point of Pines region, and suggests that young women probably tended to die in childbirth. In addition, at Turkey Creek Pueblo and at Point of Pines Pueblo more females than males were recovered (Robinson and Sprague 1965: 446). This relative lack of male skeletal material may mean that more males than females died away from the villages, while hunting, trading, or fighting, at distances too far to make home burial convenient.

Also interesting is that only 10 percent of Turkey Creek adults lived past age 46 (Stein 1962: 8). The potential for large three generation households would have been limited by this short life span.

Household Level Activities

The architectural study and the limited study of portable artifacts suggest that activities within dwellings include food preparation (rectangular cooking hearths, metates); storage of water, food, and other items (jars, bins, storage rooms); food consumption (bowls); manufacturing (manufacturing tools); and infant burial (under floors). If circular hearths are primarily for warming people rather than for cooking, the miscellaneous activity rooms might provide sleeping space, perhaps supplemental to that of the habitation rooms. These rooms also provide space for manufacturing and food preparation. That food is produced as well as processed at the household level is suggested by the proximity of many of the storage rooms to habitation and miscellaneous activity rooms and by the lack of hatch access to storage rooms. Finally, the mottled patterning of the sterile-trash dichotomy (Fig. 5.1) and the Sherd Density Index (Fig. 5.4) suggests that both aggregation and abandonment frequently occurred by household.

SUPRADWELLING DIVISIONS: INFERENCES ABOUT SUPRAHOUSEHOLD UNITS

Definition of supradwelling architectural units that might reflect roughly equivalent social units requires combining certain of the original 20 room groups (Fig. 5.2). Also, some of the larger groups might be broken down into two groups. Even with such adjustments, a number of systems for combining rooms into supradwelling divisions are equally reasonable. Fortunately, the establishment of supradwelling divisions precisely reflective of social realities is not essential to present purposes.

What might the suprahousehold groups, however formulated, represent in terms of the social organization and growth of the pueblo? A possible scenario is that these groups originally occupied discrete villages in the preaggregation situation (see Graves and others 1982, for a similar suggestion for the Grasshopper region). During the Reserve phase in the Point of Pines region, people lived in small settlements with a maximum of about 30 rooms. Groups of these discrete villages were united ceremonially by shared Great Kivas in their areas (Olson 1959: 484). Each village group probably exchanged food and other items, intermarried, and cooperated when threatened by outsiders or faced with other problems.

When circumstances made aggregation into a larger community beneficial, these already affiliated villages may have simply united into one large village where the households of each small village rebuilt their houses within specified subdivisions of the larger village. The relationships in the former group of villages might have continued with more or less the same cooperative arrangements as before aggregation, but with increased spatial closeness. Cushing (1979: 185) suggests that this type of aggregation occurred at Zuni, that the seven subdivisions of Zuni are survivals of the original aggregation of seven towns.

Suprahousehold Level Activities

Activities of the postulated suprahousehold groups are not clear. The three small kivas identified at Turkey Creek are covered over by dwellings, as are the four pit houses. If these were early ceremonial structures associated with ritual at the second level of organization, all or most of them ceased to function later in the occupation of the pueblo.

The suprahousehold room groups demonstrate variability in the comparative numbers and physical arrangement of room types. The households of some groups may share more functions than those of other groups. Storage rooms, especially, are good candidates for shared space among some suprahousehold units (Group E). In other suprahousehold divisions (Group H), storage rooms appear to be tied to specific habitation and miscellaneous activity rooms, suggesting that in these units, individual households tend to maintain their own storage facilities. Since the number of trash-burial mounds (eight) is too few to reflect household units and too many to reflect dual units, it is possible that each mound was tied to particular suprahousehold units, and that adult burial and trash disposal took place at the suprahousehold level.

THE DUAL DIVISION OF TURKEY CREEK PUEBLO: INFERENCES ABOUT DUAL ORGANIZATION

The dual division of Turkey Creek Pueblo suggests that its social organization may be similar to the dual organization or moiety systems of the Keresans or the Tanoans (Ortiz 1969; Parsons 1929; Dozier 1970). Dual organization among historical Pueblo groups forms a continuum of functional importance. At one end of the continuum, dual organization provides a strictly ceremonial division, especially among Keresan pueblos like Santa Ana (Strong 1979: 401). At the other end, dual division provides the basis for political as well as for ceremonial activities. For example, among the Tewa, village leadership shifts between the moieties according to season (Parsons 1929: 89).

Among various historic Pueblo groups, dual organization is sometimes reflected in residence on different sides (north or south) of a village (Jorgensen 1980: 191–192, 239; Parsons 1929: 91), in dual plazas, and in dual kivas (Dozier 1970: 155;

Parsons 1929: 89). In some Pueblos just one kiva is used by both moieties (Jorgensen 1980: 239), but the duality is physically expressed in other ways. At Nambe, for instance, the north bench of a single large kiva is used by the Winter People, and the south bench by the Summer People (Parsons 1929: 101).

At Isleta, too, there is just one kiva, but each moiety has its own special house for retreats (Ellis 1979: 358). It is possible, but would be hard to demonstrate, that the Kiva Room Groups K and P at Turkey Creek Pueblo represent moiety houses such as those at Isleta. These room groups appear to be dwellings that also were used for ritual activities. Each has eight rooms, suggesting occupation by large, comparatively wealthy households. The presence of cooking hearths, metates, and other domestic features indicates that the normal range of female-related food preparation activities took place in them. On the other hand, their connection to the Great Kiva, unusual architectural characteristics, multiple burials, and the male-related artifacts on their floors (especially, projectile points) suggest that these room groups doubled as ceremonial structures. In sum, the Kiva Room Groups may reflect both domestic activities at the household level and ceremonial activities at the dual level.

There is some evidence for residential duality at Turkey Creek Pueblo. The north-south room analysis suggests subtle temporal contrasts, minor contrasts in construction style, and perhaps contrasts in the organization of domestic space between the two groups. These contrasts may reflect preaggregation ties. The earlier Reserve phase settlement system consisted of groups of small villages affiliated with areal Great Kivas. It is possible that two such groups, with slightly different ways of doing things, aggregated at Turkey Creek.

Dual Unit Activities

Because each side of the pueblo connects to the Great Kiva through its own Kiva Room Group (K or P), it is proposed that ritual is an important function at the dual level. Ritual and food sharing are closely allied functions ethnographically and may be interwoven here. Also ethnographically, close ties exist between ritual and political leadership. It is possible that this level is also politically important, that each side of the dual division has its own leaders, perhaps residing in the Kiva Room Groups.

Room Groups K and P may be dwellings used for both ritual and domestic activities. As indicated above, each has eight rooms, comparable ritual and domestic traits, and may reflect activities at two hierarchical levels, the household level and the dual-division level.

THE VILLAGE UNIT

Beyond the fact of aggregation itself, the Great Kiva is the clearest architectural reflection of unity at the village level. Ceremony is clearly a unifying activity of the total village. Ethnographic data suggest that the village plazas, as well as the kiva, may be places in which both ceremony and food exchange occur (Stevenson 1904). Importantly, there is no evidence for the actual storage, or control, of food at this level.

Ethnographically, kivas are also places for general councils of males to meet (Cushing and others 1922: 256; Hammond and Rey 1940: 253; Klett 1874: 585; V. Mindeleff 1891: 130), and the Great Kiva at Turkey Creek may also have served in this capacity. Other possible kiva activities for which there is, however, no clear archaeological evidence are external trade (Simmons 1942: 61); occasional sleeping, for males (Cushing and others 1922: 256; Hammond and Rey 1940: 254; Hammond and Rey 1966: 172; Stevenson 1904: 89, 112; Titiev 1944: 7, 16, 30); and male manufacturing activities (Beaglehole 1937; Cushing and others 1922; V. Mindeleff 1891; Stephen 1936).

Turkey Creek Pueblo Aggregation

The pattern presented by the sterile-trash dichotomy suggests that Turkey Creek Pueblo growth was by the accretion of households or small villages. The possibility for the stockpiling of wood suggests that full village moves may have been planned ahead, even if they did not take place all at once. It is likely that the northwest basalt room groups were at Turkey Creek Pueblo first and perhaps constituted a small village that was joined by households from other villages.

Why did aggregation into large pueblos begin at this time in the Point of Pines region? The nature of aggregation in the Pueblo Southwest is a popular and hotly debated topic (Cordell 1984). Reasons for aggregation suggested in the literature include climate shifts that make certain areas particularly desirable for agriculture (Graves and others 1982) and improved opportunities for external trade through centralization (Graves and others 1982; Plog 1983; Upham 1982).

A third reason for aggregation is defense (LeBlanc 1978; Woodbury 1959). Defense as a primary motive for pueblo aggregation is not currently a fashionable inference. However, the historic Pueblo literature indicates that aggregation is often defensive (Bunzel 1933: 30; Cushing 1920: 260–262; Kroeber 1917: 122; C. Mindeleff 1897: 641–642; V. Mindeleff 1891: 223), and that the waxing and waning of defense needs are common explanations for village moves (Table 7.2). One does not need to postulate an early influx of Athabascans to find enemies for prehistoric Pueblo groups. Pueblo villages had serious conflicts with each other both in historic and in immediately prehistoric times. For instance, according to oral history, the Hopi village of Walpi and neighboring Sikyatki quarreled over land boundaries and water rights. Eventually, Walpi warriors invaded Sikyatki, massacred their warriors, and captured their women (Fewkes 1896, 1897). In a historic Hopi conflict, pro-Spanish Awatovi had received a friar into their village. Sometime around 1700, angry anti-Spanish Walpi warriors joined with other Hopi warriors in a raid against Awatovi. They destroyed this village, burned the kivas, killed the men, and captured the women and children (Brew 1979:

Table 7.2. Reasons for Village Moves

Reason for move	Source
Disease	Donaldson 1893: 7; V. Mindeleff 1891: 15, 31, 38; Stephen 1936: 1175
Dirt and offal	Donaldson 1893: 7
Defensive position needed	Bandelier 1892: 99; Eggan 1950: 125; Fewkes 1897: 580; V. Mindeleff 1891: 15, 20, 23, 26, 33; Parsons 1939: 15; Simmons 1979a: 193
Defensive position no longer needed	Bandelier 1892: 101; V. Mindeleff 1891: 227; Parsons 1939: 15; Simmons 1979b: 211
Defensive aggregation needed	Bunzel 1933: 30; Cushing 1920: 260–262; Kroeber 1917: 122; Titiev 1944: 97
Destruction by enemies	Brew 1979: 522; Fewkes 1894: 396, 397; Fewkes 1897: 580; V. Mindeleff 1891: 34–35; Titiev 1944: 71
Factionalism	Benavides 1954: 34; Fewkes 1894: 397, 413, 414; Cushing, Fewkes, and Parsons 1922: 286; Parsons 1939: 15; Titiev 1944: 98–99
Environmental problems (drought, famine)	Aberle 1948: 11, 61; Bunzel 1933: 59; Eggan 1950: 125; Parsons 1939: 16; C. Mindeleff 1897: 645, 646; V. Mindeleff 1891: 15, 26, 30
Crowding (related to seasonal moves)	Eggan 1950: 111, 125; V. Mindeleff 1891: 31, 38; Nagata 1970: 245; Titiev 1972: 326
Seasonal moves become permanent	Fewkes 1894: 400; C. Mindeleff 1897: 643–646; V. Mindeleff 1891: 79; Nagata 1970
Earthquakes (?)	Cushing 1979: 192
Omens	C. Mindeleff 1897: 646; V. Mindeleff 1891: 15

522; V. Mindeleff 1891: 34–35; Titiev 1944: 71). At contact with the western world, old Zuni men talked of a precontact war between Zuni and Marata, a group of pueblos to the southeast (Bandelier 1892: 6).

From the twelfth century until contact with the West, the archaeological record indicates that large areas occupied by Pueblo peoples were abandoned and other areas experienced population increases. It is reasonable to assume that some Pueblo groups perceived of other Pueblo groups as threatening, particularly since many groups were on the move, culturally different, and spoke different languages.

Such a situation would open up opportunities for trade as well as for conflict among groups. The relationships among diverse prehistoric Pueblo groups might have been parallel to historically known relationships between Pueblo and Athabascan groups. These groups alternately raided each other and relied on each other for the peaceful exchange of trade goods. Turkey Creek Pueblo clearly has exchange contacts. Its collection of artifacts includes exotic pottery and nonlocal goods such as copper bells and shell.

Turkey Creek also has material evidence for defensibility as derived from the ethnographic and historic literature (Table 7.3). It is an aggregated community, perhaps with farming shelters located some distance away. It has a courtyard layout, with protected inner plazas. Access from the exterior into the large common areas of Turkey Creek Pueblo is restricted. Access to Plaza 1 is through a single opening to the east, and access to the Great Kiva is through this plaza. Plaza 2, the western plaza, is reached only through the corridor running from Plaza 1. Another possible route of access into the pueblo is through Area B, which may once have formed part of an early plaza. Exterior walls without doors provide a barrier to the outside. Access into individual dwellings presumably is provided by ladders to the roofs and hatch entry into rooms. Because ladders can be easily pulled up, access into dwellings is protective in nature. Turkey Creek also has many sealed doors, a trait with a number of alternate explanations, one of which is defense. Finally, the village is located in an open area that would make it difficult to attack by surprise, assuming that regular watch was kept from its roof. It could be defended from the roof with arrows and rocks, in the manner in which the Zuni attempted to defend their villages from the Spanish (Bandelier 1892: 32–34).

In the Point of Pines region aggregated settlements began in the Tularosa phase (about A.D. 1150–1265; Haury 1989) and continued until the Point of Pines phase (about 1400–1450). At that time large settlements broke down once more into small villages, and groups of these small villages apparently shared areal kivas, as was done back in Reserve times (Smiley 1952). A study of changes in architectural features and trade goods over time, as well as environmental change, might reveal reasons behind the waxing and waning of aggregated settlement in the area, beyond simply defense. However, the data available to date suggest that the advantage of improved defense may have been the primary motive for aggregation at Turkey Creek Pueblo.

The Abandonment of Turkey Creek Pueblo

Turkey Creek abandonment, like its aggregation, appears to have been gradual and probably occurred by household. North households tended to leave Turkey Creek Pueblo before its final abandonment, and the abundance of floor artifacts in

Table 7.3. Evidence for Defense and Conflict

Evidence	Source
Aggregation	C. Mindeleff 1897: 641–642; V. Mindeleff 1891: 98, 223
Aggregation with farming shelters	C. Mindeleff 1897: 642
Courtyard architecture with high walls	Bandelier 1892: 32–34; Hammond and Rey 1940: 222, 252, 323; V. Mindeleff 1891: 62, 68–69
Defensive site	V. Mindeleff 1891: 59, 76, 89, 223
Walls	Hammond and Rey 1940: 170; V. Mindeleff 1891: 24, 59, 94, 95
Covered passages	V. Mindeleff 1891: 72, 76, 180; Stevenson 1904: 349
Defensive trails	Cushing, Fewkes, and Parsons 1922: 279
No ground floor doors, with ladder and hatch entry to ground floor rooms	Bandelier 1892: 38, 40; Curtis 1883: 13; Cushing, Fewkes, and Parsons 1922: 271; James 1919: 35; Klett 1874: 580; V. Mindeleff 1891: 104, 143, 156; Powell 1972: 18; Simmons 1979b: 211
Sealed doors	Cushing, Fewkes, and Parsons 1922: 279
Burials scalped or beheaded	Beaglehole and Beaglehole 1935: 22, 23
Males (warriors) cremated	Smith and Roberts 1954: 157
War tools	Beaglehole and Beaglehole 1935: 19; Wright 1979: 49
Fire	V. Mindeleff 1891: 34; Stephen 1936: 1179

the north rooms relative to the south rooms suggests that at least some of these people moved far enough away that they did not take much with them. These people may have had comparatively low status, as do ethnographically known households that abandon still functioning communities (Nagata 1970). The relative abundance of habitation rooms to the north suggests that more nuclear family households occupied the north than the south. Since cross-culturally, smaller households tend to be poorer households, the early abandoners of Turkey Creek Pueblo may have tended to live in both smaller and poorer households than the later abandoners.

The last households to leave tended to clear their floors of artifacts, suggesting that they moved nearby, perhaps to Point of Pines Pueblo. After abandonment, Turkey Creek Pueblo was scavenged of wall stones and perhaps other items such as hatch slabs, for new construction in the area. The abandonment pattern of this pueblo, located in a region that thrived for at least another 150 years, contrasts greatly with the patterns of villages abandoned at the same time that whole regions were vacated. The final abandonment of the Point of Pines and Grasshopper regions left large quantities of de facto refuse on the room floors of the latest occupied villages (Ciolek-Torrello 1985; Cordell 1984; Reid and Shimada 1982; Schiffer 1985; Wendorf 1950).

Why was Turkey Creek Pueblo abandoned? Table 7.2 lists some of the reasons for village moves suggested by the Hopi and Zuni literature. There is no solid evidence backing any single explanation for the abandonment of Turkey Creek. It is possible that heightened defense needs, increasingly important and complex trade patterns, or both, made it advantageous to move to Point of Pines Pueblo, a far larger community (about 800 rooms at its peak) than Turkey Creek. The Kayenta migration to Point of Pines Pueblo (Haury 1958) occurred at about the time Turkey Creek Pueblo was abandoned. Future research should help clarify the nature of the abandonment of Turkey Creek and other thirteenth-century happenings in the Point of Pines region.

CONCLUSIONS

This report on Turkey Creek Pueblo has been guided by one overarching concern: how can archaeologists, with their particular kind of data, both learn from and contribute to the exciting new social science research on the organization and function of the household, the most basic unit of human social organization? Architecture and other material characteristics of a culture are both responsive to and reflective of social organization, in general, and household organization, in particular. Since the built environment can constrain as well as reflect social organization, the direction of causality between material remains and household organization is not always clear. In spite of this and other difficulties, it is necessary for archaeologists to understand how the social organization of people may be reflected in the preservable material remains of their organization in space.

Clearly this architectural study demonstrates the value of a household focus in the analysis of prehistoric social organization. At Turkey Creek, however, the household dwelling is architecturally elusive. To circumvent this difficulty a typology of domestic rooms was developed and the dwelling was treated as an abstract entity that could be bracketed between rooms and supradwelling divisions, both of which are architecturally more distinct than dwellings. Through this approach, inferences about dwelling size, function, and variability were possible.

Analysis of the functional, temporal, and spatial variability in room attributes showed that Turkey Creek Pueblo was organized in a four-level hierarchy of social units, with the household at the base. Households were grouped into suprahousehold divisions and these, in turn, were grouped into north and south divisions, each with its special room group associated with the Great Kiva. The largest social unit was the total village, united by the Great Kiva. The dual division, or moiety system, was the most unexpected organizational feature to emerge from the analysis.

At the lower two levels of organization, activities apparently included food preparation, manufacturing, trash disposal, burial, food storage, and, by implication, food production. Also people appeared to move into and abandon the village by household or by suprahousehold. At the dual and village levels activities included ceremony and defense. Ceremony at these higher levels implies food exchange and perhaps political leadership as well. The ceremonial activities of the dual and village units may have unified otherwise independent household and suprahousehold units. Such unity might function to ease food stress, provide protection from outsiders, or both.

Although archaeological data are weak for studying some of the factors involving households, they are strong for studying others. The weaknesses include the nonpreservable cognitive and social aspects of past cultures. Thus, household value systems and precise household configurations and inheritance systems are elusive cultural characteristics, given prehistoric data. The particular strengths of prehistoric data are their time depth and their good information on the preservable aspects of economic adaptations and the built environment. Insofar as archaeologists direct their research toward the strengths of the archaeological record, they have much to contribute to the general effort of social scientists to understand how the human household organizes itself and functions. Continued recognition of the importance of the household promises to sharpen inferences concerning crucial aspects of prehistory and to lead archaeologists in informative new directions of inquiry.

APPENDIX A

Definitions of Variables

Variable	Definition
	Variables of the Turkey Creek Pueblo Analysis
Room Size (Size)	Size 1: area<=6 square meters
	Size 2: 6<area<=11
	Size 3: 11<area<=34
Hearth	Presence (quantity in Appendix B) or absence of a hearth of any type
Circular Hearth (C. Hearth)	Presence (quantity in Appendix B) or absence of a circular hearth or hearths
Rectangular Hearth (R. Hearth)	Presence (quantity in Appendix B) or absence of a rectangular hearth or hearths
Storage Pit (Pit)	Presence or absence of a storage pit or pits
Hatch	Presence or absence of a slab or slabs that may have been part of a hatch entry
Storage Bin (Bin)	Presence or absence of a storage bin or bins
Vent	Presence or absence of a wall vent or vents
Burial	Presence or absence of a subfloor burial or burials
Pounds of Sherds (Lbs)	Estimated pounds of sherds per square meter of floor space
Sherd Density Index (SDI)	Pounds of sherds divided by wall height
Sherd Density Index Group (SDIGP)	If SDI<=0.5 then SDIGP=1
	If 0.5<SDI<=1.0 then SDIGP=2
	If 1.0<SDI<=1.5 then SDIGO=3
	If 1.5<SDI<=2.0 then SDIGP=4
	If 2.0<SDI<=2.5 then SDIGP=5
	If 2.5<SDI then SDIGP=6
Multiple Plaster (Multiplaster)	Number of coats of plaster present (0–5)
Room Shape (Shape)	Average wall length divided by average wall width, collapsed into discrete categories: 1–3 (1 = most square; 3 = least square)
Room Group (Group)	A-T: 20 spatially clustered groups of contiguous rooms, grouped on the basis of long walls that define large areas filled in with rooms
Room Placement (Place)	Location of the room in relation to the following attributes: I, interior; E, borders exterior; O, borders Plaza 1 (One); T, borders Plaza 2 (Two); K, borders Great Kiva
Room Area (Area)	Average wall length times average wall width in square meters
Room Area Group (Areagp)	If area<=4.0 then areagp=1
	If 4.0<area<=7.0 then areagp=2
	If 7.0<area<=10.0 then areagp=3
	If 10.0<area<=13.0 then areagp=4
	If 13.0<area<=16.0 then areagp=5
	If 16.0<area<=19.0 then areagp=6
	If 19.0<area<=22.0 then areagp=7
	If 22.0<area<=25.0 then areagp=8
	If 25.0<area then areagp=9

Variables of the Turkey Creek Pueblo Analysis *(continued)*

Variable	Definition
Wall Height (Height)	Average wall height in courses
Basalt-based Wall (Basalt)	Presence or absence of a basalt-based wall or walls
Plaster	Presence (number of coats in Appendix B) or absence of plaster on a wall or walls
Floor	Number of floor surfaces
Sterile	Presence or absence of native or mixed native soil (no trash) under the floor
Posthole (Post)	Presence or absence of a posthole or postholes
Door	Presence or absence of a door or doors
Size of Circular Hearth Room (Csize)	Csize 2 = Size 2 rooms with circular hearth or hearths Csize 3 = Size 3 rooms with circular hearth or hearths
Size of Rectangular Hearth Room (Rsize)	Rsize 2 = Size 2 rooms with rectangular hearth or hearths Rsize 3 = Size 3 rooms with rectangular hearth or hearths
Room Class (Class)	Class 1 = Presence of circular hearth or hearths only (no rectangular hearth) Class 2 = Presence of rectangular hearth or hearths only (no circular hearth) Class 3 = Presence of both circular hearth(s) and rectangular hearth(s)
Room Side (Side)	North side of pueblo = Groups A-L South side of pueblo = Groups M-T
Trough Metate (Trough)	Presence or absence of a trough metate in any provenience within a room
Vessel	Presence or absence of jar(s) or bowl(s) or both on room floor
Jar	Presence or absence of a jar or jars on floor
Bowl	Presence or absence of a bowl or bowls on floor
Floor Artifact (Artifact)	Presence or absence of shaft straightener, axe, antler flaker, awl, hoe, knife, drill, or projectile point listed on the floor
Shaft Straightener (SS) (limited room sample)	Presence or absence of a shaft straightener on the floor in rooms with artifacts listed on floor
Axe (l.r.s.)	Presence or absence of an axe on the floor, in rooms with artifacts listed on floor
Antler Flaker (Ant. Flak.) (l.r.s.)	Presence or absence of an antler flaker on the floor, in rooms with artifacts listed on floor
Awl (l.r.s.)	Presence or absence of an awl on the floor, in rooms with artifacts listed on floor
Hoe (l.r.s.)	Presence or absence of a hoe on the floor, in rooms with artifacts listed on floor
Knife (l.r.s.)	Presence or absence of a knife on the floor, in rooms with artifacts listed on floor
Drill (l.r.s.)	Presence or absence of a drill on the floor, in rooms with artifacts listed on floor
Projectile Point (PP) (l.r.s.)	Presence or absence of a projectile point on the floor, in rooms with artifacts listed on floor
Shaft Straightener (total room sample)	Presence or absence of a shaft straightener listed on the floor
Axe (t.r.s.)	Presence or absence of an axe listed on the floor
Antler flaker (t.r.s.)	Presence or absence of an antler flaker listed on the floor
Awl (t.r.s.)	Presence or absence of an awl listed on the floor
Hoe (t.r.s.)	Presence or absence of a hoe listed on the floor
Knife (t.r.s.)	Presence or absence of a knife listed on the floor
Drill (t.r.s.)	Presence or absence of a drill listed on the floor
Projectile Point (t.r.s.)	Presence or absence of a projectile point listed on the floor

APPENDIX B

Turkey Creek Pueblo Data by Room Number and Room Group

Appendix B. Turkey Creek Pueblo Data by Room Number and Group

Room #	1	2	3	10	11	16	17	18	21	27	30	31	40	42	46	67	68	72	86	96	12	13
Group	A	A	A	A	A	A	A	A	A	A	A	A	A	A	A	A	A	A	A	A	B	B
Place	E	E	I	E	E	E	E	E	I	I	I	I	I	I	I	I	I	I	E	I	E	E
Height	4.0	3.8	3.2	3.8	3.5				4.5	4.8	1.0	5.0	4.0	4.8	5.0	3.2	3.2	3.5	1.5	4.5	2.5	2.8
Basalt	1	1	1	1	0	1	1	1	0	0	1	0	0	0	0	1	0	1	1	0	1	1
Plaster	0	0	1	0	0	0	0	0	1	3	0	2	2	1	1	0	1	0	0	1	0	0
Floor	1	2	1	1	1	1	1	1	1	1	1	1	3	2	1	1	1	1	1	2	1	1
Door	1	0	0	0		0		0	0	1	0	0	0		0	0	0	0		0	0	0
Post	0	1	1	0	0	0	0	0	1	1	1	1	0	1	1	1	1	1		1	0	1
Hatch	0	1	1	1	0	0	0	0	0	1	0	0	0	0	0	0	0	0			1	1
Bin	1	0	0	0	0	0	0	0	0	0	0	0	0	1	0	0	0	0		0	0	0
Vent	0	0	0	0	1	0		0	0	0	0	0	0	0	0	0	0	0		0	0	0
Burial	0	0	0	0	0			0	0	0	1	0	0	0	0	0	0	0		0	0	0
Pit	0	1	0	0		0		0	0	0	1	0	0	1	0	0	0	0		0	0	0
Jar		0							1					0	1					1		0
Bowl		1							1					1	1					0		0
S.S.			0	0						1								0		0		0
Axe			1	0						1								1		1		0
A.Flak.			0	0						0								0		0		0
Awl			0	0						0								0		0		1
Hoe			0	0						0								0		0		1
Knife			0	1						0								0		1		0
Drill			0	0						0								0		0		0
P.P.			0	0						0								0		0		0
Sterile	1	1			1	1	1	1	1	0	1	1	1		1	0	0	1	1		1	1
Area	20.0	13.9	10.5	10.2	6.4				10.8	17.1	10.2	11.6	32.8	9.7	7.6	7.5	4.0	14.2		7.6	5.7	7.6
SDI	0.6	1.9	3.0	0.8	0.5				2.0	2.4	2.4	0.9	0.6	1.1	2.0		1.9	4.0		5.6	2.1	4.0
Shape	3.1	1.3	1.6	1.0	1.2				1.1	1.2	1.1	1.6	1.8	1.6	1.0	1.3	1.1	1.8		1.1	1.2	2.2
C.Hrth.	0	0	0	1	1	0		0	1	0	1	0	1	0	1	1	0	1		1	0	1
R.Hrth.	0	1	0	0	0	0		0	0	1	0	0	1	0	1	0	2	0		0	0	0
Hrth.	0	1	0	1	1	0		0	1	1	1	1	1	1	1	2	2	1		1	0	1
Trough	1	1	1	1	0	0		0	3	1	1	0	1	0	1	0	1	0		0	0	1

Room #	14	15	36	43	54	57	66	73	78	79	89	107	108	160	175	28	37	45	49	52	53	58
Group	B	B	B	B	B	B	B	B	B	B	B	B	B	B	B	C	C	C	C	C	C	C
Place	E	I	I	E	I	I	I	I	I	I	I	I	I	I	E	E	E	E	E	E	E	E
Height	3.5	3.5	3.5	2.8	2.5	3.2	1.7	1.8	2.8	2.5	5.5	4.0	4.2	4.0	4.2	2.5	2.2	2.2	2.0	2.2	2.8	2.8
Basalt	0	0	1	0	0	0	0	0	0	0	0	1	0	0	0	1	0	0	0	0	0	1
Plaster		0	0	0	0	0	0	0	0	0	0	1	1	0	0	0	0	0	0	0	1	0
Floor	1	1	2	1	1	1	3	1	1	1	1	1	2	1	1	1	1	1	1	1	1	1
Door	0		0	0	0	0	0	0	0	0		1	0	0	0	0	0	0	0	0		0
Post	1	1	1	1	1	0	0	0	0	1	1	0	1	0	1	0	0			0		
Hatch	0	0	1	0	0	0	0	0	0	0	0	1	0	1	0	0				0		
Bin	0	0	0	0	0	0	0	0	1	0	0	0	0	1	0	0	0			0		
Vent	0	0	0	0	1	0	0	0	0	0	0	1	0	0	0	0				0		
Burial	0	0	0	0	0	0	0	0	0	0	0	0	0	0	0	0	0			1		
Pit	0	0	0	0	0	0	1	0	0	0	0	0	0	0	0	0	1			0		
Jar	0												1									
Bowl	0												0									
S.S.	0												1					0				
Axe	0												1					0				
A.Flak.	0												1					0				
Awl	0												1					0				
Hoe	0												1					0				
Knife	0												1					0				
Drill	0												0					0				
P.P.	1												1					0				
Sterile		1		1	1	0	0	1	0	0	0	0	0	0	0	0		0	0	0	0	0
Area	4.4	3.9	9.4	7.5	6.3	7.0	3.8	3.1	4.9	4.8	2.5	2.5	17.5	10.3	16.0	8.9	11.4	6.8	6.4	10.0	9.3	2.7
SDI		0.6	2.3	0.7	0.6	0.9	2.4	3.5	0.7	1.6		1.0	2.9	0.6	0.9	0.4	1.4				0.6	
Shape	1.2	1.0	1.1	1.3	1.2	1.1	1.9	1.8	1.7	1.0	1.2	2.0	1.1	1.6	1.8	1.6	1.5	1.3	1.1	2.1	1.5	1.2
C.Hrth.	0	0	1	0	1	0	1	0	1	0	0	0	0	1	2	1	0			1		
R.Hrth.	0	0	0	2	1	0	0	0	0	0	0	1	0	0	0	0	0			0		
Hrth.	0	0	1	3	1	0	1	0	1	0	0	1	1	2	0	1	0			1		
Trough	0	0	0	1	1	1	0	1	0	0	0	0	1	1	0	0	0			0		

See Appendix A for definitions of variables.

Appendix B (continued). Turkey Creek Pueblo Room Data

Room #	59	60	5	6	7	8	20	22	23	24	25	29	32	35	38	9	39	41	44	47	48	50
Group	C	C	D	D	D	D	D	D	D	D	D	D	D	D	D	E	E	E	E	E	E	E
Place	E	E	E	E	O	O	E	O	E	E	I	E	E	I	E	O	I	I	I	I	I	I
Height	3.5	2.0	1.5	3.0	3.0	3.0	1.5	2.5	4.0	6.0	4.0	2.5	5.2	4.0	5.0	2.2	4.8	6.2	5.0	5.8	3.8	3.0
Basalt	0	0	1	1	1	0	1	1	1	0	1	0	0	0	0	1	0	0	0	0	0	0
Plaster	0	0	0	0	0	0	0	0	1	1	1	0	0	0	1	0	0	1	0	3	0	1
Floor	1	1	1	1	1	3	1	1	1	1	1	1	1	1	1	2	1	1	1	2	1	2
Door	0	0	0	0	0	0	0	0	0	0	0	0	0	0	0	0	0	0	0	0	0	0
Post			1	1	1	0	0	0	1	1	1	1	1	0	0	0	1	0	1	1	1	1
Hatch			0	0	1	1	0	1	0	0	0	0	0	0	0	0	0	0	0	0	0	0
Bin			0	0	0	0	0	0	0	0	0	0	0	0	0	0	0	0	0	0	0	0
Vent			0	0	0	0	0	0	0	1	0	0	0	0	0	0	0	0	0	1	0	0
Burial			0	1	0	0	0	0	0	0	0	0	0	0	0	0	0	0	0	0	0	1
Pit			0	0	0	0	0	0	0	1	0	0	1	0	0	0	0	0	0	0	0	0
Jar			1	1		1			1										1			
Bowl			0	0		1			1										1			
S.S.			0	0		0												0	1			0
Axe			0	0		0												0	0			1
A.Flak.			0	1		0												0	0			1
Awl			0	0		1												0	1			0
Hoe			0	0		0												1	0			1
Knife			0	1		0												0	0			0
Drill			0	0		0												0	0			0
P.P.			1	0		0												0	1			0
Sterile	0	0			0	0		0	0	0	1	0	0	0	0	0	0	0	0	1	0	0
Area	4.3	6.5	11.5	24.4	6.9	19.7	10.3	4.5	12.2	4.4	11.1	3.5	5.0	4.6	3.6	14.6	5.3	5.0	4.1	17.8	2.1	3.7
SDI				4.1	2.4	2.9		1.4	4.1	0.8	0.3	0.2	0.4	0.8	3.7	1.1	0.6	1.8	0.8	0.6	0.2	3.1
Shape	1.4	1.9	1.2	2.3	1.9	1.4	1.2	2.7	1.0	1.2	1.2	1.8	1.8	2.4	1.0	1.9	1.2	1.1	1.0	1.0	1.2	1.3
C.Hrth.		1	0	0	0	0	0	1	0	0	0	0	0	0	0	0	0	0	0	0	0	0
R.Hrth.		0	1	0	0	0	0	0	0	1	0	0	0	0	0	0	0	0	0	2	0	0
Hrth.		1	1	1	0	0	0	1	0	1	0	0	0	0	0	0	0	0	0	2	0	0
Trough		1	1	0	0	2	1	0	0	0	0	0	1	0	0	0	0	0	0	2	0	0

Room #	51	61	62	63	65	69	75	76	77	80	88	91	106	117	109	110	145	150	151	152
Group	E	E	E	E	E	E	E	E	E	E	E	E	E	E	F	F	F	F	F	F
Place	I	I	I	I	I	I	I	I	I	I	I	I	O	O	I	I	I	I	I	I
Height	5.2	3.2	3.5	3.2	4.5	2.5	3.8	4.5	4.0	5.2	3.5	3.2	4.8	3.2	4.5	4.5	5.0	4.2	2.7	4.0
Basalt	1	0	0	0	0	0	0	0	0	0	0	0	0	0	0	0	0	0	0	1
Plaster	0	0	0	1	2	0	1	0	1	2	0	1	0	1	3	3	1	0	0	0
Floor	1	1	1	1	1	1	2	1	1	1	1	1	1	1	1	1	3	1	1	1
Door	0	0	0	0	0	0	0	0	0	0	0	0	0	0	0	0	1	0	0	0
Post	1	0	1	1	1	0	1	0	0	1	0	1	1	0	1	1	1	1	0	0
Hatch	0	0	0		1	0	1		0	1	0	1	0	0	0	1	1	0	0	
Bin	0	0	0	0	0	0	0	0	0	0	0	1	0	0	0	1	0	0	0	0
Vent	0	0	0	0	0	0	0	0	0	0	0	0	0	0	0	0	0	0	0	0
Burial	0	0	0	0	0	0	0	0	0	1	0	0	0	0	0	0	0	0	0	0
Pit	0	0	0		0	0	0	0	0	0	0	0	0	0	0	0		1	0	0
Jar							1					1			1					
Bowl							0					0			0					
S.S.					0							0			1	0				
Axe					1							0			0	0				
A.Flak.					1							1			0	0				
Awl					0							1			1	1				
Hoe					0							0			0	0				
Knife					0							0			0	0				
Drill					0							0			0	0				
P.P.					1							1			0	0				
Sterile	0		0	0	0	0	1	0	1	0	1	0	0		0	0	1	1	0	
Area	3.8		4.4	8.0	13.8	2.2	13.8	4.6	3.2	7.1	2.8	10.5	1.7	1.3	15.5	15.4	8.9	3.2		11.6
SDI	0.3		0.6		0.8	2.7	2.4	3.6	1.2	3.8	1.5	1.3	0.3	3.6	1.6	0.5	2.8	1.9		0.6
Shape	1.3		1.2	1.1	1.3	1.7	1.1	1.1	2.2	1.1	1.4	1.1	1.1	1.1	1.4	1.6	1.3	1.7		1.3
C.Hrth.	0	0	0	0	1	0	0	0	0	0	0	1	0	0	0	1	1	0	0	1
R.Hrth.	0	0	0	1	1	0	1	0	0	1	0	0	0	0	1	0	1	0	0	0
Hrth.	0	0	0	1	2	0	1	0	0	1	0	1	0	0	1	1	1	?	0	1
Trough	0	0	0	1	1	0	1	0	0	0	0	0	0	0	1	1	1	0	0	1

Appendix B (continued). Turkey Creek Pueblo Room Data

Room #	153	178	177	184	185	189	19	26	33	34	55	56	74	81	82	83	84	85
Group	F	F	F	F	F	F	G	G	G	G	G	G	G	G	G	G	G	G
Place	I	I	I	I	I	E	I	E	E	E	E	E	I	I	I	I	I	I
Height	4.0	3.0	4.5	5.0	5.0	4.7	3.5	2.5			2.3	1.2	3.2	2.5	3.0	1.7	2.5	5.8
Basalt	0	0	0	0	0	0	1	1	0	1	0	0	0	0	0	0	1	0
Plaster	1	0	1	1	1	1	0	0	0	0	0	0	0	0	0	0	0	0
Floor	1	1	2	1	1	1	1	1	1	1	1	1	1	1	1	1	1	3
Door	0	0	0	0	0	0	0	0	0	0	0	0	0	0	0			0
Post	0	0	0	1	0	1	1				1	1	1	0	1	1	1	1
Hatch			1	1		0	1				0	0	0					
Bin	0	0	0	0	0	1	0				0	0	0	0	0	0	0	0
Vent	0	0	0	1	0	0	0				0	0	0	0	0	0	1	0
Burial	0	0	0	1	0	0	1				0	0	0	1	0	0	0	1
Pit	0	0	0	0	0	1	0				1	0	0	0	0	0	0	0
Jar		1														0		
Bowl	0															1		
S.S.	0																	
Axe	0																	
A.Flak.	1																	
Awl	0																	
Hoe	0																	
Knife	0																	
Drill	0																	
P.P.	0																	
Sterile	0	0	0	0	0		1	1	0	1	0	0	0	0	0	0	1	1
Area	7.1	10.7	12.6	20.5	4.6	19.8	7.3		15.2		7.2	5.0	8.0	12.8	10.4	7.9	21.7	6.3
SDI	1.8	0.5	1.4	0.7	0.5	1.0	1.9				2.1	2.5	0.8	1.6	0.3	0.8	0.4	0.9
Shape	2.7	1.5	1.1	1.3	1.6	1.4	1.1		1.6		1.4	1.1	1.2	1.5	1.4	1.3	1.7	1.4
C.Hrth.	0	0	0	0	0	0	1				0	0	1	0	0	0	0	1
R.Hrth.	1	1	2	1	0	1	0				1	0	0	0	1	0	1	1
Hrth.	1	1	2	1	0	2	1				1	0	1	1	1	1	1	2
Trough	0	1		1	0	1	1				0	0	0	1	0	0	0	1

Room #	90	98	100	101	102	103	104	116	126	64	70	71	87	92	93	94	97	105
Group	G	G	G	G	G	G	G	G	G	H	H	H	H	H	H	H	H	H
Place	I	E	I	I	T	I	I	T	T	I	I	I	I	I	I	I	I	I
Height	2.5		3.2	5.2	4.0	2.0	2.5	2.5	2.5	4.0	2.8	3.5	4.8	5.5	5.0	3.0	3.8	5.0
Basalt	0	1	0	0	0	1	1	0	0	0	0	0	0	0	0	0	0	0
Plaster	0	0	0	1	0	0	1	0	0	0	3	0	2	1	1	1	0	2
Floor	1		2	1	1	1	1	1	2	1	1	1	1	1	1	1	2	1
Door	0		1	0	0	0		0	0	0	0	0	0	0	0	0	0	0
Post	1		1	1	0	0	1	1	1	0	1	1	0	0	1	1	1	1
Hatch	0		1	0	0	0	0	0	1	1	1		1		1	1	0	
Bin	0		1	0	0	0	0	0	0	0	0	0	0	0	0	0	0	0
Vent	0		0	0	0	0	0	0	1	0	0	0	0	0	0	0	0	0
Burial	0		0	0	0	1	0	1	0	0	0	0	0	0	0	1	0	0
Pit	0		0	0	0	0	0	0	0	0	0	0	0	0	0	0	0	0
Jar																		
Bowl																		
S.S.											0					0		
Axe											0					0		
A.Flak.											0					0		
Awl											1					1		
Hoe											1					0		
Knife											0					1		
Drill											0					1		
P.P.											0					0		
Sterile	0		0	0	0	1	0	1	0	1	1	1	1	0	1			0
Area	4.3		10.6	2.9	3.5	4.8	6.1	1.8	11.8	15.0	10.3	13.0	5.5	2.6	5.1	7.2	9.0	3.7
SDI	1.0		0.6		0.7		2.0	16.3	1.0	0.5	5.5	1.1	8.3	0.3	0.4	2.8	1.9	1.3
Shape	2.2		1.5	1.2	1.2	1.3	1.5	1.8	1.3	1.0	1.0	1.6	1.9	1.7	1.7	1.3	1.7	1.1
C.Hrth.	1		0	0	0	0	0	0	0	0	1	0	0	0	0	0	0	0
R.Hrth.	0		1	0	0	0	0	0	0	0	0	1	0	0	0	0	2	0
Hrth.	1		1	0	0	1	0	0	0	0	1	1	0	0	0	0	2	1
Trough	0		1	0	0	0	0	0	0	0	0	0	0	1	0	0	1	0

Appendix B (continued). Turkey Creek Pueblo Room Data

Room #	111	112	114	115	118	121	122	123	127	128	129	131	132	138	143	144	95	99
Group	H	H	H	H	H	H	H	H	H	H	H	H	H	H	H	H	I	I
Place	I	I	I	O	O	I	I	O	I	I	I	I	I	I	T	T	I	I
Height	4.0	4.5	3.8	4.2	4.5	3.5	4.0	4.2	4.5	3.2	4.0	4.0	3.8	3.2	4.2	4.0	2.7	3.5
Basalt	0	0	0	0	0	0	0	0	0	0	0	0	0	0	0	0	1	0
Plaster	0	0	0	0	1	0	0	0	1	1	0	0	0	1	1	0	0	0
Floor	1	1	1	1	1	1	1	1	1	1	1	1	2	1	1	2	1	1
Door	0	0	0	0	0	0	0	0	0	0	0	0	0	0	0	0	0	0
Post	1	1	0	1	1	0	1	1	0	1	1	1	1	0	1	1	0	0
Hatch	1	0	0	1	1	0	0	0	1	1	1	0	1	0			0	0
Bin	0	0	0	0	0	0	0	0	0	0	0	0	0	0	0	0		
Vent	0	0	0	0	0	0	0	0	0	1	0	0	0	0	0	0	0	0
Burial	0	0	0	0	1	0	0	0	0	0	1	0	0	0	1	0	0	0
Pit	0	0	0	0	0	0	0	0	0	0	0	0	0	0	0	0	0	0
Jar	0									1					1			
Bowl	1									0					0			
S.S.	0													0				
Axe	1													0				
A.Flak.	0													0				
Awl	0													1				
Hoe	0													0				
Knife	1													0				
Drill	0													0				
P.P.	0													0				
Sterile	0	0		0	0	0	1	0	1	0	0	0	0	0		0	0	0
Area	4.7	1.5	8.7	14.1	12.4	5.3	3.6	7.7	2.4	8.4	10.9	6.5	6.7	2.7	9.8	12.6	1.7	1.8
SDI	1.6	0.3	0.3	1.2	1.7	0.5	1.8	1.1	0.5	2.8	1.7	0.6	1.9	0.9	2.4	0.9	3.2	1.6
Shape	1.9	1.2	1.7	1.0	1.6	1.5	1.2	1.7	1.2	1.5	1.3	1.8	1.3	1.7	1.8	1.2	2.7	3.2
C.Hrth.	1	0	0	0	0	0	0	0	0	1	1	1	2	0	1	0	0	0
R.Hrth.	0	0	1	1	1	1	0	1	0	0	0	0	0	0	0	1	0	0
Hrth.	1	0	1	1	1	1	0	1	0	1	1	1	2	0	1	1	0	0
Trough	0	0	1	1	1	1	0	0	0	1	1	0	0	0	1	0	0	0

Room #	113	119	120	130	124	125	133	136	137	139	140	141	142	147	148	149	155	156
Group	I	I	I	I	I	I	I	I	I	I	I	I	I	I	I	I	I	I
Place	I	I	I	I	E	E	I	E	I	I	I	I	I	I	E	I	I	I
Height	2.0	2.0	2.0	2.0	1.0	1.0	3.5	1.8	3.0	2.5	3.8	4.0	2.8	2.2	2.8	4.3	3.8	5.0
Basalt	1	0	1	0	1		1	1	1	1	0	0	1	1	0	1	1	0
Plaster	0	0	0	0			0	0	1	0	0	2	0	1	0	0	0	0
Floor	2	1	1	1				1	1	1	1	2	1	1	1	1	1	1
Door											0	0	0		0	0	0	0
Post	1	1	0					1	1	1	0	1	1	1		1	0	0
Hatch	0	0	0	0				0	0	0	0	0	0	0	0	0		
Bin	0	0	0	0				0	0	0	0	0	0	0	0	0	0	0
Vent	0	0	0	0				0	0	0	0	0	0	0	0	0	0	0
Burial	0	0	0	1				0	0	0	0	0	0	0	0	0	0	0
Pit	0	0	0	0				0	0	0	0	0	0	1	0	0	0	0
Jar																1		
Bowl																0		
S.S.																0		
Axe																0		
A.Flak.																1		
Awl																1		
Hoe																0		
Knife																0		
Drill																0		
P.P.																0		
Sterile	0	0	0	0				1	0	1	1	0	1	1	1	1	0	0
Area	2.8	8.3	4.8	4.2				5.1	2.3	2.7	4.8	8.4	2.0	2.9	2.8	8.8	2.8	3.9
SDI	1.8	0.3	2.1	0.6				0.7	1.4	1.5	1.1	1.0	1.8	2.4		1.9	3.1	1.3
Shape	1.1	1.3	2.7	2.1				1.1	1.1	1.4	1.5	1.5	1.6	1.5	1.2	1.3	1.4	1.7
C.Hrth.	0	1	0	0				1	0	1	0	0	0	1	0	1	0	0
R.Hrth.	0	0	0	0				0	0	0	1	0	0	0	0	0	0	0
Hrth.	0	1	0	1				1	0	1	0	1	0	1	0	1	0	0
Trough	0	0	1	0				0	0	0	0	1	0	1	0	0	0	0

Appendix B (continued). Turkey Creek Pueblo Room Data

Room #	159	161	162	163	164	165	166	167	173	180	134	146	172	174	176	183	187	190
Group	I	I	I	I	I	I	I	I	I	I	J	J	J	J	J	J	J	J
Place	I	I	I	I	I	I	E	E	E	E	T	T	I	T	T	T	T	I
Height	4.0	3.8	4.0	3.5	3.8	5.0	3.0	2.2	2.5	3.2	3.2	3.0	3.0	3.2	3.0	3.0	3.2	3.5
Basalt	0	0	0	1	0	0	0	0	0	0	0	0	0	0	0	0	1	0
Plaster	0	0	0		0	0	0	0	0	0	0	0	0	0	0	0	0	0
Floor	1	1	1	1	1	1	1	1	1	2	1	1	1	1	1	1	1	1
Door	0	0	0	0	0	0	0	0	0	0	0	0	0	0	0	0	0	0
Post	0	0	0	0	0	0	0							1	0	0	0	0
Hatch	0	0	0		0	1	0	0		0	0	0	0			0		
Bin	0	0	0	0	0	0	0	0	0	0	0	0	0	0	0	0	0	0
Vent	0	0	0	0	0	0	0	0	0	0	0	0	0	0	0	0	0	0
Burial	0	0	0	0	0	1	0	0	0	0	0	0	0	1	0	0	1	0
Pit	0	0	0		0	0	0	0	0	0	0	0	0	0	0	0	0	0
Jar																	0	
Bowl																	1	
S.S.														0				
Axe														0				
A.Flak.														0				
Awl														1				
Hoe														0				
Knife														0				
Drill														0				
P.P.														0				
Sterile	0	1	1	1	0	0	0	0	0	0	0			0	0	0	0	0
Area	3.4	3.0	2.7	4.2	2.9	7.9	5.4	2.0	2.9	4.8	8.8	1.5	3.3	1.9	6.9	7.0	8.9	5.0
SDI		1.3	0.3		0.6	1.3	0.6	0.1	1.4	0.5	2.3	0.6	0.2	0.4	4.8	0.9	1.1	
Shape	1.2	1.3	1.6	2.0	1.6	2.1	1.9	1.6	1.1	1.2	2.2	1.6	1.3	1.2	1.9	1.6	1.3	1.4
C.Hrth.	1	0	0	1	0	1	1	0	1	0	0	0	0	0	0	1	1	1
R.Hrth.	0	0	0	0	0	0	0	0	0	0	0	0	0	0	0	0	0	0
Hrth.	1	0	0	1	0	1	1	0	1	0	0	0	0	0	0	1	1	1
Trough	0	0	0	0	0	1	1	0	1	1	0	0	0	0	1	1	0	0

Room #	191	194	213	157	158	168	169	188	193	217	220	170	181	192	222	226	227	228
Group	J	J	J	K	K	K	K	K	K	K	K	L	L	L	L	L	L	L
Place	I	I	I	K	K	T	K	I	I	I	I	K	K	I	E	I	I	E
Height	2.8	4.2	5.5	3.8	4.2	4.8	3.6	5.3	3.5	5.5	4.2	2.5	2.0	3.5	3.2	5.2	4.5	5.0
Basalt	0	0	0	0	0		0	0	0			1	1	1		0	0	0
Plaster	0	1	2	1	1	1	1	1	1		1	0	0	0	1	1	1	1
Floor	1	2	3	1	1	2	2	2	2		2	2	2	2	3	2	2	2
Door	0		1	0			0	0	0		0	0	0	0	0	0	0	1
Post	0	1	1	1	0		0	1	1		0	0	0	0	1	0	0	1
Hatch	0	1	1	1	1	1	1	1	1			0			1	1		
Bin	0	0	1	0	0	0	0	0	0		0	0	1	0	0	0	0	0
Vent	0	1	0	0	0	0	0	0	0		0	0	0	0	1	0	0	0
Burial	0	0	0	0	0	1	1	0	0		0	1	1	0		0	0	0
Pit	0	0		0	1	1	0	0	0		0	0	0			0	0	0
Jar		1		1	1	1	1		0									
Bowl				1	1	1	0		1									
S.S.		0	1	0	0	0	0		0		0					0	1	0
Axe		0	1	0	0	0	1		0		1					0	0	1
A.Flak.		0	0	0	1	1	1		1		1					0	0	0
Awl		1	0	0	1	1	0		1		0					0	1	0
Hoe		1	0	0	0	0	0		1		0					0	1	0
Knife		0	0	1	0	1	0		0		0					0	0	0
Drill		0	1	1	1	0	0		0		0					0	0	0
P.P.		1	0	1	1	1	1		1		0					1	0	0
Sterile	0		0		1	1	1	0	0		0			1	0			
Area	3.8	14.0	14.0	7.6	13.5	6.9	8.0	6.8	14.1	1.8	3.0	3.4	2.6	2.9	23.1	10.6	7.0	7.3
SDI	0.5	0.4	1.0	3.5	1.1		2.6	1.3	0.5		0.8					0.4	2.3	
Shape	1.6	1.1	1.2	1.0	1.4	1.7	1.0	1.5	1.3	1.2	1.3	1.5	1.2	1.7	1.9	2.2	1.6	2.5
C.Hrth.	0	0	0	1	1	2	0	5	1	0	2	0	0	0	0	1	1	2
R.Hrth.	0	1	1	0	1	0	1	1	1	0	0	0	0	0	0	0	1	0
Hrth.	0	1	1	1	2	3	1	6	2	0	2	0	1	1	1	1	2	2
Trough	0	0	0	2	0		0	0	0	0	0	0	0	0	0	1	0	0

Appendix B (continued). Turkey Creek Pueblo Room Data

Room #	230	231	236	240	241	242	243	244	265	271	276	171	238	251	253	256	257	267
Group	L	L	L	L	L	L	L	L	L	L	L	M	M	M	M	M	M	M
Place	E	E	I	E	I	E	I	I	I	I	E	E	E	I	E	I	E	E
Height	4.0	3.5	7.0	4.0	5.0	5.2	6.2	3.2	5.2	6.2	6.8	3.5	3.0	4.2	5.2	4.5	6.5	4.7
Basalt			0		0	0	0	0	0	0	0	0	0	0	0	0	0	0
Plaster	1	1	1	1	1	1	1	1	1	3	1	0	0	1	1	1	1	1
Floor	1	1	1	1	3	1	1	1	2		3	2	1	1	1	1	1	2
Door	0	0	0	0	1	0	0	1	0	0	0	0	0	0	0	0	1	1
Post	0	0	0	0	0	0	1	0	0	0	0	0	0	1	0	1	1	0
Hatch	1	1	0	1	1	0	1	0	0	0	0	1	0	1	1	1	1	0
Bin	0	0	0	0	0	0	0	1	0	0	0	0	0	0	0	0	1	0
Vent	0	0	0	0	0	0	0	1	0	0	0	0	0	0	0	1	0	0
Burial	0	0	0	0	0	0	0	0	0	0	1	0	0	1	0	0	0	0
Pit	0	0	0	0	0	0		0	0	0	0	0	0	0	0	0	0	0
Jar											1			1				
Bowl											1			0				
S.S.					0									0				
Axe					0									0				
A.Flak.					0									0				
Awl					0									1				
Hoe					0									0				
Knife					1									0				
Drill					0									0				
P.P.					0									0				
Sterile	0	0	0	0	1	0	1			1	0	1	0	0	1		1	
Area	12.3	15.8	5.3	10.9	27.7	10.2	11.4	11.7	7.2	6.8	24.3	8.2	3.6	13.0	4.9	7.3	10.2	3.8
SDI	0.5	1.8	0.1	0.7	1.4	0.2	0.3	0.4		1.8	1.1	3.5	0.9	1.4	1.0	0.8	1.2	0.7
Shape	1.2	1.2	1.2	1.7	2.5	1.1	1.2	1.1	1.2	1.4	1.1	1.4	1.5	1.9	1.2	1.2	1.0	1.7
C.Hrth.	0	0	0	0	0	0	0	0	0	0	0	0	0	1	0	1	0	0
R.Hrth.	1	1	0	0	0	0	0	1	0	0	1	0	0	1	0	0	0	0
Hrth.	1	1	0	1	1	0	0	1	0	0	1	0	0	2	0	1	0	1
Trough	1	1	0	0	1	0	1	0	0	0	0	0	0	1	0	1	1	0

Room #	289	291	301	303	306	254	270	280	282	283	288	292	296	302	309	310	179	182
Group	N	N	N	N	N	O	O	O	O	O	O	O	O	O	O	O	P	P
Place	E	I	I	I	I	I	I	I	I	I	I	I	I	I	I	I	K	K
Height	7.0	5.5	7.0	5.0	4.8	7.0	5.5	3.2	6.8	7.0	4.5	6.2	5.8	5.5	7.8	2.5	5.5	5.8
Basalt	0	0	0	0	0	0	0	0	0	0	1	0	0	0	0	0	0	0
Plaster	1	1	1	1	1	1	1	1	1	1	0	1	5	1	0	1	1	1
Floor	1	1	1	1	1	1	1	1	1	1	2	1	2	1	2	1	2	1
Door	1	0	0	0	0	1	0	0	0	1	0	1	1	0	1	0	0	0
Post	0	1	0	0	0	1	0	0	0	0	0	1	0	0	0	1	1	1
Hatch	1	1	0	0	0	1	0	0	0	1	1	0	1	0	0	0	0	1
Bin	0	0	0	0	1	0	0	0	0	0	0	0	1	0	0	0	0	0
Vent	1	1	1	1	1	1	0	0	0	1	0	0	1	0	1	0	1	0
Burial	0	0	0	1	0	0	0	0	0	0	0	0	0	0	0	0	0	1
Pit	0	0	0	0	0	0	0	0	0	0	0	0	0	0	0	0	0	0
Jar																		
Bowl																		
S.S.																	0	
Axe																	0	
A.Flak.																	0	
Awl																	0	
Hoe																	0	
Knife																	0	
Drill																	0	
P.P.																	1	
Sterile	0	0	0	0	0	0	0		0	0		0	1			0	0	0
Area	19.1	12.3	6.0	9.9	7.4	11.3	8.1	4.2	6.5	6.3	4.5	5.9	10.3	2.9	10.6	1.8	10.3	8.4
SDI	0.4	0.1	0.2	0.2	1.4	0.4	1.1	0.4	0.9	1.7	2.5	0.3	1.3		0.2		1.4	0.3
Shape	1.1	1.3	1.8	1.2	1.4	1.0	1.2	1.2	1.1	1.2	1.8	1.3	1.2	1.9	2.2	1.8	1.3	1.7
C.Hrth.	0	1	0	1	2	0	0	0	0	0	0	0	1	0	0	0	3	1
R.Hrth.	0	0	1	0	0	0	0	0	0	0	0	0	0	0	0	0	1	1
Hrth.	0	1	1	1	2	1	0	0	0	0	0	0	1	0	1	0	5	2
Trough	0	0	1	0	0	1	0	0	0	0	0	0	1	0	0	0	1	1

Appendix B (continued). Turkey Creek Pueblo Room Data

Room #	186	198	234	239	245	250	195	199	262	268	277	278	279	285	293	295	299	300
Group	P	P	P	P	P	P	Q	Q	Q	Q	Q	Q	Q	Q	Q	Q	Q	Q
Place	K	I	I	I	I	I	O	O	I	I	I	I	I	I	I	I	I	I
Height	6.0	6.0	8.0	5.0	5.0	6.2	4.5	5.0	5.8	6.7	5.5	5.8	5.5	6.2	5.0	5.3	4.0	6.8
Basalt	0	0	0	0	0	0	0	0	0	0	0	0	0	0	0	0	0	0
Plaster	1	1	1	0	1	1	1	1	1	1	1	1	1	1	1	1	1	1
Floor	2	2	1	3	1	1	1	1	1	4	1	1	1	1	1	1	1	1
Door	1	0	1	1	1	1	0	1	0	1	1	0	0	1	1	0	0	0
Post	1	1	1	0	0	0	0	0	0	0	0	0	0	0	1	0	1	0
Hatch		1		0	1	1	0		1	0	1	0	0	0	1	0	0	1
Bin	0	0	0	0	0	0	0	0	0	1	0	0	0	0	1	0	0	0
Vent	0	0	0	0	0	0	0	0	0	1	1	0	0	0	1	0	0	1
Burial	0	0	0	0	0	0	0	0	0	0	0	0	0	0	0	0	0	1
Pit	0	0	0	0	0	0	0	0	0	0	0	0	0	0	0	0	0	0
Jar															1			
Bowl															0			
S.S.	0														0			
Axe	0														1			
A.Flak.	0														0			
Awl	0														0			
Hoe	0														0			
Knife	0														0			
Drill	0														0			
P.P.	1														0			
Sterile	1	1	1	0	0		1	1	0	0	0			0				0
Area	13.1	6.4	6.2	5.7	8.1	3.9	3.5	19.4	5.8	6.3	6.1	3.1	1.2	5.1	14.1	2.2	6.2	11.1
SDI	1.0	1.0	1.5	0.2	1.8	1.0		0.7	0.6	1.2		0.7		0.8	0.9	0.2	1.4	0.3
Shape	1.3	2.3	1.5	1.8	1.2	1.1	1.2	1.4	1.1	1.6	1.9	1.5	1.5	1.7	1.1	1.4	1.8	1.1
C.Hrth.	2	1	4	0	0	0	0	1	0	0	0	0	0	0	1	0	0	0
R.Hrth.	0	0	0	0	0	0	0	0	1	0	0	0	0	0	0	0	0	1
Hrth.	2	1	4	0	0	0	0	1	1	0	0	0	0	0	1	0	0	1
Trough	0		1	0	0	0	0	1	1	0		0		0	2	1	0	0

Room #	304	307	308	4	196	197	200	201	202	203	204	205	207	208	209	211	212	214
Group	Q	Q	Q	R	R	R	R	R	R	R	R	R	R	R	R	R	R	R
Place	I	I	I	E	O	E	E	E	E	E	E	E	E	I	E	E	I	I
Height	7.0	7.0	5.0	2.8	4.5	3.5	2.0	2.5	4.2	3.5	2.5	3.8	2.3	4.0	4.0	3.5	3.2	4.0
Basalt	0	0	0	1	0	0	0	1	1	1			1	0			1	
Plaster	2	1	1	0	1	1	0	0	0	0	0	0	0	1	0	0	0	0
Floor	1	1	1	1		1	1	1	1	1	2	1	1	1	1	1	1	1
Door	0	0	0	0	0	0	0	0	0	0	0	0	0	1	0	0	0	0
Post	0	0	0	0	0	0	0	0	0	0	0	0	0	0	0	0	0	0
Hatch		1		0	0	0	0	0	1				1	1	1			
Bin	0	1	0	0	1	0	0	0	0	0	0	0	0	0	0	0	0	0
Vent	1	1	0	0	0	0	0	0	1	0	0	0	0	0	0	1	0	0
Burial	0	0	0	0	0	0	0	0	0	0	0	0	0	0	1	0	0	0
Pit	0	0	0	0	0	0	0	0	0	0	0	0	0	0	0	0	0	0
Jar		0																1
Bowl		1																0
S.S.					1		0											
Axe					1		0											
A.Flak.					0		0											
Awl					0		0											
Hoe					0		0											
Knife					0		0											
Drill					0		1											
P.P.					0		0											
Sterile	0	0	0		0	0	0	0	0	0	0	0	0	0		0	0	0
Area	9.2	5.7	4.4	5.4	12.5	6.8	24.0	3.2	5.0	5.8	25.1	4.5	6.4	20.4	9.8	2.0	4.2	10.5
SDI	0.2	0.2	0.3		0.8	0.4	0.7	1.1	0.5	0.9	0.5	0.1	0.3	1.0	0.2			2.4
Shape	1.4	2.5	2.2	1.1	1.9	1.2	1.5	2.1	1.5	1.0	2.1	1.4	1.2	1.1	1.9	1.8	1.5	1.7
C.Hrth.	1	0	0	0	0	1	2	0	0	1	1	0	2	0	1	0	0	0
R.Hrth.	0	0	0	0	0	1	0	0	0	0	0	0	0	1	0	0	0	0
Hrth.	1	0	0	0	0	2	2	0	0	1	1	0	2	1	1	0	0	0
Trough	0	0	0	0	0	0	0	1		0	1	0	0	1	1			0

Appendix B (continued). Turkey Creek Pueblo Room Data

Room #	215	223	224	225	229	233	249	259	260	263	274	286	287	237	246	247	248	252
Group	R	R	R	R	R	R	R	R	R	R	R	R	R	S	S	S	S	S
Place	I	I	I	I	I	I	I	I	I	I	I	I	I	E	E	E	E	E
Height	5.2	5.2	4.0	4.5	4.7	4.5	4.2	5.2	5.5	6.0	5.2	5.7	5.8	4.5	4.2	4.5	4.3	3.8
Basalt		0	0		0	0	0	0	0	0	0	0	0		0			0
Plaster	2	1	1	1	1	1	0	1	1	1	1	1	2	1	1	1	1	1
Floor	1	1	1	1	1	1	1	1	1	1	1	2	1	3	1	1	2	1
Door	0	0	0	0	0	0	0	0	0	0	0	0	0	0	0	0	0	0
Post	0	0	1	0		1	0	0	1	0	0	0	0	0	0	0	0	0
Hatch	1	1	1			1	0	0		1	0	1	1	1		0		1
Bin	0	1	1	0	0	0	0	0	0	0	0	1	0	1	0	0	1	0
Vent	0	0	1	0	0	1	0	0	0	1	0	1	1	0	0	0	1	0
Burial	0	0	1	0	1	0	0	0	0	1	0	0	0	0	0	0	0	0
Pit	0	0	0	0		0	0	0	0	0	0	0	0	0	0	0	0	0
Jar			1			1				1								
Bowl			1			0				0								
S.S.			0															
Axe			1															
A.Flak.			1															
Awl			1															
Hoe			0															
Knife			1															
Drill			1															
P.P.			0															
Sterile	0	0		0	1	0	1	0	0	0	1	0	0		0	0	0	1
Area	5.6	15.1	11.7	2.3	9.1	17.6	4.0	15.3	7.0	12.1	4.2	9.5	8.1	14.0	2.2	3.4	9.7	5.0
SDI	2.6	0.6	0.7	1.9		0.9	0.3	0.4	0.2	1.8		0.5	0.1	4.2	0.0	1.3	1.4	0.8
Shape	1.2	2.1	1.3	1.7	1.2	1.2	1.7	1.2	1.3	1.1	1.9	1.7	1.2	1.6	1.2	1.4	1.2	1.5
C.Hrth.	0	0	1	0	0	0	0	1	1	0	0	0	2	0	0	0	2	1
R.Hrth.	1	0	0	0	1	0	0	0	0	0	0	1	0	0	0	0	0	0
Hrth.	1	0	1	0	1	0	0	1	1	0	0	1	2	0	0	2	1	
Trough		1	1	0		1	0	0	0	1		1	0		0	1	1	0

Room #	255	264	272	273	281	206	216	218	219	221	258	266	269	275	294	297	298
Group	S	S	S	S	S	T	T	T	T	T	T	T	T	T	T	T	T
Place	I	I	I	I	I	E	E	E	I	E	I	I	I	I	I	I	I
Height	4.0	4.8	5.3	6.3	5.7	2.0	7.0	2.8	4.0	2.5	4.3	2.8	5.5	7.0	4.2	5.2	5.0
Basalt	0	0	0	0	0		0				0	0		0	0	0	0
Plaster	1	0	2	1	1	0	1	0	0	0	1	0	1	1	1	1	1
Floor	1	1	1	1	1	1	1	1	1	1	1	1		2	1	1	1
Door	0	0	0	1	0	0	0	0	0	0	0	0	1	1	0	0	0
Post	0	0	0	1	0	0	1	0	0	0	0	0	0	0	0	0	0
Hatch	1		1	0	0	1	1	0	0	1	1	0	0	0	0	0	0
Bin	0	0	0	0	0	0	0	0	0	0	0	0	0	0	0	0	0
Vent	0	0	1	1	1	0	1	0	0	0	1	0	0	1	0	0	0
Burial	0	0	0	0	0		0	0	0	0	1	0	0	0	0	0	0
Pit	0	0	0	0	0		0	0	0	0	0	0	0	0	0	0	0
Sterile	1	1	0	0	0	0	0	0	1	0	0	0		0			0
Area	9.5	5.1	8.4	20.0	11.1	18.2	10.4	2.8	9.9	7.8	6.1	15.0	2.5	24.0	2.2	3.0	5.3
SDI	1.6	0.8	0.3	0.3	0.5			1.9	3.8	3.1	1.9	0.7	1.1	0.6	1.6	3.8	0.6
Shape	1.5	1.6	1.3	1.2	1.4	1.5	1.3	1.5	1.2	1.0	1.9	1.4	1.0	2.1	1.1	1.1	1.9
C.Hrth.	1	0	1	1	1	0	1	0	0	1	0	0	0	0	0	0	0
R.Hrth.	0	0	0	0	0	1	0	0	0	0	0	0	0	0	0	0	0
Hrth.	1	0	1	1	1	1	1	0	0	1	0	0	0	0	0	0	0
Trough	0	0	1	0	0		1	0	0	0	1	0	0	1	1	0	0

Frequency Table For Turkey Creek Room Variables

APPENDIX C

TURKEY CREEK PUEBLO ROOM VARIABLES

Variable	Frequency	Percent
Hearth		
No Info.	19	
Absent	132	46.8
Present	150	53.2
Circular Hearth		
No Info.	20	
Absent	193	68.7
Present	88	31.3
Rectangular Hearth		
No Info.	20	
Absent	222	79.0
Present	59	21.0
Storage Pit		
No Info.	29	
Absent	259	95.2
Present	13	4.8
Hatch		
No Info.	66	
Absent	145	61.7
Present	90	38.3
Storage Bin		
No Info.	17	
Absent	261	91.9
Present	23	8.1
Vent		
No Info.	18	
Absent	240	84.8
Present	43	15.2
Burial		
No Info.	18	
Absent	250	88.3
Present	33	11.7
Plaster		
No Info.	9	
Absent	146	50.0
1 Coat	127	43.5

TURKEY CREEK PUEBLO ROOM VARIABLES (continued)

Variable	Frequency	Percent
2 Coats	12	4.1
3 Coats	6	2.1
5 Coats	1	0.3
Shape		
No Info.	12	
1 (most square)	179	61.9
2	102	35.3
3 (least square)	8	2.8
Place		
Exterior	78	25.9
Interior	189	62.8
Kiva	8	2.7
Plaza 1	13	4.3
Plaza 2	13	4.3
Room Area Group		
1 (smallest)	81	26.8
2	77	25.6
3	55	18.3
4	44	14.6
5	21	7.0
6	6	2.0
7	9	3.0
8	5	1.7
9 (largest)	3	1.0
Wall Height		
No Info.	6	
1 Course	4	1.4
2 Courses	25	8.5
3 Courses	69	23.4
4 Courses	83	28.1
5 Courses	66	22.4
6 Courses	32	10.8
7 Courses	14	4.7
8 Courses	2	0.7
Basalt-based Walls		
No Info.	24	
Absent	218	78.7
Present	59	21.3

TURKEY CREEK PUEBLO ROOM VARIABLES *(continued)*

Variable	Frequency	Percent
Sterile		
No Info.	49	
Absent	177	70.2
Present	75	29.8
Posthole		
No Info.	21	
Absent	164	58.6
Present	116	41.4
Door		
No Info.	30	
Absent	240	88.6
Present	31	11.4
Room Side		
North	178	66.9
South	88	33.1
Sherd Density Index Group		
1 (lowest)	78	29.3
2	67	25.2
3	38	14.3
4	34	12.8
5	17	6.4
6 (highest)	32	12.0
Room Size		
1 (small)	133	44.2
2 (medium)	101	33.5
3 (large)	67	22.3
Room Class		
1 (C. Hearth only)	76	56.3
2 (R. Hearth only)	47	34.8
3 (Both C. and R. Hearths)	12	8.9
Vessel		
Present	34	
Bowls	18	
Jars	28	

TURKEY CREEK PUEBLO ROOM VARIABLES *(continued)*

Variable	Frequency	Percent
Trough Metate		
No Info.	38	
Absent	174	66.2
Present	89	33.8

INDIVIDUAL FLOOR ARTIFACTS-LIMITED ROOM SAMPLE*

Variable	Frequency	Percent
Antler Flaker		
Absent	32	71.1
Present	13	28.9
Awl		
Absent	26	57.8
Present	19	42.2
Axe		
Absent	29	64.4
Present	16	35.6
Drill		
Absent	39	86.7
Present	6	13.3
Hoe		
Absent	37	82.2
Present	8	17.8
Knife		
Absent	35	77.8
Present	10	22.2
Projectile Point		
Absent	31	68.9
Present	14	31.1
Shaft Straightener		
Absent	39	86.7
Present	6	13.3

* For all "limited room sample" artifacts, only the 45 rooms with individual artifacts listed explicitly on the floor are included.

APPENDIX D

Contingency Test Results

Symbols Used in Summary Tables of Contingency Test Results*			
1.	R	=	An apparent relationship between variables
2.	R+	=	An apparent positive relationship between variables
3.	R-	=	An apparent negative relationship between variables
4.	M	=	More than expected
5.	F	=	Fewer than expected
6.	A	=	As expected
7.	H	=	High
8.	N	=	North
9.	S	=	South
10.		=	No information or not appropriate
11.	X	=	No apparent relationship between variables

* Contingency test results presented in tables in the text are excluded from the summary tables of this appendix.

Table D.1. Contingency Test Results for Fixed Attributes

	Area Group	C-size	R-size	Sterile	SDIGP	Room Group	Ba-salt	Height	Plaster	Multi-plast.	Door	Hatch	Post	Shape	Burial	Vent	Bin	Pit	Side
				N-M	N-H		N-M	S-H	S-M	R	S-M	S-M	N-M	R		S-M			N-M
Side	X	X	X	N-M	N-H	R	N-M	S-H	S-M	R	S-M	S-M	N-M	R	X	S-M	X	X	N-M
Pit	X	X	X	X	M(3--5)	X	X	X	X	X	X	X	R+	X	X	X	X	X	
Bin	R+	X	X	X	M(2--3)	R	X	X	R+	R+	R+	R+	X	X	X	R+			
Vent	R+	X	X	R-	M(1)	R	R-	X	R+	R+	R+	R+	X	X	X				
Burial	R+	X	X	X	X	X	X	R+	X	X	X	X	X						
Shape	X	X	X	X	X	X	X	X	X	X	X	X	1-M						
Post	R+	X	X	X	X	R	X	X	X	X	X	R+							
Hatch	R+	X	X	X	X	R	X	R+	R+	X	X								
Door	R+	X	X	X	X	R	X	R+	R+	R+									
Mltiplst.	X			X	X	R	X	R+	R+										
Plaster	R+	X	X	X	X	R	R-	R+											
Height	X	X	X	X	X	R	R-												
Basalt	X	F(2--3)	X	R+	M(5--6)	R	R-												
Group	X	R		R	R														
SDIGP	X	X		X															
Sterile	X	X																	
Rsize																			
Csize																			
Class	2--H																		
Area																			
Group																			

Table D.2. Contingency Test Results for Portable Artifacts with Fixed Attributes

	Trough Metate	Vessel	Bowl	Jar	Artifact
Side	X	X	N-M	X	N-M
Pit	X	X	R+	X	X
Bin	R+	X	X	X	X
Vent	R+	X	X	X	X
Burial	R+	R+	X	R+	X
Shape	X	X			X
Post	R+	R+	R+	R+	R+
Hatch	R+	R+	R+	R+	R+
Door	X	X	X	X	X
Multiplaster	X				
Plaster	X	R+	R+	R+	R+
Height	X	X	X	X	X
Basalt	X	X	X	X	X
Group	X	R	R	R	R
SDIGP	X	R+	X	R+	R+
Sterile	X	X	X	X	X
Rsize	X	R+			X
Csize	X	X			R+
Class	X	X	X	X	X
Area group	(1–2)-F	R+			R+

Table D.3. Contingency Test Results for Portable Artifacts with Individual Artifacts

	Trough Metate	Vessel	Bowl	Jar
Limited Room Sample:				
Projectile Point	X	X		
Drill				
Knife	X	X		
Hoe	X			
Awl	X	X		
Antler Flaker	X	R+		
Axe	X	X		
Shaft Straightener				
Total Room Sample:				
Projectile Point	X		R+	R+
Drill			R+	R+
Knife	X		R+	R+
Hoe			X	X
Awl	X		R+	R+
Antler Flaker	X	R+	R+	R+
Axe	X	R+	X	R+
Shaft Straightener			R+	X
Artifact	X	R+		
Jar	R+		R+	
Bowl	X			
Vessel	R+			

Table D.4. Contingency Test Results for Individual Artifacts with other Individual Artifacts, using the Total Room Sample (N = 301 Rooms)

	N	Shaft Straightener 6	Axe 16	Antler Flaker 13	Awl 19	Hoe 8	Knife 10	Drill 6	Projectile Point 14
Projectile Point		X	R+	R+	R+	R+	R+	R+	
Drill		X	X	R+	R+	X	R+		
Knife		X	R+	R+	R+	X			
Hoe		R+	X	R+	R+				
Awl		R+	X	R+					
Antler Flaker		X	R+						
Axe		R+							

Table D.5. Contingency Test Results for Individual Artifacts with other Individual Artifacts, using the Limited Room Sample (N = 45 rooms)

	Shaft Straightener	Axe	Antler Flaker	Awl	Hoe	Knife	Drill	Projectile Point
Projectile Point	X	X	X	X	X	X	X	
Drill	X	X	X	X	X	R+		
Knife	X	X	X	X	X			
Hoe	X	X	X	R+				
Awl	X	R–	X					
Antler Flaker	X	X						
Axe	X							

Table D.6. Contingency Test Results for Individual Portable Artifacts with Fixed Attributes, using the Total Room Sample (N = 301 Rooms)

	Antler Flaker	Awl	Axe	Drill	Hoe	Knife	Projectile Point	Shaft Straightener
Hearth	R+	R+	X	X	X	R+	R+	X
C. Hearth	X	R+	X	R+	X	X	R+	X
R. Hearth	R+	R+	X	X	X	X	R+	R+
Group	K, E-M	X	X			X	P, K-M	
Basalt	X	X	X			X	X	
Plaster	R+	R+	R+			X	R+	
Post	X	R+	R+			R+	R+	
Hatch	R+	R+	R+			R+	R+	
Bin	X	X	R+			X	X	
Vent	X	X	X			X	X	
Burial	R+	X	X			R+	X	
Pit	X	X	X			X	X	
Class	X	X	X			X	3–M	
Size	R+	R+	3–M			X	R+	
Door	X	X	X			X	X	
SDIGP	R+	X	R+	X	X	R+	X	X
Sterile	X	X	X	X	X	X	X	
Side	N-M	N-M	X	X	N-M	X	X	X

Table D.7. Contingency Test Results for Individual Portable Artifacts with Fixed Attributes, using the Limited Room Sample (N = 45 Rooms)

	Antler Flaker	Awl	Axe	Drill	Hoe	Knife	Projectile Point	Shaft Straightener
Hearth	X	X	X	X	X	X	X	X
C. Hearth	X	X	X	X	X	X	X	R−
R. Hearth	X	X	X	X	X	X	X	R+
Group	R	X	X	X	X	X	R	X
Areagp	X	X	X			X	X	R+
Height	R	X	X			X	X	X
Basalt	X	X	X			X	X	X
Plaster	X	X	X			X	X	X
Post	X	X	X			X	X	X
Hatch	X	X	X			X	X	X
Bin	X	X	X			X	X	X
Vent	X	X	X			X	X	X
Burial	R+	X	X			X	X	X
Shape	X	X	X			X	X	X
Pit	X	X	X			X	X	X
Class	X	X	X			X	3–M	
Size	X	X	X			X	X	
Door	R−	R−	X			X	X	
Sterile	X	X	X	X				

References

Aberle, Sophie D.
    1948   The Pueblo Indians of New Mexico: Their Land, Economy and Civil Organization. *American Anthropologist* 50(4), Part 2, Memoir 70.

Adams, E. Charles
    1983   The Architectural Analogue to Hopi Social Organization and Room Use, and Implications for Prehistoric Northern Southwestern Culture. *American Antiquity* 48(1): 44–61.

Allen, William L., and James B. Richardson III
    1971   The Reconstruction of Kinship from Archaeological Data: The Concepts, the Methods, and the Feasibility. *American Antiquity* 36(1): 41–53.

Bandelier, Adolph
    1892   An Outline of the Documentary History of the Zuni Tribe. *Journal of American Ethnology and Archaeology* 3: 1–115.

Bannister, Bryant, and William J. Robinson
    1971   *Tree-Ring Dates from Arizona U-W Gila-Salt Rivers Area.* Laboratory of Tree-Ring Research. Tucson: University of Arizona.

Beaglehole, Ernest
    1937   Notes on Hopi Economic Life. *Yale University Publications in Anthropology* 15: 1–88.

Beaglehole, Ernest, and Pearl Beaglehole
    1935   Hopi of the Second Mesa. *Memoirs of the American Anthropological Association* 44: 5–65.

Beals, Ralph L., George W. Brainerd, and Watson Smith
    1945   Archaeological Studies in Northeast Arizona. *University of California Publications in American Archaeology and Ethnology*, Vol. 44, No. 1. Berkeley and Los Angeles: University of California Press.

Benavides, Fray Alonso de
    1954   *Benavides' Memorial of 1630*, edited by C. J. Lynch. Washington: Academy of American Franciscan History.

Bennett, Kenneth A.
    1973   The Indians of Point of Pines, Arizona: A Comparative Study of Their Physical Characteristics. *Anthropological Papers of The University of Arizona* 23. Tucson: University of Arizona Press.

Berkner, Lutz K.
    1972   The Stem Family and the Developmental Cycle of the Peasant Household: An Eighteenth-century Austrian Example. *The American Historical Review* 77(2): 398–418.

Bohannan, Paul
    1963   *Social Anthropology.* New York: Holt, Rinehart, and Winston.

Breternitz, David A.
    1959   Excavations at Nantack Village, Point of Pines, Arizona. *Anthropological Papers of The University of Arizona* 1. Tucson: University of Arizona Press.

Breternitz, David A., James C. Gifford, and Alan P. Olson
    1957   Point of Pines Phase Sequence and Utility Pottery Type Revisions. *American Antiquity* 22(4): 412–416.

Brew, John O.
    1979   Hopi Prehistory and History to 1850. In "Southwest," edited by Alfonso Ortiz, Vol. 9, *Handbook of North American Indians*, edited by William C. Sturtevant, pp. 514–523. Washington: Smithsonian Institution.

Brown, Susan E.
    1977   Household Composition and Variation in a Rural Dominican Village. *Journal of Comparative Family Studies* 8(2): 257–267.

Bunzel, Ruth L.
    1933   Zuni Texts. *Publications of the American Ethnological Society* 15: 1–285.

Carlson, Roy L.
    1970   White Mountain Redware. *Anthropological Papers of The University of Arizona* 19. Tucson: University of Arizona Press.

Chang, Kwang-Chih
    1958   Study of the Neolithic Social Grouping: Examples from the New World. *American Anthropologist* 60: 298–334.

Ciolek-Torrello, Richard
    1978   A Statistical Analysis of Activity Organization: Grasshopper Pueblo, Arizona. MS, Doctoral dissertation, Department of Anthropology, University of Arizona, Tucson.
    1985   A Typology of Room Function at Grasshopper Pueblo. *Journal of Field Archaeology* 12: 41–63.

Ciolek-Torrello, Richard, and J. Jefferson Reid
    1974   Change in Household Size at Grasshopper. *The Kiva* 40(1–2): 39–47.

Colton, Harold S.
    1936   The Rise and Fall of the Prehistoric Population of Northern Arizona. *Science* 84(2181): 337–343.

Cook, Edwin A.
    1961   A New Mogollon Structure. *The Kiva* 26(3): 24–32.

Cordell, Linda S.
    1984   *Prehistory of the Southwest.* New York: Academic Press.

Cummings, Byron
    1915   Kivas of the San Juan Drainage. *American Anthropologist* 17: 272–282.

Curtis, William E.
    1883   *Children of the Sun.* Chicago: Inter-Ocean Publishing.

Cushing, Frank H.
    1920   Zuni Breadstuff. *Indian Notes and Monographs* 8. New York: Museum of the American Indian, Heye Foundation.
    1979   *Zuni: Selected Writings of Frank Hamilton Cushing*, edited by J. Green. Lincoln and London: University of Nebraska Press.

Cushing, Frank H., J. Walter Fewkes, and Elsie C. Parsons
- 1922 Contributions to Hopi History. *American Anthropologist* 24: 253–298.

Dean, Jeffrey S.
- 1969 Chronological Analysis of Tsegi Phase Sites in Northeastern Arizona. *Papers of the Laboratory of Tree-Ring Research*, No. 3. Tucson: University of Arizona Press.
- 1970 Aspects of Tsegi Phase Social Organization: A Trial Reconstruction. In *Reconstructing Prehistoric Pueblo Societies*, edited by William A. Longacre, pp. 140–173. Albuquerque: University of New Mexico Press.
- 1986 Delineating the Anasazi. In *Emil W. Haury's Prehistory of the American Southwest*, edited by J. Jefferson Reid and David E. Doyel, pp. 407–413. Tucson: University of Arizona Press.

Dean, Jeffery S., and William J. Robinson
- 1982 Dendrochronology of Grasshopper Pueblo. In "Multidisciplinary Research at Grasshopper Pueblo, Arizona," edited by William A. Longacre, Sally J. Holbrook, and Michael W. Graves, pp. 46–60. *Anthropological Papers of The University of Arizona* 40. Tucson: University of Arizona Press.

Donaldson, Thomas C.
- 1893 Extra Census Bulletin: Moqui Pueblo Indians of Arizona and Pueblo Indians of New Mexico. *Eleventh Census of the United States* (1890). Washington: U.S. Census Printing Office.

Dozier, Edward P.
- 1970 *The Pueblo Indians of North America*. New York: Holt, Rinehart, and Winston.

Eggan, Fred R.
- 1950 *Social Organization of the Western Pueblos*. Chicago: University of Chicago Press.

Ellis, Florence Hawley
- 1951 Pueblo Social Organization and Southwestern Archaeology. *American Antiquity* 17: 148–151.
- 1964 A Reconstruction of the Basic Jemez Pattern of Social Organization, with Comparisons to Other Tanoan Social Structures. *University of New Mexico Publications in Anthropology* 11. Albuquerque: University of New Mexico Press.
- 1979 Southern Tewa. In "Southwest," edited by Alfonso Ortiz, Vol. 9, *Handbook of North American Indians*, edited by William C. Sturtevant, pp. 351–365. Washington: Smithsonian Institution.

Feinberg, Stephen
- 1977 *The Analysis of Cross Classified Data*. Cambridge: M.I.T. Press.

Fewkes, J. Walter
- 1894 The Kinship of the Tusayan Villagers. *American Anthropologist* 7: 394–417.
- 1896 The Prehistoric Culture of Tusayan. *American Anthropologist* 9: 151–174.
- 1897 Tusayan Totemic Signatures. *American Anthropologist* (Old Series) 10(1): 1–11.
- 1900a Pueblo Ruins Near Flagstaff, Arizona: A Preliminary Notice. *American Anthropologist* 2: 422–450.
- 1900b Tusayan Migration Traditions. *Nineteenth Annual Report of the Bureau of American Ethnology, 1897–1898*, pp. 573–633. Washington.

Forde, C. Daryll
- 1934 *Habitat, Economy and Society: A Geographical Introduction to Ethnology*. London: Methuen.

Freeman, J. D.
- 1971 The Family System of the Iban of Borneo. In *The Developmental Cycle in Domestic Groups*, edited by Jack Goody, pp. 15–52. Cambridge: Cambridge University Press.

Geertz, Hildred, and Clifford Geertz
- 1975 *Kinship in Bali*. Chicago: University of Chicago Press.

Gladwin, Harold Sterling
- 1957 *A History of the Ancient Southwest*. Portland: The Bond Wheelwright Company.

Goody, Jack
- 1971 The Fission of Domestic Groups among the Lodagaba. In *The Developmental Cycle in Domestic Groups*, edited by Jack Goody, pp. 53–91. Cambridge: Cambridge University Press.
- 1972 Domestic Groups. *An Addison-Wesley Module in Anthropology* 28. Reading, Massachusetts: Addison-Wesley.

Graves, Michael W.
- 1983 Growth and Aggregation at Canyon Creek Ruin: Implications for Evolutionary Change in East-Central Arizona. *American Antiquity* 48(2): 290–315.
- 1984 Temporal Variation among White Mountain Redware Design Styles. *The Kiva* 50(1): 3–24.

Graves, Michael W., William A. Longacre, and Sally Holbrook
- 1982 Aggregation and Abandonment at Grasshopper Pueblo, Arizona. *Journal of Field Archaeology* 9: 193–206.

Hammel, Eugene A.
- 1972 The Zadruga as Process. In *Household and Family in Past Time*, edited by Peter Laslett and R. Wall, pp. 335–373. Cambridge: Cambridge University Press.
- 1984 On the *** of Studying Household Form and Function. In *Households: Comparative and Historical Studies of the Domestic Group*, edited by Robert McC. Netting, Richard R. Wilk, and Eric J. Arnould, pp. 29–43. Berkeley: University of California Press.

Hammel, Eugene A., and Peter Laslett
- 1974 Comparing Household Structure over Time and between Cultures. *Comparative Studies in Society and History* 16(1): 73–109.

Hammond, George P., and Agapito Rey, editors
- 1940 *Narratives of the Coronado Expedition 1540–1542*. Albuquerque: University of New Mexico Press.
- 1966 *The Rediscovery of New Mexico: 1580–1594: The Explorations of Chamuscado, Espejo, Castano de Sosa, Morlete, and Leyva de Bonilla and Humana*. Albuquerque: University of New Mexico Press.

Haury, Emil W.
- 1957 Archaeological Studies of Culture History of the Point of Pines Region in East Central Arizona. MS, National Science Foundation Grant Proposal, Arizona State Museum, University of Arizona, Tucson.
- 1958 Evidence at Point of Pines for a Prehistoric Migration from Northern Arizona. In "Migrations in New World Culture History," edited by Raymond H. Thompson. *University of Arizona Bulletin* 29(2), *Social Science Bulletin* 27: 1–8. Tucson: University of Arizona.
- 1989 Point of Pines, Arizona: A History of The University of Arizona Archaeological Field School. *Anthropological Papers of The University of Arizona* 50. Tucson: University of Arizona Press.

Hawley, Florence M.
- 1937 Pueblo Social Organization as a Lead to Pueblo History. *American Anthropologist* 39: 504–521.

Heindl, Leo A.
- 1955 "Clean Fill" at Point of Pines, Arizona. *The Kiva* 20(4): 1–8.

Hill, James N.
  1966 A Prehistoric Community in Eastern Arizona. *Southwestern Journal of Anthropology* 22: 9–30.
  1970a Prehistoric Social Organization in the American Southwest: Theory and Method. In *Reconstructing Prehistoric Pueblo Societies*, edited by William A. Longacre, pp. 11–56. Albuquerque: University of New Mexico Press.
  1970b Broken K Pueblo: Prehistoric Social Organization in the American Southwest. *Anthropological Papers of The University of Arizona* 18. Tucson: University of Arizona Press.

Hough, Walter
  1915 *The Hopi*. Cedar Rapids, Iowa: The Torch Press.

Horne, Lee
  1982 The Household in Space: Dispersed Holdings in an Iranian Village. *American Behavioral Scientist* 25(6): 677–685.

James, George W.
  1919 *The Indians of the Painted Desert Region, Wallapais, Havasupais*. Boston: Little, Brown.

Johnson, Alfred E.
  1964 Excavations at Turkey Creek Pueblo, Arizona, 1958–1960. MS, Arizona State Museum Archives, University of Arizona, Tucson.
  1965 The Development of Western Pueblo Culture. MS, Doctoral dissertation, Department of Anthropology, University of Arizona, Tucson.

Jorgensen, Joseph G.
  1980 *Western Indians: Comparative Environments, Languages, and Cultures of 172 Western American Indian Tribes*. San Francisco: W. H. Freeman.

Jorgensen, Julia
  1975 A Room Use Analysis of Table Rock Pueblo, Arizona. *Anthropological Research* 31: 149–161.

Kidder, Alfred Vincent
  1924 An Introduction to the Study of Southwestern Archaeology With a Preliminary Account of the Excavations at Pecos. *Papers of the Phillips Academy Southwestern Expedition* 1. New Haven: Yale University Press.

Klett, Frances
  1874 The Zuni Indians of New Mexico. *The Popular Science Monthly* 5: 580–591.

Kolb, Charles C.
  1985 Demographic Estimates in Archaeology: Contributions from Ethnoarchaeology on Mesoamerican Peasants. *Current Anthropology* 26(5): 581–599.

Kramer, Carol
  1979 An Archaeological View of a Contemporary Kurdish Village: Domestic Architecture, Household Size, and Wealth. In *Ethnoarchaeology: Implications of Ethnography for Archaeology*, pp. 139–163. New York: Columbia University Press.
  1982 Ethnographic Households and Archaeological Interpretation: A Case from Iranian Kurdistan. *American Behavioral Scientist* 25(6): 663–675.

Kroeber, Alfred L.
  1917 Zuni Kin and Clan. *Anthropological Papers of the American Museum of Natural History* 18(2): 39–206.

Laslett, Peter
  1968 *The World We have Lost*. London: Methuen.
  1972 Preface and Introduction: The History of the Family. In *Household and Family in Past Time*, edited by Peter Laslett and R. Wall, pp. ix–xii; 1–89. Cambridge: Cambridge University Press.

LeBlanc, Steven
  1971 An Addition to Naroll's Suggested Floor Area and Settlement Population Relationship. *American Antiquity* 36(2): 210–211.
  1978 Settlement Patterns in the El Morro Valley, New Mexico. In *Investigations of the Southwestern Anthropological Research Group: The Proceedings of the 1976 Conference*, edited by Robert C. Euler and George J. Gumerman, pp. 45–51. Flagstaff: Museum of Northern Arizona.

Lindsay, Alexander J., Jr.
  1969 *The Tsegi Phase of the Kayenta Cultural Tradition in Northeastern Arizona*. Doctoral dissertation, The University of Arizona. Ann Arbor: University Microfilms.

Lofgren, Orvar
  1974 Family and Household among Scandinavian Peasants: An Exploratory Essay. *Ethnologia Scandinavica* 74: 17–52.

Longacre, William A.
  1964 Archaeology as Anthropology: A Case Study. *Science* 144: 1454–1455.
  1966 Changing Patterns of Social Integration: A Prehistoric Example from the American Southwest. *American Anthropologist* 68: 94–102.
  1970a Archaeology as Anthropology. *Anthropological Papers of The University of Arizona* 17. Tucson: University of Arizona Press.
  1970b (Editor) *Reconstructing Prehistoric Pueblo Societies*. Albuquerque: University of New Mexico Press.
  1974 Kalinga Pottery-making: The Evolution of a Research Design. In *Frontiers of Anthropology*, edited by M. J. Leaf, pp. 151–159. New York: D. Van Nostrand.
  1981 Kalinga Pottery: An Ethnoarchaeological Study. In *Patterns of the Past: Studies in Honour of David Clarke*, edited by Ian Hodder, Glynn Isaac, and Norman Hammond, pp. 49–67. Cambridge: Cambridge University Press.

Lowell, Julie C.
  1987 *The Structure and Function of the Prehistoric Household in the Pueblo Southwest: A Case Study from Turkey Creek Pueblo*. Doctoral dissertation, Department of Anthropology, University of Arizona, Tucson. Ann Arbor: University Microfilms.

Martin, Paul S., and John B. Rinaldo
  1950 Sites of the Reserve Phase, Pine Lawn Valley, Western New Mexico. *Fieldiana: Anthropology* 30(3). Chicago: Chicago Natural History Museum.

Martin, Paul S., John B. Rinaldo, William A. Longacre, and others
  1964 Chapters in the Prehistory of Eastern Arizona, II. *Fieldiana: Anthropology* 55. Chicago: Chicago Natural History Museum.

Mc.Gregor, John C.
  1941 *Southwestern Archaeology*. New York: John Wiley and Sons.

Merbs, Charles F.
  1967 Cremated Remains from Point of Pines, Arizona: A New Approach. *American Antiquity* 32(4): 498–506.

Mindeleff, Cosmos
  1895 Cliff Ruins of Canyon de Chelly, Arizona. *American Anthropologist* (Old Series) 8(2): 153–174.
  1900 Localization of Tusayan Clans. *Bureau of American Ethnology, Nineteenth Annual Report, 1897–1898*: 635–653.

Mindeleff, Victor
  1891 A Study of Pueblo Architecture: Tusayan and Cibola.

Eighth Annual Report of the Bureau of Ethnology to the Secretary of the Smithsonian Institution 1886–1887: 3–298.

Morgan, Lewis H.
1881 Houses and House-life of the American Aborigines. *Contributions to North American Ethnology* IV. Washington.

Morris, Elizabeth A.
1957 Stratigraphic Evidence for a Cultural Continuum at the Point of Pines Ruin. MS, Master's thesis, Department of Anthropology, University of Arizona, Tucson.

Murdock, George Peter
1949 *Social Structure*. New York: MacMillan.

Nagata, Shuichi
1970 *Modern Transformations of Moenkopi Pueblo*. Urbana: University of Illinois Press.

Naroll, Raoul
1962 Floor Area and Settlement. *American Antiquity* 27(4): 587–589.

Nelson, Ben A.
1981 Ethnoarchaeology and Paleodemography: A Test of Turner and Lofgren's Hypothesis. *Journal of Anthropological Research* 37(2): 107–129.

Netting, Robert McC.
1982 Some Home Truths on Household Size and Wealth. *American Behavioral Scientist* 25(6): 641–661.

Netting, Robert McC., Richard R. Wilk, and Eric J. Arnould
1984 Introduction. In *Households*, edited by Robert McC. Netting, Richard R. Wilk, and Eric J. Arnould, pp. xiii–xxxviii. Los Angeles: University of California Press.

Olson, Alan P.
1959 An Evaluation of the Phase Concept in Southwestern Archaeology: As Applied to the Eleventh and Twelfth Century Occupations at Point of Pines, East Central Arizona. MS, Doctoral dissertation, Department of Anthropology, University of Arizona, Tucson.
1960 The Dry Prong Site, East Central Arizona. *American Antiquity* 26(2): 185–204.

Ortiz, Alfonso
1969 *The Tewa World: Space, Time, Being, and Becoming in a Pueblo Society*. Chicago: University of Chicago Press.

Parsons, Elsie C.
1917 Notes on Zuni. *Memoirs of the American Anthropological Association* 4(1): 151–327.
1929 The Social Organization of the Tewa of New Mexico. *Memoirs of the American Anthropological Association* 36.
1939 *Pueblo Indian Religion*. Chicago: University of Chicago Press.

Plog, Fred T.
1983 Political and Economic Alliances on the Colorado Plateaus, A.D. 400–1450. In *Advances in World Archaeology* 2, edited by Fred Wendorf and Angela E. Close, pp. 289–330. New York: Academic Press.

Plog, Stephen
1976 The Inference of Prehistoric Social Organization from Ceramic Design Variability. *Michigan Discussions in Anthropology* 1: 1–47.

Powell, John Wesley
1972 *The Hopi Villages: The Ancient Province of Tusayan*. Palmer Lake, Colorado: Filter Press.

Prudden, T. Mitchell
1903 The Prehistoric Ruins of the San Juan Watershed in Utah, Arizona, Colorado, and New Mexico. *American Anthropologist* 5: 224–288.
1914 The Circular Kivas of Small Ruins in the San Juan Watershed. *American Anthropologist* 16: 33–58.
1918 A Further Study of Prehistoric Small House Ruins in the San Juan Watershed. *Memoirs of the American Anthropological Association* 5: 3–50.

Rapoport, Amos
1969 *House Form and Culture*. Englewood Cliffs, New Jersey: Prentice-Hall.

Rathje, Willian L.
1980 To the Salt of the Earth: Some Comments on Household Archaeology among the Maya. Paper prepared in advance for participants in Burg Wartenstein Symposium no. 86. "Prehistoric Settlement Pattern Studies: Retrospect and Prospect."

Reed, Erik K.
1950 Eastern-central Arizona Archaeology in Relation to the Western Pueblos. *Southwestern Journal of Anthropology* 6: 120–138.

Reid, J. Jefferson
1973 *Growth and Response to Stress at Grasshopper Pueblo, Arizona*. Doctoral dissertation, Department of Anthropology, University of Arizona, Tucson. Ann Arbor: University Microfilms.

Reid, J. Jefferson, and Izumi Shimada
1982 Pueblo Growth at Grasshopper: Methods and Models. In "Multidisciplinary Research at Grasshopper Pueblo, Arizona," edited by William A. Longacre, Sally J. Holbrook, and Michael W. Graves, pp. 12–18. *Anthropological Papers of The University of Arizona* 40. Tucson: University of Arizona Press.

Reid, J. Jefferson, and Stephanie M. Whittlesey
1982 Households at Grasshopper Pueblo. *American Behavioral Scientist* 25(6): 687–703.

Roberts, Frank H. H., Jr.
1930 Early Pueblo Ruins in the Piedra District, Southwestern Colorado. *Bureau of American Ethnology Bulletin 96*. Washington.
1931 The Ruins at Kiatuthlanna, Eastern Arizona. *Bureau of American Ethnology Bulletin 100*. Washington.
1935 A Survey of Southwestern Archaeology. *American Anthropologist* 37: 1–35.

Robinson, William J., and Roderick Sprague
1965 Disposal of the Dead at Point of Pines, Arizona. *American Antiquity* 30(4): 442–453.

Rohn, Arthur H.
1965 Postulation of Socio-economic Groups from Archaeological Evidence. *Society for American Archaeology Memoirs* 19: 65–69.
1971 *Mug House*. Washington: National Park Service.

Roseberry, William
1985 A Unit for Social Analysis. Review of *Households: Comparative and Historical Studies of the Domestic Group*, edited by Robert McC. Netting, Richard R. Wilk, and Eric J. Arnould. Berkeley: University of California Press, 1984. *Science* 228: 1081–1082.

Sahlins, Marshall D.
1957 Land Use and Extended Family in Moala, Fiji. *American Anthropologist* 59: 449–462.

Sanjek, Roger
1982 The Organization of Households in Adabraka: Toward a Wider Comparative Perspective. *Comparative Studies in Society and History* 24(1): 57–103.

Schiffer, Michael B.
1985 Is There a "Pompeii Premise" in Archaeology? *Journal of Anthropological Research* 41(1): 18–41.

1987 *Formation Processes of the Archaeological Record.* Albuquerque: University of New Mexico Press.

Schroeder, Albert H.
1979 Pecos Pueblo. In "Southwest," edited by Alfonso Ortiz, Vol. 9, *Handbook of North American Indians*, edited by William C. Sturtevant, pp. 430–437. Washington: Smithsonian Institution.

Shafer, Harry J.
1982 Classic Mimbres Phase Households and Room Use Patterns. *The Kiva* 48(1–2): 17–37.

Simmons, Leo W., editor
1942 *Sun Chief: The Autobiography of a Hopi Indian.* New Haven: Yale University Press.

Simmons, Marc
1979a History of Pueblo-Spanish Relations to 1821. In "Southwest," edited by Alfonso Ortiz, Vol. 9, *Handbook of North American Indians*, edited by William C. Sturtevant, pp. 178–193. Washington: Smithsonian Institution.
1979b History of the Pueblos since 1821. In "Southwest," edited by Alfonso Ortiz, Vol. 9, *Handbook of North American Indians*, edited by William C. Sturtevant, pp. 206–223. Washington: Smithsonian Institution.

Smiley, Terah L.
1952 Four Late Prehistoric Kivas at Point of Pines, Arizona. *University of Arizona Bulletin* 23(3). *Social Science Bulletin* 21. Tucson: University of Arizona.

Smith, Watson, and John M. Roberts
1954 Zuni Law: A Field of Values. *Papers of the Peabody Museum of American Archaeology and Ethnology, Harvard University* 43(1). *Reports of the Rimrock Project Values Series* 4: 3–175. Cambridge: Harvard University.

Stein, Mercedes R.
1962 An Analysis of the Human Skeletal Material from Turkey Creek Ruin. MS, Master's thesis, Department of Anthropology, University of Arizona, Tucson.

Stein, Walter T.
1963 Mammal Remains from Archaeological Sites in the Point of Pines Region, Arizona. *American Antiquity* 29(2): 213–220.

Stephen, Alexander M.
1936 *Hopi Journal of Alexander M. Stephen*, edited by Elsie C. Parsons. New York: AMS Press.

Stevenson, Matilda C.
1904 The Zuni Indians: Their Mythology, Esoteric Fraternities, and Ceremonies. *Bureau of American Ethnology, Annual Report* 23: 1–634. Washington.

Steward, Julian H.
1937 Ecological Aspects of Southwestern Society. *Anthropos* 32: 87–104.
1955 *Theory of Culture Change.* Urbana: University of Illinois Press.

Strong, Pauline T.
1979 Santa Ana Pueblo. In "Southwest," edited by Alfonso Ortiz, Vol. 9, *Handbook of North American Indians*, edited by William C. Sturtevant, pp. 398–406. Washington: Smithsonian Institution.

Sullivan, Alan P., III
1974 Problems in the Estimation of Original Room Function: A Tentative Solution from the Grasshopper Ruin. *The Kiva* 40(1–2): 93–100.

Titiev, Mischa
1944 Old Oraibi: A Study of the Hopi Indians of Third Mesa. *Papers of the Peabody Museum of American Archaeology and Ethnology, Harvard University* 22(1): 1–277. Cambridge: Harvard University.
1972 *The Hopi Indians of Old Oraibi: Change and Continuity.* Ann Arbor: University of Michigan Press.

Tuggle, H. David, and J. Jefferson Reid
1982 Cross-dating Cibola White Wares. In "Cholla Project Archaeology" 5, "Ceramic Studies", edited by J. Jefferson Reid. *Arizona State Museum Archaeological Series* 161: 8–17. Tucson: Arizona State Museum, University of Arizona.

Turner, Christy G., II, and L. Lofgren
1966 Household Size of Prehistoric Western Pueblo Indians. *Southwestern Journal of Anthropology* 22(1): 117–132.

Upham, Steadman
1982 *Polities and Power: An Economic and Political History of the Western Pueblo.* New York: Academic Press.

Upham, Steadman, Kent G. Lightfoot, and Roberta A. Jewett, Editors
1989 *The Sociopolitical Structure of Prehistoric Southwestern Societies.* Boulder: Westview Press.

Wasley, William W.
1952 The Late Pueblo Occupation at Point of Pines, East-central Arizona. MS, Master's thesis, Department of Anthropology, University of Arizona, Tucson.

Watson, Patty Jo
1978 Architectural Differentiation in Some Near Eastern Communities, Prehistoric and Contemporary. In *Social Archeology: Beyond Subsistence and Dating*, edited by Charles L. Redman, M. J. Berman, E. V. Curtin, W. T. Langhorne, Jr., N. M. Versaggi, and J. C. Wanser, pp. 131–158. New York: Academic Press.

Wendorf, Fred
1950 A Report on the Excavation of a Small Ruin Near Point of Pines, East Central Arizona. *University of Arizona Bulletin* 21(3). *Social Science Bulletin* 19. Tucson: University of Arizona.

Wheat, Joe Ben
1952 Prehistoric Water Sources of the Point of Pines Area. *American Antiquity* 17(3): 185–196.

Wheaton, Robert
1975 Family and Kinship in Western Europe: The Problem of the Joint Family Household. *Journal of Interdisciplinary History* 4: 601–628.

Wilcox, David R.
1975 A Strategy for Perceiving Social Groups in Puebloan Sites. In "Chapters in the Prehistory of Eastern Arizona IV," by Paul S. Martin, Ezra B. W. Zubrow, Daniel C. Bowman, David A. Gregory, John A. Hanson, Michael B. Schiffer, and David R. Wilcox, pp. 120–159. *Fieldiana: Anthropology* 65.
1981 Changing Perspectives on the Protohistoric Pueblos, AD 1350–1700. In "The Prehistoric Period in the North American Southwest, AD 1450–1700," edited by David R. Wilcox and W. Bruce Masse, pp. 378–409. *Arizona State University Anthropological Research Papers* 24. Tempe: Arizona State University.
1982 A Set-Theory Approach to Sampling Pueblos: The Implications of Room-set Additions at Grasshopper Pueblo. In "Multidisciplinary Research at Grasshopper Pueblo, Arizona," edited by William A. Longacre, Sally J. Holbrook, and Michael W. Graves, pp. 19–27. *Anthropological Papers of The University of Arizona* 40. Tucson: University of Arizona Press.

Wilk, Richard R., and Robert McC. Netting
1981 Notes on the History of the Household Concept. Paper

prepared in advance for participants in the Wenner-Gren Foundation Symposium: "Households: Changing Form and Function."

1984 Households: Changing Forms and Functions. In *Households: Comparative and Historical Studies of the Domestic Group*, edited by Robert McC. Netting, Richard R. Wilk, and Eric J. Arnould, pp. 1–28. Berkeley: University of California Press.

Wilk, Richard R., and William L. Rathje
1982 Household Archaeology. *American Behavioral Scientist* 25(6): 617–639.

Woodbury, Richard
1959 A Reconsideration of Pueblo Warfare in the Southwestern United States. *Actas Del 33 Congreso Internacional De Americanistas* II: 124–133.

1961 Prehistoric Agriculture at Point of Pines, Arizona. *Memoirs of the Society for American Archaeology* 17, edited by Raymond H. Thompson. *American Antiquity* 26(3), Part 2.

Woodford-Berger, Prudence
1981 Women in Houses: The Organization of Residence and Work in Rural Ghana. *Anthropologiska Studies* 30–31: 3–35.

Wright, Barton
1979 *Hopi Material Culture: Artifacts Gathered by H. R. Voth in the Fred Harvey Collection*. Flagstaff: Northland Press.

Yanagisako, Sylvia J.
1979 Family and Household: The Analysis of Domestic Groups. *Annual Review of Anthropology* 8: 161–205.

Index
Chris Pulliam

Abandonment
   by Pueblo peoples, 63
   of Grasshopper Pueblo, 64
   of Point of Pines Pueblo, 64
   of Turkey Creek Pueblo
      and floor artifacts, 64
      by household, 61, 63–64
      by room and room groups, 18, 29, 38–42, 43, 46, 50, 51, 53, 55, 56, 58
      indicated by sherd density, 18, 32, 38–42
      reasons for, 64
      relation to dual organization, 56, 58
      sequence of, 7, 21, 38, 40
      to Point of Pines region, 64
Abandonment patterns
   and portable artifacts, 40, 42
   at Turkey Creek Pueblo, 11, 58
Abandonment processes, 11
Access into Dwellings. *See* Doors; Hatches
Access into Turkey Creek Pueblo, 50, 56, 63
Acoma, 16
Activities
   at suprahousehold level, 60, 61, 65
   ceremonial, 52, 55, 56, 60, 61, 62, 65
   clan-related, 4
   dual unit, 62
   female-related, 53, 62
   kiva, 62
   male, 53, 55
   of domestic groups, 3, 60–62
   within dwellings, 61
   See also Space
Aggregation, 61–63
Agricultural features, 11, 15
Anasazi, ix, 16
Animal remains, 11, 15
Antler flakers, 20, 27, 28, 50, 52, 55, 58
Architectural attribute definitions, 17–19
Architectural studies, of cliff dwellings, x
Architectural units, at Mug House, 6
Architecture (domestic) at Shahabad, Iran, 7–8
Arizona State Museum, xiii, 10, 11
Artifacts
   definitions of, 20
   floor, 10, 11, 20, 25–29, 31, 40–42, 46, 50, 51, 52, 53, 55, 58, 62, 64
   male-related, 62
   portable, 19, 20, 27, 28, 29, 40, 41, 42, 46, 52, 53, 55, 58, 61
   See also Awls; Axes; Bowls; Drills; Hoes; Jars; Knives; Metates, trough; Projectile points; Shaft straighteners; Vessels
Awatovi, destruction of, 62
Awls, 20, 25, 27, 52, 58
Axes, 20, 46, 52

Basalt-based walls. *See* Walls, basalt-based
Beams, stockpiling of, 35
Betatakin, 6

Bins (storage) and bin areas, 19, 24, 29
   in Point of Pines region, 40
   rooms with, 40, 57, 58
   See also Pits, storage; Rooms, storage
Bowls, 20, 27, 29, 40–42, 52, 58. *See also* Vessels
Broken K Pueblo, 5, 6, 7
Burial population in Point of Pines region, 61
Burials at Turkey Creek Pueblo, xiii
   adult, 9, 60–61
   description of, 19
   in moiety houses, 62
   in room groups, 46, 55, 56
   infant, 25, 28, 60–61
   lack of male, 61
   locations of, 12–13, 25, 26, 60
   See also Cremations
Canyon Creek phase sites, 15
Carter Ranch, 5
Ceramic analysis, 10, 32. *See also* Sherd density and density index
Ceramic production, among the Kalinga, 8
Ceramic sequence, at Turkey Creek Pueblo, 15
Ceramic styles, 5
Ceremonial structures. *See* Great Kiva; Kivas
Chicago Museum of Natural History, x
Chronology, of Southwestern prehistory, ix
Circle Prairie, 11
Clans, ix, 4
Classification of households, 3, 5–7
Colorado Plateau, ix, 4
Computer procedures, 20–21
Construction
   dating of, 15 (*see also* Tree-ring dates)
   jacal, 43, 51, 52
   periods, 40, 43, 46, 50, 51, 52, 58
   related to dual organization, 56
   room, 32, 36, 38, 52
   sequence, 7, 32, 35–36, 38
   See also Walls, basalt-based
Conversions. *See* Remodeling of rooms
Cremations, 9, 19
Crops, 11, 15
Crowding, at Turkey Creek Pueblo, 60
Culture process, 4

Dating techniques, ix, 15. *See also* Ceramic sequence; Tree-ring dates
Dean, Jeffrey S., x
Defense, evidence for, 62–64
Descent systems, 5–6
Doors, 8, 19, 29, 30, 31, 50–53, 58, 59, 63
Drills, 20, 25, 28
Dual division, xi, 52, 61–62. *See also* Dual organization; Moiety system
Dual organization, 56–59, 61–62
Dwellings
   access into (*see* Doors; Hatches)
   activities in, 31, 61

and room types, 29, 31
as households, 21, 59 (*see also* Households)
communication within, 29, 31
identification of, 22
size variability of, 59
typical, 29, 31, 59
Zuni, 59
See also Room Groups

Eastern Pueblos, xiii
Ellis, Florence H., ix
Evolution, unilinear, 1
Exchange contacts, 63

Fertility, 60–61
Fewkes, J. Walter, ix
Flagstone floor, in kiva, 55
Formation processes, x, 6, 21

Grasshopper Pueblo
   abandonment of, 64
   circular hearths in, 26
   data from, 5, 11
   households in, 1, 5, 7
   room function at, 22
   room size at, 29
   room typology at, 6–7
Great Kiva, at Turkey Creek Pueblo, 9, 26, 27, 32, 35, 50, 52, 53, 55, 56, 58, 59, 62, 63, 65
Growth, at Turkey Creek Pueblo, 61

Hasanabad, household study at, 7
Hatches, 19, 24, 25, 28, 29, 30, 31, 46, 50, 51, 52, 55, 58, 59, 63
Haury, Emil W., xiii, 1, 9
Hearth class, 17
Hearths
   circular (*see* Rooms with circular hearths)
   definition of, 17
   in room groups, 50, 51
   rectangular (*see* Rooms with rectangular hearths)
   rooms categorized by, 22, 23, 42
   slab-lined, 27
   See also Grasshopper Pueblo; Point of Pines phase; Point of Pines region; Reserve phase; Tularosa phase
Heuristic approach, 21
Hoes, 20, 58
Hohokam, ix
Hopi, xiii, 4, 16, 21, 27, 59, 62
Household
   abandonment, 61, 63–64
   activities of, 3, 60–62
   adaptation, 1, 4
   and prehistoric social organization, 64
   archaeological approaches to, 3–8
   at Grasshopper Pueblo, 1, 5, 7
   classified by function, 5–7

definitions of, 3
descent rules, 5–6
developmental cycle of, 36, 60
extended family, 6, 60
forms, 1
function, x–xi, 3, 6–7, 8
multifamily, 60
nuclear family, 1, 6, 60, 64
size, 4–5, 60
structure, 60
Zuni, 21
See also Dwellings; Suprahousehold

Inheritance affecting household forms, 1

Jacal construction, 43, 51
Jars, 4, 20, 24, 27, 29, 40–42, 50, 51, 52. *See also* Vessels
Johnson, Alfred E., xiii, 1, 9

Kayenta area, x
Kayenta cooking jars, 4
Kayenta migration to Point of Pines, 15, 64
Kiet Siel, 6
Kin groups, 58
Kinship affecting household forms, 1
Kivas, 6, 9, 27, 35, 51, 55, 61, 62, 63. *See also* Great Kiva
Knives, 20, 25, 28, 52

Laguna, 16
Life expectancy, 60, 61
Lindsay, Alexander J., Jr., x
Longacre, William A., x, 5, 8

Marata, 63
Marriage rules affecting household forms, 1
Martin, Paul S., x
Matrilineages, 5
Matrilocal residence. *See* Residence rules
Maverick Mountain phase, Point of Pines Pueblo, 15
Mesa Verde area, x, 6
Metates, trough, 20, 25, 27, 28, 29, 31, 46, 48, 53
Mindeleff, Cosmos, ix
Mindeleff, Victor, ix
Mogollon, ix, 15
Moieties, 61–62
Moiety system
 and dual organization, 61–62
 and room groups, 53
 at Turkey Creek Pueblo, xiii, 62, 65
 in historic Eastern Pueblos, xiii
 lack of, in Hopi and Zuni, xiii
 See also Dual organization
Mortality rate, 60–61
Mounds
 burial, 9, 61 (*see also* Burials)
 trash, 9, 12–13, 60, 61
Mug House, 6
Murdock, George P., x

Nantack Ridge, 11
National Science Foundation, xiii
New archaeology, ix, x

Patayan, ix
Pine Lawn Valley, x
Pinedale Black-on-white ceramics, 15
Pinedale phase sites, 15

Pit houses (structures), 9, 10, 27, 32, 35, 43, 50, 61
Pits, storage, 19, 36, 46, 58. *See also* Bins, storage; Rooms, storage
Plaster on walls, 19, 29, 45, 50, 51, 52, 55, 58
Point of Pines phase, 27, 40, 63
Point of Pines Pueblo, 15, 42, 64
Point of Pines region, xiii, 1, 9, 11
 abandonment of, 64
 aggregation in, 62, 63
 agricultural features in, 11, 15
 bins in, 40
 burial population in, 61
 hearth types in, 27
 phase sequence in, 15
 Reserve phase in, 40, 61, 63
 room function change in, 27
 scavanging wall stones in, 53
Postabandonment process, 21, 53, 55, 58
Posts and postholes, 19, 24, 25, 26, 28, 29, 43, 46, 47, 50, 51, 52, 58
Projectile points, 20, 25, 27, 52, 53, 55, 62
Prudden, T. Mitchell, ix, 4
Pueblo groups, 63
Pueblo periods, 4, 6

Remodeling of rooms, 21, 25, 26, 31, 32, 36–38, 60
Reserve Black-on-white ceramics, 15
Reserve phase
 basalt-based wall construction, 56
 hearth types, 27
 in Point of Pines region, 40, 61, 63
 settlement system, 62
 sites, 15, 40
 villages, 61
Residence rules, 1, 5, 6
Residential duality, 62. *See also* Dual Organization
Rinaldo, John B., x
Rohn, Arthur H., x
Room area and area group, 17, 18, 22, 38
Room attributes pattern, 21
Room classes, 22, 52
Room conversions. *See* Remodeling of rooms
Room fill, deflation of, 40
Room floor transitions. *See* Remodeling of rooms
Room function, 22, 29, 36, 38
Room groups
 abandonment by, 43, 46, 50, 51, 53
 analysis of, 43, 46, 50–53, 55
 and room shape, 50
 and room size, 50
 and room types, 31, 46, 50, 51, 52
 architecture of, 46, 50, 51, 52, 53
 characteristics of, 43, 46, 50–51, 52–53
 definition of, 18–19
 function of, 51, 53
 locations of, 34
 moiety division of, 53, 54
 room types in, 31
 tree-ring dates from, 53
 wall height of, 46, 50, 51, 53, 55, 58
 with basalt-based walls, 43, 46
 See also Spatial variability
Room placement, 19, 53. *See also* Spatial variability
Room sample, 17, 20
Room shape, 19, 50

Room side, definition of, 19
Room size, 17, 22, 27–29, 42, 46, 50, 51, 52, 58, 59
Room types, 6, 24, 28, 29, 31, 42, 58, 59, 60, 61
Room use, 8
Room variables, 17–20
Rooms, burned, 40, 42, 53, 54, 55
Rooms, domestic, 53, 59
 typology of, 21, 31, 64–65
Rooms, functional typology of, 22–27
Rooms, habitation, 24, 27–28, 53, 59, 60, 61. *See also* Rooms with rectangular hearths
Rooms, miscellaneous activity, 27–28, 59, 60, 61. *See also* Rooms with circular hearths
Rooms, storage, 6, 8, 24, 29, 36, 43, 46, 50, 51, 52, 59, 60, 61. *See also* Bins; Pits, storage; Rooms without hearths
Rooms with circular hearths, 17, 18, 22, 36
 activities in, 25–26, 27, 60
 architectural attributes of, 25
 burials in, 25
 characteristics of, 24–26
 conversions involving, 38
 floor artifacts in, 25
 frequency of, 25, 29, 46, 50, 51, 52, 53, 55, 58
 portable artifacts in, 25
 spatial patterning of, 24–25
Rooms with rectangular hearths, 17, 18, 22, 36
 activities in, 27, 60
 characteristics of, 26–27
 conversions involving, 38
 floor artifacts in, 27
 lack of temporal trends in, 26
 frequency of, 29, 46, 50, 51, 53, 58, 60
 functions of, 26–27, 60
 portable artifacts in, 27
Rooms without hearths, 22, 36, 43, 59
 architectural attributes of, 24
 characteristics of, 24
 conversions involving, 36, 38
 frequency of, 50, 51, 58
 function of, 24
 portable artifacts in, 24
 temporal patterning of, 24
San Carlos Apache Reservation, xiii, 1, 9
San Juan area, ix
Scavenging of wall stones, postabandonment, 40, 50, 53, 55, 64
School of American Research, x
Seriation, Graves', 15
Shaft straighteners, 20, 27, 28
Sherd density and density index, 18, 21, 24, 32, 38–42, 43, 46, 51, 52, 53, 56, 61
Sikyatki, 62
Skeletal materials. *See* Burials
Social groups, at Turkey Creek Pueblo, 59
Social organization, ix–xi, 1–4, 61, 64. *See also* Household
Social units, x, 4, 59, 65
Space
 activities in, 3, 7–8, 21
 domestic organization of, 55, 62
 dual organization of, 58
 use of, xiii
Spatial variability, 43–58
Sterile soil. *See* Sterile-Trash dichotomy
Sterile-Trash dichotomy, 18, 21, 25, 32, 36, 38, 40, 43, 46, 50, 51, 52, 56, 61, 62
Steward, Julian H., ix
Storage rooms. *See* Rooms, storage

Suprahousehold, xi, 43, 55, 59, 60, 61

Thompson, Raymond H., xiii, 1, 9
Time
    control of, 7
    measures of, 21 (*see also* Ceramic sequence; Remodeling of rooms; Sherd density and density index; Sterile-Trash dichotomy; Tree-ring dates)
Trash. *See* Sterile-Trash dichotomy
Tree-ring dates, 11, 15, 32, 35–36, 52
Tsegi Canyon, 6
Tuff, construction with, 46, 50
Tularosa Black-on-white ceramics, 15
Tularosa phase, 15
    aggregation, 63
    basalt-based wall construction, 36
    bins, 40
    hearth types, 27
Turkey Creek Pueblo
    as Western Pueblo, 16
    collections from, xiii
    cooperation at suprahousehold level, 60
    environment, 11
    excavation of, 9–10
    exchange contacts with, 63
    expansion of, 46, 50, 60
    features of, 9
    in other studies, 11
    levels of organization, xi
    location of, xiii, 1, 2, 9
    occupation time span, 15

Unit pueblo, ix, 4
University of Arizona, xiii, 9
Upham, Steadman, x

Vents, 19, 24, 28, 29, 30, 31, 40, 50, 51, 52, 53, 58
Vessels, 4–5, 20, 24, 25, 27, 29, 31, 32, 40, 41, 46, 50, 51, 52, 53
Village moves, reasons for, 62–63. *See also* Abandonment
Village unit at Turkey Creek Pueblo, 21, 59, 61–64

Walls
    basalt-based, 19, 26, 29, 31, 32, 36, 43, 46, 50, 51, 52, 55, 56, 58, 59
    bonding of, 18, 43
    height of, 18, 19, 40, 46, 49, 50, 51, 52, 53, 54, 55, 58, 59
    long, 18, 35, 43, 44, 52, 55, 59
    plastered, 19, 29, 45, 50, 51, 52, 55, 58
Walpi, 8, 62
Wealth differences, at Turkey Creek Pueblo, 60
Western Pueblos, 5, 16
White Mountain Red Ware design styles, 15
White Mountain Red Ware pottery, 11
Wood
    stockpiling of, 35–36, 62
    structural, 15

Zuni
    aggregation at, 61
    cooking facilities, 27
    dwelling size average, 59
    fraternity rooms, 53
    household, 21
    moiety system lacking at, xiii
    use of space, xiii
    war with Marata, 63

ABSTRACT

This monograph is a study of household organization and function at Turkey Creek Pueblo, a thirteenth-century ruin located in the Point of Pines region of east-central Arizona. This large pueblo has approximately 335 rooms, two plazas, and a rectangular Great Kiva. During the summers of 1958 through 1960, a remarkable 314 of its rooms were excavated by the University of Arizona Archaeological Field School. The broad and consistently reported architectural data from this excavation provide an extraordinary opportunity for understanding the social use of space in a prehistoric pueblo community, a subject of lively current interest among archaeologists.

The patterning of room attributes at Turkey Creek Pueblo is inferred by a statistical analysis of 31 room variables in 301 rooms. These variables include such attributes as room size, hearth style, floor pottery, wall style, burials, and doors. Their patterning is influenced by room function, temporal change, and intrapueblo areal differentiation.

It was found that dwellings, the architectural units associated with households, are composed of three room types. Storage rooms tend to be small with no hearths or other features. Habitation rooms tend to be large with rectangular hearths. Miscellaneous activity rooms tend to be mid-sized with circular hearths. A typical dwelling has one habitation room, one or two miscellaneous activity rooms, and two or three storage rooms. However, considerable variability exists in the size and organization of these dwellings, reflecting variability in household size and configuration.

Architectural analysis further suggests that the households of Turkey Creek Pueblo formed the first level of a four-level organizational hierarchy. At the second level, all households are grouped into suprahouseholds, which are architecturally reflected by groups of rooms distinguished from each other by long unbroken walls. The third level is a north-south dual division or moiety. This moiety division is reflected in the presence of two distinct sets of domestic rooms that are physically united only through the Great Kiva. The most dramatic structural indication of dual organization are two unusual room groups that were partly ceremonial in function and attached to the kiva. The fourth and most inclusive social unit is the village itself. Food production, food processing, and storage are major functions of the lower two levels, and food exchange, ceremony, and defense are primary functions of the higher two levels.

Also discussed are village aggregation and abandonment, room remodeling patterns, and site formation processes. In addition, both the raw data and the results of the computer procedures are organized into appendixes and tables to serve as references for comparisons with other pueblos. A series of maps shows the spatial distribution of the most important variables.

RESUMEN

Este monográfico es un estudio de la organización y función de los hogares del pueblo Turkey Creek, una ruina del siglo 13 situada en la región Point of Pines de la parte este-central de Arizona. Este gran pueblo contiene aproximadamente 335 cuartos, dos plazas, y una Gran Kiva en forma rectángula. Durante los veranos de 1958 hasta 1960, se excavaron el notable número de 314 de los cuartos por la Escuela de Campo Arqueológica de la Universidad de Arizona. Los extensos y constantemente relatados datos sobre la architectura de esta excavación presentan una oportunidad extraordinaria para poder entender el uso social del espacio en la comunidad de un pueblo prehistórico, actualmente un sugeto de mucho interés entre los arqueológicos.

La distribución de los atributos en los cuartos del pueblo Turkey Creek se deduce por un análisis estadístico de 31 variables en 301 cuartos. Estos variables incluyen semejantes atributos como el tamaño del cuarto, el estilo de la chiminea, la cerámica en el suelo, el estilo de la pared, los entierros, y las puertas. La distribución está influida por el uso del cuarto, cambios temporales, y diferencias regionales entre los pueblos.

Se descubrió que las viviendas, las unidades arquitectónicas asociadas con los hogares, se componen de tres tipos de cuarto. Los cuartos de almacén en general son chicos y sin chimineas u otros atributos. Los cuartos de habitación en general son grandes con chimineas rectángulas. Los cuartos de actividad general típicamente son de tamaño regular con chimineas redondas. Una vivienda típica consiste de un cuarto de habitación, uno o dos de activiadad general, y dos o tres cuartos de almacén. Sin embargo, existe bastante variedad en el tamaño y organización de estas viviendas, reflejando la variedad en el tamaño y configuración de los hogares.

El análisis arquitectónico además indica que los hogares de Turkey Creek formaban el primer nivel de una organización jerárquica de cuatro niveles. En el segundo nivel, todos los hogares están agrupados hacia superhogares, los cuales se reflejan en grupos de cuartos que se distinguen unos a los otros por largos y continuos muros. El trecer nivel se una división doble separando el norte y el sur o es decir en facciones. Esta división de facciones se refleja en la presencia de dos grupos distintivos de cuartos domésticos los cuales se unen físicamente solamente por medio de la Gran Kiva. La mas dramática estructural indicación de esta dual organización se encuentra en dos inusuales grupos de cuartos los cuales eran en parte de uso ceremonial y que estaban sujetados a la Kiva. El cuarto y la mas inclusivo grupo social es el mismo pueblo. La producción, preparación, y almacenaje de la comida son las funciones mayores de los mas bajos niveles, y el intercambio de la comida, ceremonias y defensa son las funciones mas importantes de los dos niveles mas altos.

También se discute la junta y el abandono del pueblo, la norma empleada para renovar los cuartos, y los procesos empleados para formar el sitio. Además, los datos brutos como también los resultados de los procesos de computadora se han organizado hacia apéndices y tablas para así servir como referencias en comparaciones con otros pueblos. Una serie de mapas demuestra la distribución espacial de los mas importantes variables.